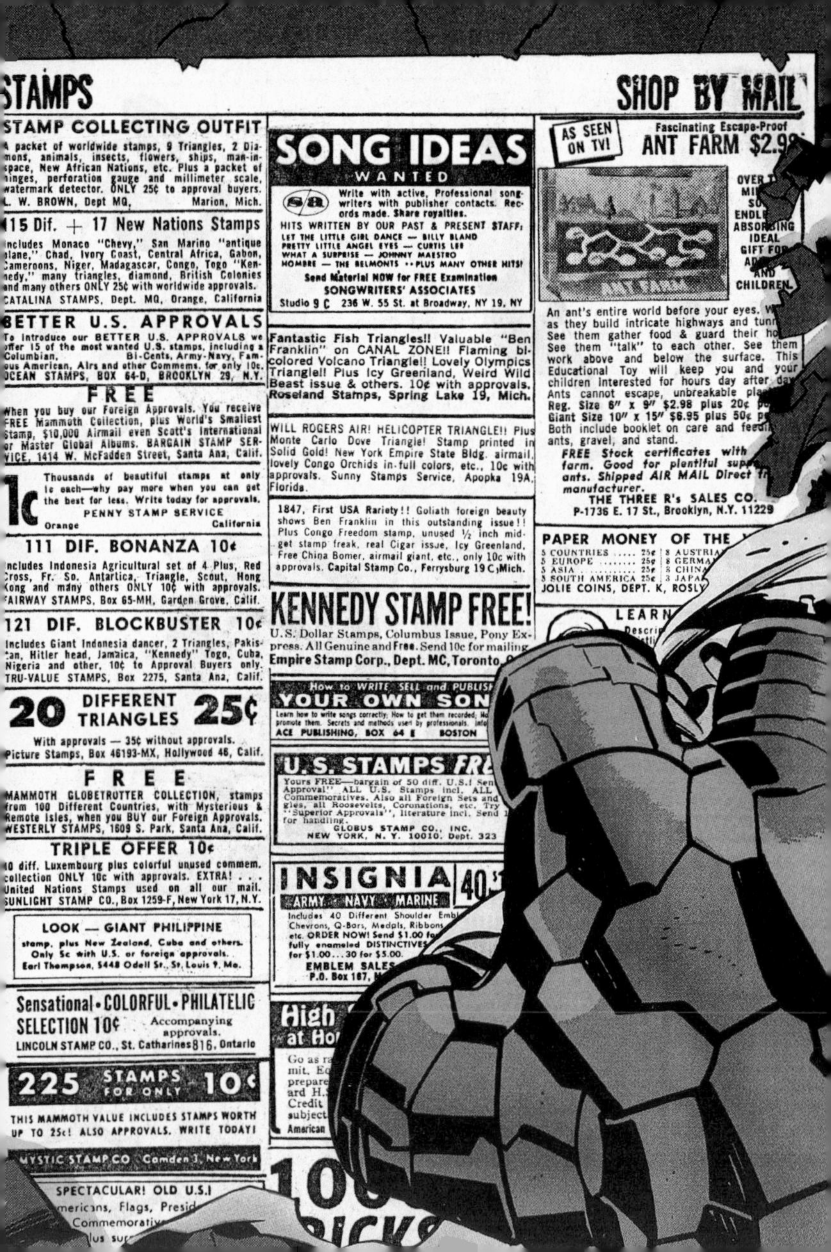

STAMPS

STAMP COLLECTING OUTFIT

A packet of worldwide stamps, 9 Triangles, 2 Diamons, animals, insects, flowers, ships, man-in-space, New African Nations, etc. Plus a packet of hinges, perforation gauge and millimeter scale, watermark detector. ONLY 25¢ to approval buyers.
L. W. BROWN, Dept MQ, Marion, Mich.

115 Dif. + 17 New Nations Stamps

Includes Monaco "Chevy," San Marino "antique plane," Chad, Ivory Coast, Central Africa, Gabon, Cameroons, Niger, Madagascar, Congo, Togo "Kennedy," many triangles, diamond, British Colonies and many others ONLY 25¢ with worldwide approvals.
CATALINA STAMPS, Dept. MQ, Orange, California

BETTER U.S. APPROVALS

To introduce our BETTER U.S. APPROVALS we offer 15 of the most wanted U.S. stamps, including a Columbian, Bi-Cents, Army-Navy, Famous American, Airs and other Commems. for only 10c.
OCEAN STAMPS, BOX 64-D, BROOKLYN 29, N.Y.

FREE

When you buy our Foreign Approvals. You receive FREE Mammoth Collection, plus World's Smallest Stamp, $10,000 Airmail even Scott's International or Master Global Albums. BARGAIN STAMP SERVICE, 1414 W. McFadden Street, Santa Ana, Calif.

1c

Thousands of beautiful stamps at only 1c each—why pay more when you can get the best for less. Write today for approvals.
PENNY STAMP SERVICE
Orange California

111 DIF. BONANZA 10¢

Includes Indonesia Agricultural set of 4 Plus, Red Cross, Fr. So. Antartica, Triangle, Scout, Hong Kong and many others ONLY 10¢ with approvals.
FAIRWAY STAMPS, Box 65-MH, Garden Grove, Calif.

121 DIF. BLOCKBUSTER 10¢

Includes Giant Indonesia dancer, 2 Triangles, Pakistan, Hitler head, Jamaica, "Kennedy" Togo, Cuba, Nigeria and other, 10¢ to Approval Buyers only.
TRU-VALUE STAMPS, Box 2275, Santa Ana, Calif.

20 DIFFERENT TRIANGLES 25¢

With approvals — 35¢ without approvals.
Picture Stamps, Box 46193-MX, Hollywood 46, Calif.

FREE

MAMMOTH GLOBETROTTER COLLECTION, stamps from 100 Different Countries, with Mysterious & Remote Isles, when you BUY our Foreign Approvals.
WESTERLY STAMPS, 1609 S. Park, Santa Ana, Calif.

TRIPLE OFFER 10¢

10 diff. Luxembourg plus colorful unused commem. collection ONLY 10c with approvals. EXTRA! . . . United Nations Stamps used on all our mail.
SUNLIGHT STAMP CO., Box 1259-F, New York 17, N.Y.

LOOK — GIANT PHILIPPINE

stamp, plus New Zealand, Cuba and others. Only 5c with U.S. or foreign approvals.
Earl Thompson, 5448 Odell St., St. Louis 9, Mo.

Sensational • COLORFUL • PHILATELIC SELECTION 10¢

Accompanying approvals.
LINCOLN STAMP CO., St. Catharines 816, Ontario

225 STAMPS FOR ONLY 10¢

THIS MAMMOTH VALUE INCLUDES STAMPS WORTH UP TO 25c! ALSO APPROVALS. WRITE TODAY!
MYSTIC STAMP CO. Camden 3, New York

SPECTACULAR! OLD U.S.!

mericans, Flags, Presid
Commemorativ
lus sur

SONG IDEAS WANTED

Write with active, Professional songwriters with publisher contacts. Records made. Share royalties.
HITS WRITTEN BY OUR PAST & PRESENT STAFF:
LET THE LITTLE GIRL DANCE — BILLY BLAND
PRETTY LITTLE ANGEL EYES — CURTIS LEE
WHAT A SURPRISE — JOHNNY MAESTRO
HOMBRE — THE BELMONTS • • PLUS MANY OTHER HITS!
Send Material NOW for FREE Examination
SONGWRITERS' ASSOCIATES
Studio 9 C 236 W. 55 St. at Broadway, NY 19, NY

Fantastic Fish Triangles!! Valuable "Ben Franklin" on CANAL ZONE!! Flaming bi-colored Volcano Triangle!! Lovely Olympics Triangle!! Plus Icy Greenland, Weird Wild Beast issue & others. 10¢ with approvals.
Roseland Stamps, Spring Lake 19, Mich.

WILL ROGERS AIR! HELICOPTER TRIANGLE!! Plus Monte Carlo Dove Triangle! Stamp printed in Solid Gold! New York Empire State Bldg. airmail, lovely Congo Orchids in full colors, etc., 10c with approvals. Sunny Stamps Service, Apopka 19A, Florida.

1847, First USA Rariety!! Goliath foreign beauty shows Ben Franklin in this outstanding issue!! Plus Congo Freedom stamp, unused ½ inch midget stamp freak, real Cigar issue, Icy Greenland, Free China Bomer, airmail giant, etc., only 10c with approvals. Capital Stamp Co., Ferrysburg 19 C, Mich.

KENNEDY STAMP FREE!

U.S. Dollar Stamps, Columbus Issue, Pony Express. All Genuine and Free. Send 10c for mailing
Empire Stamp Corp., Dept. MC, Toronto, O

How to WRITE, SELL and PUBLISH YOUR OWN SON

Learn how to write songs correctly; How to get them recorded; Ho promote them. Secrets and methods used by professionals. Info
ACE PUBLISHING, BOX 64 E BOSTON

U.S. STAMPS FRE

Yours FREE—bargain of 50 diff. U.S.! Sen Approval'' ALL U.S. Stamps incl. ALL Commemoratives. Also all Foreign Sets and gles, all Roosevelts, Coronations, etc. Try ''Superior Approvals'', literature incl. Send 1 for handling.
GLOBUS STAMP CO., INC.
NEW YORK, N. Y. 10010. Dept. 323

INSIGNIA 40

ARMY • NAVY • MARINE
Includes 40 Different Shoulder Embl
Chevrons, Q-Bars, Medals, Ribbons
etc. ORDER NOW! Send $1.00 fo
fully enameled DISTINCTIVES
for $1.00...30 for $5.00.
EMBLEM SALES
P.O. Box 187,

High at Ho

Go as ra
mit. Ed
prepare
ard H.
Credit
subject
American

100
RICKS

SHOP BY MAIL

AS SEEN ON TV! Fascinating Escape-Proof ANT FARM $2.9

OVER
MI
SO
ENDL
ABSORBING
IDEAL
GIFT FOR
AD
AND
CHILDREN.

An ant's entire world before your eyes. W as they build intricate highways and tunn See them gather food & guard their ho See them "talk" to each other. See them work above and below the surface. This Educational Toy will keep you and your children interested for hours day after da Ants cannot escape, unbreakable pla
Reg. Size 6" x 9" $2.98 plus 20¢ p
Giant Size 10" x 15" $6.95 plus 50¢ p
Both include booklet on care and feedi ants, gravel, and stand.
FREE Stock certificates with farm. Good for plentiful sup ants. Shipped AIR MAIL Direct fr manufacturer.
THE THREE R's SALES CO.
P-1736 E. 17 St., Brooklyn, N.Y. 11229

PAPER MONEY OF THE

5 COUNTRIES ..... 25¢	8 AUSTRIA
5 EUROPE .... 25¢	8 GERMA
5 ASIA .... 25¢	8 CHINA
5 SOUTH AMERICA 25¢	3 JAPA

JOLIE COINS, DEPT. K, ROSLY

LEARN
Descri

MARVEL

THE LITTLE BOOK OF

Fantastic Four

Roy Thomas

TASCHEN

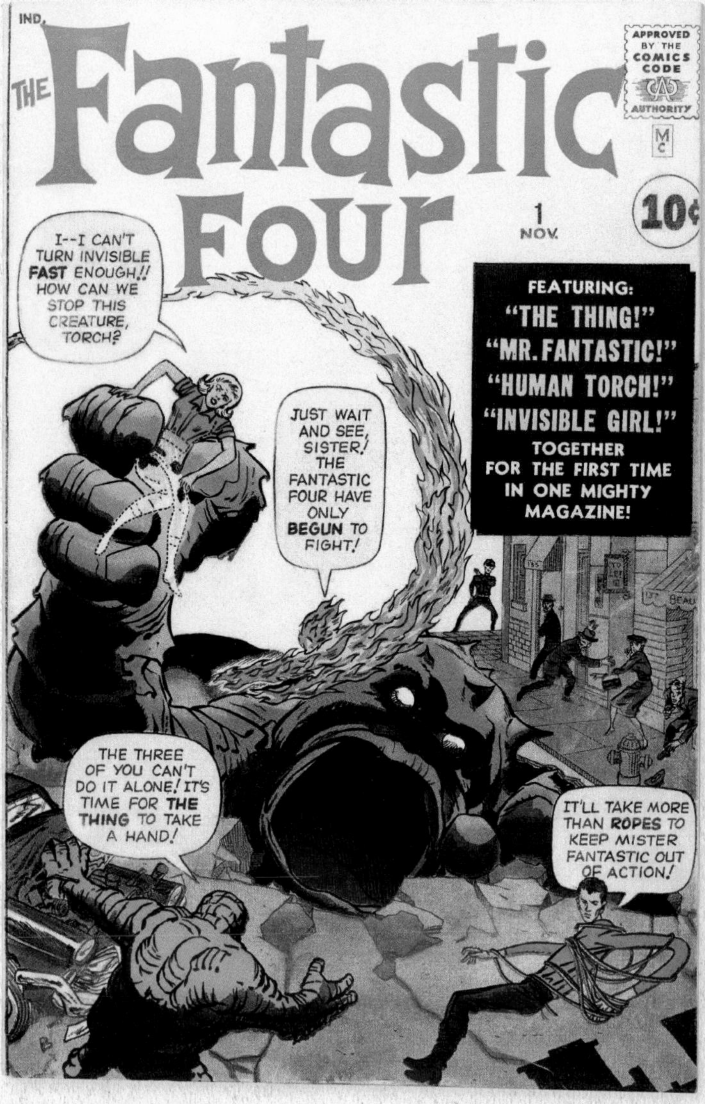
IND.
THE Fantastic FOUR
APPROVED BY THE COMICS CODE AUTHORITY
MC
10¢
1 NOV.
I--I CAN'T TURN INVISIBLE FAST ENOUGH!! HOW CAN WE STOP THIS CREATURE, TORCH?
FEATURING: "THE THING!" "MR. FANTASTIC!" "HUMAN TORCH!" "INVISIBLE GIRL!" TOGETHER FOR THE FIRST TIME IN ONE MIGHTY MAGAZINE!
JUST WAIT AND SEE, SISTER! THE FANTASTIC FOUR HAVE ONLY BEGUN TO FIGHT!
THE THREE OF YOU CAN'T DO IT ALONE! IT'S TIME FOR THE THING TO TAKE A HAND!
IT'LL TAKE MORE THAN ROPES TO KEEP MISTER FANTASTIC OUT OF ACTION!

WHAT'S SO GREAT ABOUT THE FANTASTIC FOUR?

"The World's Greatest Comic Magazine!"

That's the tagline that accompanied the *Fantastic Four* logo for decades, beginning three issues in. And the *FF*, as editor/writer Stan Lee nicknamed it, was definitely at least a strong contender for the "Greatest" crown.

Sure, *Amazing Spider-Man* passed *FF* in sales by 1967...by the '90s, *X-Men* temporarily elbowed the wall-crawler aside as Marvel's best-selling title...*Wolverine* became super-popular during the 2000s...and since 2012, bolstered by several billion dollars' worth of movie-ticket sales, *The Avengers* have swept all before them.

But none of these would have *existed* if not for the startling, block-buster success of *Fantastic Four*.

When the Fantastic Four exploded on the scene in August 1961, they hit like an A-bomb. Pre-teen, teen, and twenty-something readers alike had been getting their super hero kicks from DC's *Flash*, *Green Lantern*, and *Justice League of America*...all A-1 concepts. But the FF was something...different.

They were a team, like the JLA — but *these* super-powered humans were different. They were, well, more *real* than previous comics heroes. A couple of them actually *hated* each other. If the JLA were the local Rotarians in colorful costumes, the FF were a dysfunctional family,

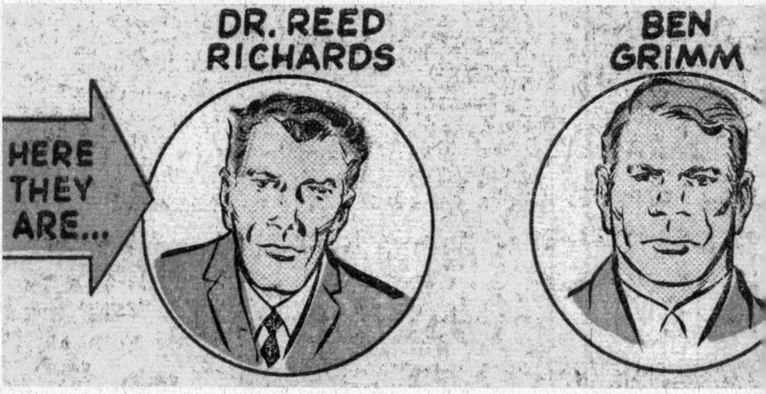
HERE THEY ARE...
DR. REED RICHARDS
BEN GRIMM

with Reed Richards ("Mr. Fantastic") and Sue Storm ("Invisible Girl") the reluctant parental figures, and Johnny Storm and Ben Grimm behaving like hostile siblings. Three seconds after Grimm had been turned into a super-strong but repulsive and rock-hided Thing, he ripped up a tree and tried to smash Richards with it. Johnny, transformed into a Human Torch, set a forest ablaze.

What's more, they didn't even wear costumes, just flight suits. Nor did they make any attempt to hide their true identities from the world. Locked up for crimes they hadn't committed, they didn't hesitate to smash their way out, with the Torch setting a federal prison afire.

But, let's face it—the Fantastic Four were not created equal. The Thing was the mag's breakout star. Nothing quite like him had ever been seen in comics—or anywhere else. He was half Frankenstein's monster, half Lennie from John Steinbeck's novella *Of Mice and Men*.

Publisher Martin Goodman ordered Lee to create a super hero team to rival DC's *Justice League*. Instead of copying it, he called in his top artist, Jack Kirby, and between them they deconstructed the very *idea* of a super hero team and put it back together again in a new

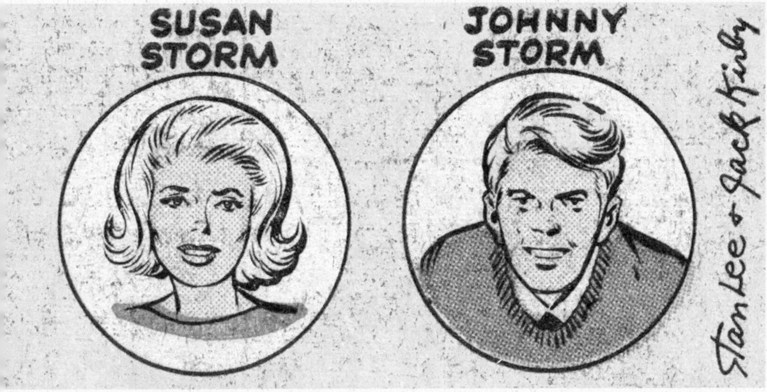
SUSAN STORM
JOHNNY STORM
Stan Lee + Jack Kirby

way. Super hero dynamics would never be the same again—not at the company soon to be christened Marvel Comics, but not at any *other* comics company, either!

Oh, sure…by No. 3, Lee bowed to readers' requests and put the team in uniforms, if not quite costumes. (The Thing instantly ripped his to shreds.) But otherwise, they remained the fascinating misfits they'd been from the outset.

The Fantastic Four were *born* great. They *also* had greatness thrust *upon* them.

For one thing, their opponents were great, too: Mole Man, a half-sympathetic foe in an era when most super-baddies were mere bank robbers…Sub-Mariner, a subsea prince…the incomparable Dr. Doom…the Frightful Four…the planet-devouring Galactus…antagonists like the Inhumans, Silver Surfer, and Black Panther, all of whom quickly evolved into series-worthy heroes.

From time to time, other characters temporarily replaced one or another of the FF: Crystal and Medusa of the Inhumans (in for a pregnant Sue Richards), Power Man, the She-Hulk, a female Thing,

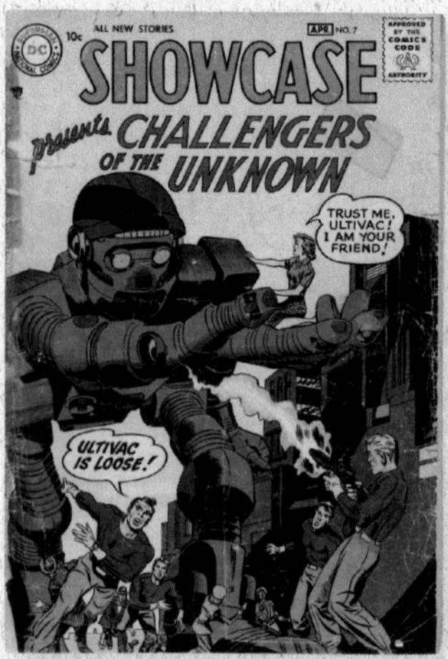
ALL NEW STORIES
10c
APR NO. 7
SHOWCASE
presents CHALLENGERS OF THE UNKNOWN
TRUST ME, ULTIVAC! I AM YOUR FRIEND!
ULTIVAC IS LOOSE!

FANTASTIC FOUR No. 1

Page 4: *Cover; pencils, Jack Kirby; inks, attributed George Klein; November 1961.*

FANTASTIC FOUR No. 1

Pages 6–7: *Interior, "The Fantastic Four"; script, Stan Lee; pencils, Jack Kirby; inks, attributed George Klein; November 1961.*

SHOWCASE No. 7

Left: *Cover; pencils and inks, Jack Kirby; DC Comics; April 1957.*

AMAZING SPIDER-MAN No. 1

Opposite: *Cover; pencils, Jack Kirby; inks, Steve Ditko; March 1963.* "Marvel Comics. Not so much a name as a special state of mind. Not so much a group of magazines as a mood, a movement, a mild and momentary madness." —Stan Lee

whoever...but the original team always got back together, as well they should have.

Others besides Lee and Kirby handled the comic after 1971—but its essence always remained what one 1960s credits-box proclaimed: "A Stan Lee/Jack Kirby powerhouse production!"

Over the years, the Fantastic Four conquered TV and video games, and even graced the silver screen. But even if they had remained merely on the comic book page, their greatness would have been assured. For they launched a revolution that's still unfolding—one with echoes in every super hero (solo star or group) since.

And, for at least a decade—and, in the minds of many, far longer than that—*Fantastic Four* was arguably "the world's greatest comic magazine!"

—ROY THOMAS

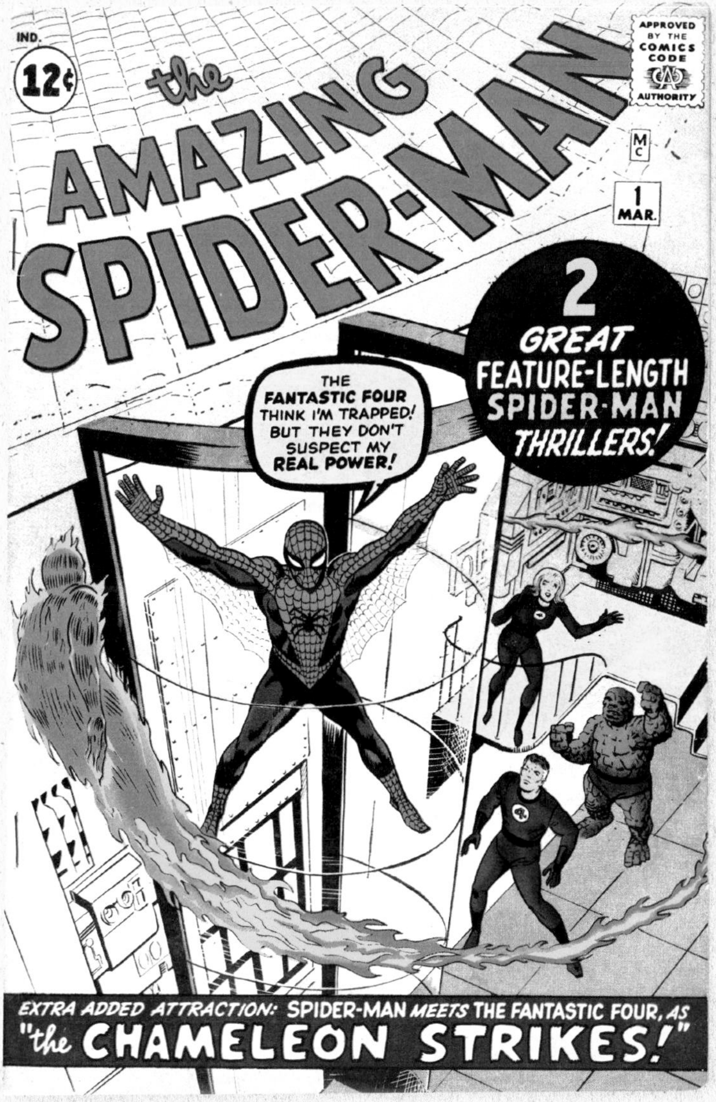

IND.
12¢
the AMAZING SPIDER-MAN
APPROVED BY THE COMICS CODE AUTHORITY
MC
1 MAR.
2 GREAT FEATURE-LENGTH SPIDER-MAN THRILLERS!
THE FANTASTIC FOUR THINK I'M TRAPPED! BUT THEY DON'T SUSPECT MY REAL POWER!
EXTRA ADDED ATTRACTION: SPIDER-MAN MEETS THE FANTASTIC FOUR, AS
"the CHAMELEON STRIKES!"

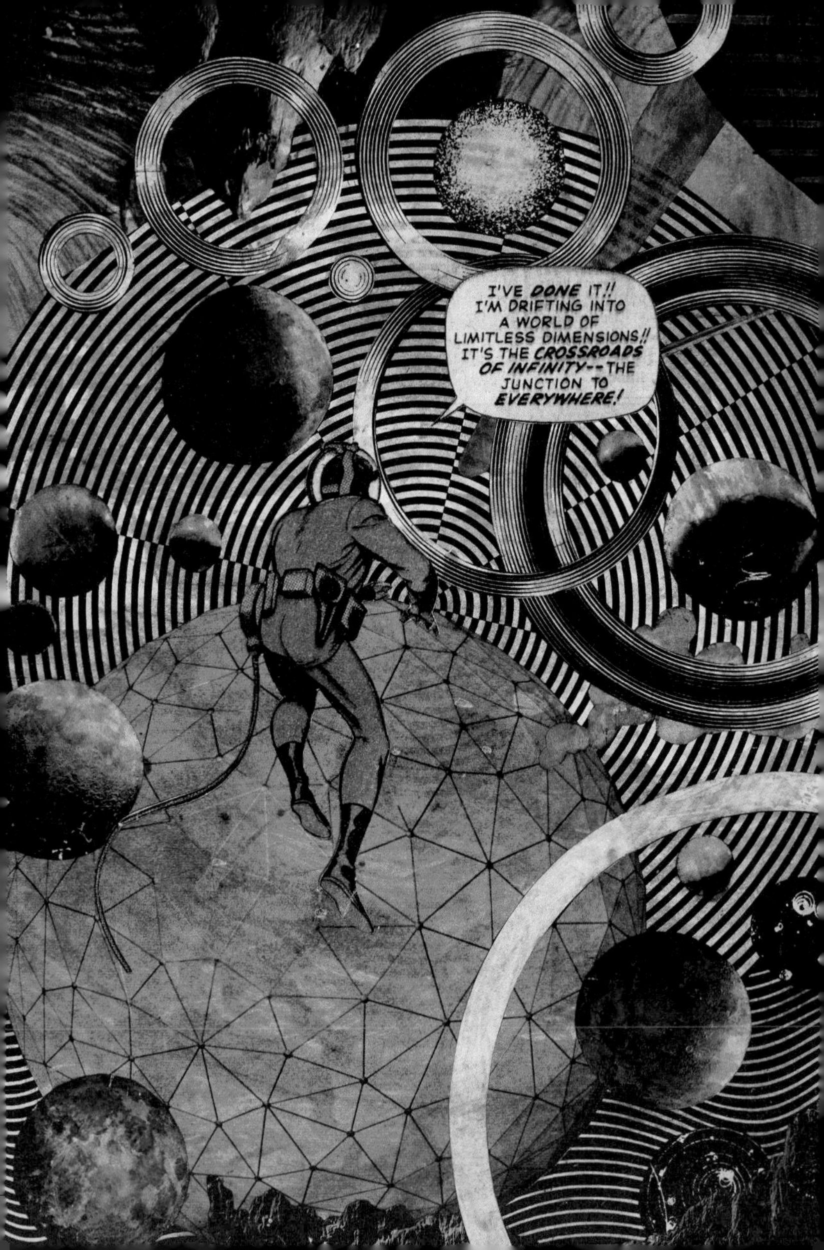
I'VE DONE IT!! I'M DRIFTING INTO A WORLD OF LIMITLESS DIMENSIONS!! IT'S THE CROSSROADS OF INFINITY--THE JUNCTION TO EVERYWHERE!

WAS IST SO GROSSARTIG AN
DEN FANTASTIC FOUR?

„Das größte Comic-Magazin der Welt!"

Ab der dritten Ausgabe stand jahrzehntelang dieser Satz über dem Titelschriftzug von *The Fantastic Four*. Und *FF*, wie Redakteur und Autor Stan Lee die Serie gerne nannte, hatte definitiv einen Anspruch auf diesen Thron.

Nun gut, 1967 mauserte sich *Amazing Spider-Man* zu Marvels bestverkaufter Serie ... in den 1990er-Jahren war es wiederum *X-Men*, das den Wandkrabbler von Platz 1 der Verkaufscharts verdrängte ... in den 2000er-Jahren wurde *Wolverine* extrem erfolgreich ... und seit 2012 lässt *The Avengers* – unterstützt durch weltweite Kinoerfolge – alle anderen Marvel-Comics hinter sich.

Doch keine dieser Serien hätte es überhaupt gegeben ohne den überraschenden, überwältigenden Erfolg von *Fantastic Four*.

Als die Fantastic Four im August 1961 über die Comic-Welt hereinbrachen, schlugen sie wie eine Bombe ein. Kinder, Jugendliche und junge Erwachsene mochten DCs Superheldenserien *Flash*, *Green Lantern* und *Justice League of America* – es waren erstklassige Konzepte. Doch die FF hatten irgendetwas ... Neues.

Sie waren ein Team wie die JLA – dennoch waren diese vier mit Superkräften begabten Menschen anders. Irgendwie waren sie *realer* als die bisherigen Comic-Helden. Manche Mitglieder der FF *hassten* sich sogar. Während die JLA Tugendhelden in bunten Kostümen waren, wirkten die FF wie eine zerstrittene Familie: Reed Richards (alias Mr. Fantastic) und Sue Storm (Invisible Girl) waren die unwilligen Elternfiguren, während Johnny Storm und Ben Grimm sich wie verfeindete Geschwister aufführten. Drei Sekunden nachdem sich Grimm in ein superstarkes, aber abgrundtief hässliches Thing verwandelt hatte, riss er einen Baum aus, um Richards damit zu erschlagen. Johnny, der sich in die Human Torch verwandelte, fackelte einen Wald ab.

Hinzu kam: Sie trugen nicht einmal Kostüme, sondern Pilotenanzüge. Und sie machten keine Anstalten, ihre wahren Identitäten vor der Welt geheim zu halten. Als man sie zu Unrecht eingesperrt hatte, bahnten sie sich mit Gewalt einen Weg nach draußen, und die Torch steckte ein staatliches Gefängnis in Brand.

Aber um ehrlich zu sein: Nicht jeder der Fantastic Four war gleich beliebt. Denn der Star der Serie war zweifellos das Thing. Etwas wie ihn hatte man in den Comics – oder sonst irgendwo – noch nie gesehen. Er war wie eine Mischung aus Frankensteins Monster und dem Farmarbeiter Lennie aus John Steinbecks Novelle *Von Mäusen und Menschen*.

Herausgeber Martin Goodman hatte Lee den Auftrag erteilt, ein Superheldenteam zu erschaffen, das DCs *Justice League* Konkurrenz machen konnte. Doch anstatt jene Helden zu kopieren, rief Lee seinen besten Künstler Jack Kirby zu sich. Gemeinsam nahmen sie das Konzept der Superheldencomics auseinander und setzten es neu zusammen. Die Superhelden sollten sich grundlegend verändern – nicht nur bei dem Verlag, der sich bald darauf Marvel Comics nannte, sondern auch bei allen anderen Comic-Verlagen!

Nun gut ... in Heft 3 beugte sich Lee den Leserwünschen und verpasste dem Team zwar keine Kostüme, aber immerhin eine Uniform. (Das Thing riss die seine sofort in Fetzen.) Davon abgesehen blieben sie die faszinierenden Sonderlinge, die sie von Anfang an gewesen waren.

Die Fantastic Four wurden bereits großartig geboren. Und sie konnten nur *noch* großartiger werden, denn sie hatten auch großartige Gegner: den Mole Man, eine fast mitleiderregende Kreatur in einer Zeit, als die meisten Schurken einfache Bankräuber waren ... den Sub-Mariner, einen Prinzen aus Atlantis ... den unvergleichlichen Dr. Doom ... die Frightful Four ... Galactus, der ganze Planeten verschlang ... und Widersacher wie die Inhumans, den Silver Surfer oder den Black Panther, die später selbst zu Helden mit eigenen Serien wurden.

Zuweilen kam es vor, dass andere Figuren Mitglieder der FF ersetzten: Crystal und Medusa von den Inhumans (die für die schwangere Sue Richards einsprangen), Power Man, She-Hulk, ein weibliches Thing und einige mehr. Doch das ursprüngliche Team kam immer wieder zusammen – und das war auch gut so.

Nach 1971 wurde die Serie nicht mehr von Lee und Kirby, sondern von anderen Autoren und Zeichnern produziert. Doch in ihrem Kern blieb sie immer das, was Credits in den 1960er-Jahren einmal verkündet hatten: „Eine titanische Koproduktion von Stan Lee und Jack Kirby!"

Im Lauf der Jahre eroberten die Fantastic Four das Fernsehen und die Welt der Videospiele und schafften es sogar auf die Kinoleinwand. Aber auch wenn sie nur in den Comics weitergelebt hätten, hätte dies nichts an ihrer Großartigkeit geändert. Denn mit ihnen begann eine Revolution, die noch immer fortwirkt und deren Spuren man bis heute in jedem Superheldencomic (egal, ob mit Solohelden oder Teams) finden kann.

Zumindest ein Jahrzehnt lang – viele würden sagen, noch viel länger – war *Fantastic Four* wohl tatsächlich das größte und großartigste Comic-Magazin der Welt!

– ROY THOMAS

BEYOND THE PALE

Page 10: *Original interior art, "This Man, This Monster!,"* Fantastic Four *No. 51; script, Stan Lee; pencils, Jack Kirby; inks, Joe Sinnott; June 1966.* Kirby's photo collages were part of his attempts to push the comics form — despite its inherent production limitations — as far beyond the norm as Marvel's cosmic storylines in *FF* and *Thor.* In this instance production man Sol Brodsky managed to incorporate color on the photographed image to good effect.

FANTASTIC FOUR No. 87

Page 14: *Interior, "The Power and the Pride!"; script, Stan Lee; pencils, Jack Kirby; inks, Joe Sinnott; June 1969.*

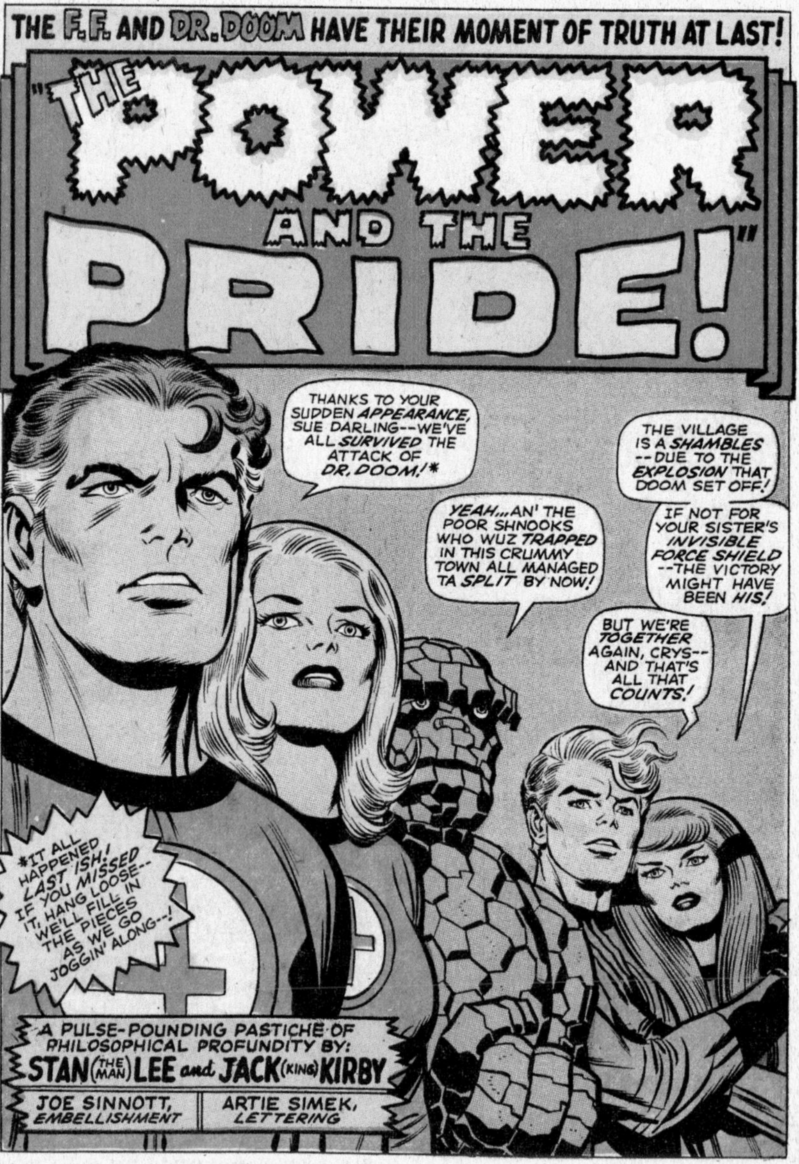
THE F.F. AND DR. DOOM HAVE THEIR MOMENT OF TRUTH AT LAST!
"THE POWER AND THE PRIDE!"
THANKS TO YOUR SUDDEN APPEARANCE, SUE DARLING--WE'VE ALL SURVIVED THE ATTACK OF DR. DOOM!*
YEAH...AN' THE POOR SHNOOKS WHO WUZ TRAPPED IN THIS CRUMMY TOWN ALL MANAGED TA SPLIT BY NOW!
THE VILLAGE IS A SHAMBLES --DUE TO THE EXPLOSION THAT DOOM SET OFF!
IF NOT FOR YOUR SISTER'S INVISIBLE FORCE SHIELD --THE VICTORY MIGHT HAVE BEEN HIS!
BUT WE'RE TOGETHER AGAIN, CRYS-- AND THAT'S ALL THAT COUNTS!
*IT ALL HAPPENED LAST ISH! IF YOU MISSED IT, HANG LOOSE-- WE'LL FILL IN THE PIECES AS WE GO JOGGIN' ALONG--!
A PULSE-POUNDING PASTICHE OF PHILOSOPHICAL PROFUNDITY BY: STAN (THE MAN) LEE and JACK (KING) KIRBY
JOE SINNOTT, EMBELLISHMENT
ARTIE SIMEK, LETTERING

MAIS QU'EST-CE QU'ILS ONT DE SI SPÉCIAL, FINALEMENT, CES QUATRE FANTASTIQUES ?

«Le meilleur magazine de BD au monde!» Pendant des dizaines d'années, et depuis son numéro 3, c'est ce que proclamait le slogan ajouté au logo de *Fantastic Four*. Et en effet *FF*, comme le surnommait Stan Lee, son rédacteur en chef et scénariste, n'était pas le moins crédible des postulants au titre suprême. Bien sûr, en 1967, la diffusion d'*Amazing Spider-Man* finira par dépasser celle de *Fantastic Four*, puis dans les années 1990, parmi les publications Marvel, *X-Men* délogera provisoirement le monte-en-l'air du sommet des ventes. Avant que *Wolverine* ne bénéficie à son tour de la ferveur populaire — pendant la décennie 2000 — et qu'à partir de 2012, boosté par les milliards de dollars de recettes glanés au cinéma par ses protagonistes, le magazine *The Avengers* ne mette tout le monde d'accord. Mais une chose est sûre : sans l'incroyable et phénoménal succès, en son temps, de *Fantastic Four*, aucune de ces réussites n'aurait pu avoir lieu.

Quand au mois d'août 1961, les Quatre Fantastiques font irruption sur la scène des comics, ils font l'effet d'une bombe atomique. Jusque-là les pré-ados, les teenagers et leurs jeunes aînés en manque de superhéros se fournissaient chez DC Comics : ça lisait *Flash*, *Green Lantern* et *Justice League of America*, excellents au demeurant. Avec l'arrivée des FF, le paysage change. Ces héros-ci forment une équipe, comme la JLA, mais leurs membres, évidemment dotés de superpouvoirs, d'un tout autre gabarit. En fait, ils sont simplement plus *réels* que les héros de BD qui les ont précédés. Déjà il y en a deux, dans le groupe, qui se détestent copieusement. Et là où les sociétaires de la Justice League faisaient plutôt figure de tranquilles notables qu'on aurait gratifiés de tenues chamarrées, les Quatre Fantastiques, eux, constituent une famille clairement dysfonctionnelle où Red Richards («Mr Fantastic») et Jane Storm («La Fille Invisible») incarnent à leur corps défendant le rôle des figures parentales tandis que Johnny Storm et Ben Grimm se conduisent en frères ennemis. Du reste, trois secondes après qu'il a été métamorphosé en une «Chose» surpuissante autant que repoussante dissimulée sous son apparence minérale, Grimm arrache un arbre et tente de s'en servir pour estourbir Richards... Changé en Torche Humaine, Johnny, lui, déclenche carrément un incendie de forêt. Pour couronner le tableau, les quatre petits nouveaux ne portent même pas de déguisement particulier, juste une combinaison de vol, pas plus qu'ils ne prennent la peine de cacher leur véritable identité au reste du monde. Arrêtés pour des crimes qu'ils n'ont pas commis, ils n'hésitent pas à se faire la belle grâce à la Torche qui met — naturellement — le feu à la prison.

Il faut néanmoins l'avouer : les Quatre Fantastiques ne sont pas tous nés égaux. La star du magazine, c'est la Chose. On n'a pratiquement jamais rien vu de tel, que ce soit en bande dessinée ou ailleurs, avant cette personnalité qui tient à demi du monstre de Frankenstein, à demi du Lennie de John Steinbeck dans son roman *Des souris et des hommes*. Au départ, c'est l'éditeur Martin Goodman qui avait exigé de Lee la création d'un groupe de superhéros à même de concurrencer la Ligue des Justiciers de DC. Au lieu de copier la concurrence, Lee s'est adjoint le concours de son dessinateur n°1, Jack Kirby, et ensemble ils ont entrepris de déconstruire le concept même d'équipe super-héroïque pour le reconstituer à neuf. À dater de ce jour, toute la dynamique du genre en fut à jamais transformée, non seulement au sein de la maison bientôt rebaptisée Marvel Comics mais aussi chez tous les éditeurs de comics. Certes, à partir du numéro 3, Lee cédera aux requêtes répétées de ses lecteurs et offrira aux héros sinon de vrais costumes, au moins des uniformes (la Chose réduira aussitôt le sien en lambeaux). À cette nuance près, ils resteront les marginaux fasci-nants qu'ils étaient à l'origine.

Car les Quatre Fantastiques sont *nés* exceptionnels. Et qui plus est, l'excellence leur fut aussi imposée, en quelque sorte, puisqu'ils avaient justement face à eux des adversaires d'exception. On citera par exemple l'Homme-Taupe, un méchant pas si antipathique que cela à une époque où la plupart des supercrapules ressemblaient généralement à de banals braqueurs de banques. Ou Submariner, le prince des abysses… Et l'incomparable Docteur Fatalis… Sans oublier les Terrifics… Puis Galactus, le destructeur de planètes… Les Inhumains… Le Surfer d'Argent… La Panthère Noire… Tous, rapidement, ont évolué vers un statut leur garantissant une série rien qu'à eux.

À l'occasion, de nouveaux personnages remplaceront temporairement l'un ou l'autre des Quatre Fantastiques ; ce sera le cas de Crystal et Médusa, issues des Inhumains — et venues relayer Jane Richards enceinte —, de Power Man, de Miss Hulk, de Miss Chose (si, si), pour ne citer qu'eux. Toujours, cependant, la formation originelle se retrouvera *in fine* réunie, comme il se doit. En dehors de Lee et Kirby, d'autres noms prendront les FF en charge après 1971, sans que jamais la qualité de leur travail ne remette en question la mention de fin qui signalait dix ans plus tôt « une production de la génératrice Stan Lee/ Jack Kirby »…

Avec les années, les Quatre Fantastiques ont conquis la télévision, le jeu vidéo et jusqu'au grand écran. Mais même s'ils n'avaient pas bougé de leurs pages dessinées, leur grandeur n'en aurait pas moins été assurée : la révolution qu'ils ont lancée continue à se déployer aujourd'hui et son écho résonne chez chaque superhéros arrivé après eux, en solo ou en groupe.

C'est un fait : pendant au moins dix ans, et bien plus longtemps encore dans la mémoire de ses nombreux lecteurs, *Fantastic Four* a vraisemblablement été « le meilleur magazine de BD au monde ».

— ROY THOMAS

FANTASTIC FOUR No. 1

Pages 18–19: *Interior, "The Fantastic Four"; script, Stan Lee; pencils, Jack Kirby; inks, attributed George Klein; November 1961.* With the Cold War space race starting to heat up at the close of the Atlas era, Reed Richards leads a crew of four to beat the Russians into space.

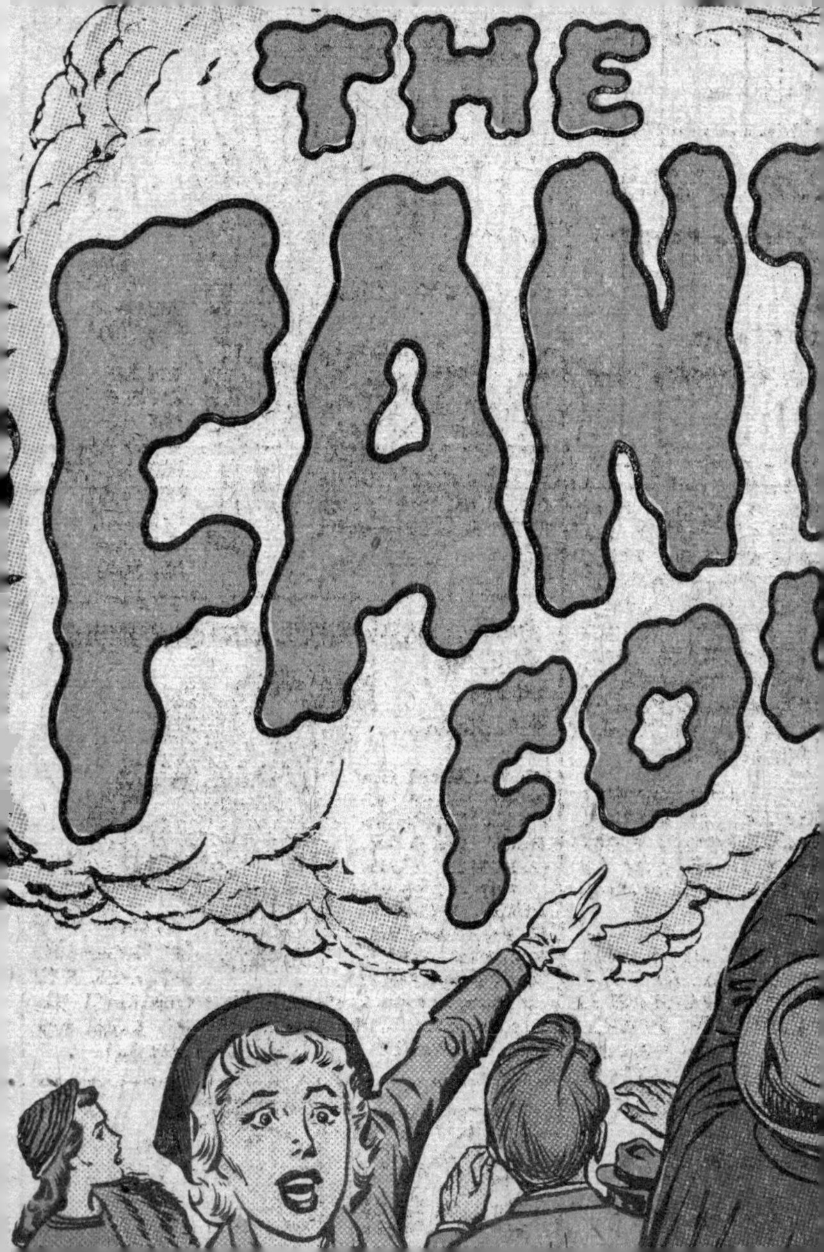
THE

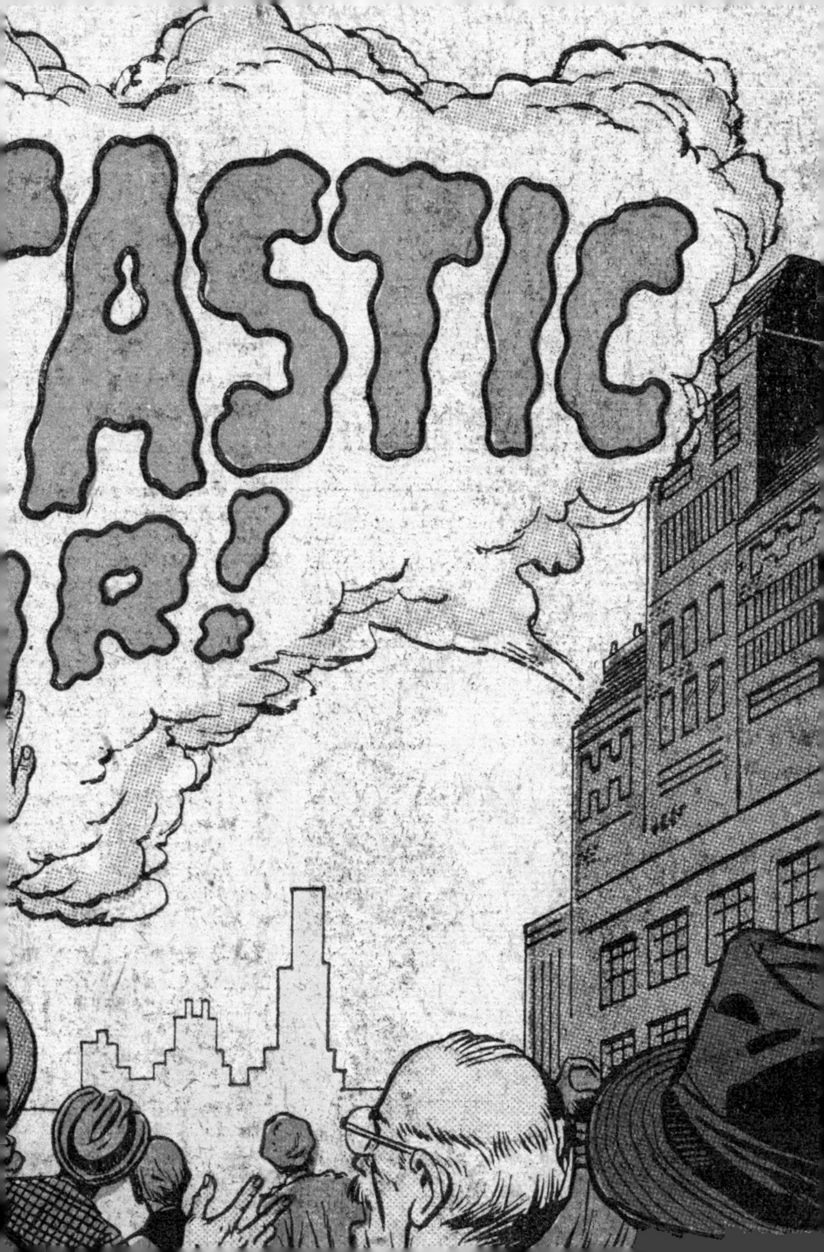
ASTIC
R!

SPACE-AGE HEROES

Above: *Photograph; Mercury astronauts Virgil Grissom, John Glenn, and Alan Shepard; 1960.* Manned spaceflights started in April of 1961, and astronauts were heroes for many at the dawn of the optimistic Kennedy era.

FANTASTIC FOUR No. 1

Opposite: *Interior, "The Fantastic Four"; script, Stan Lee; pencils, Jack Kirby; inks, attributed George Klein; November 1961.* Where once they were the quiet and reclusive warriors of two World Wars, America's heroes were changing in the early 1960s. The country looked now to a youthful president and its anointed space travelers—and Lee and Kirby used this new template to present their own vision for the future.

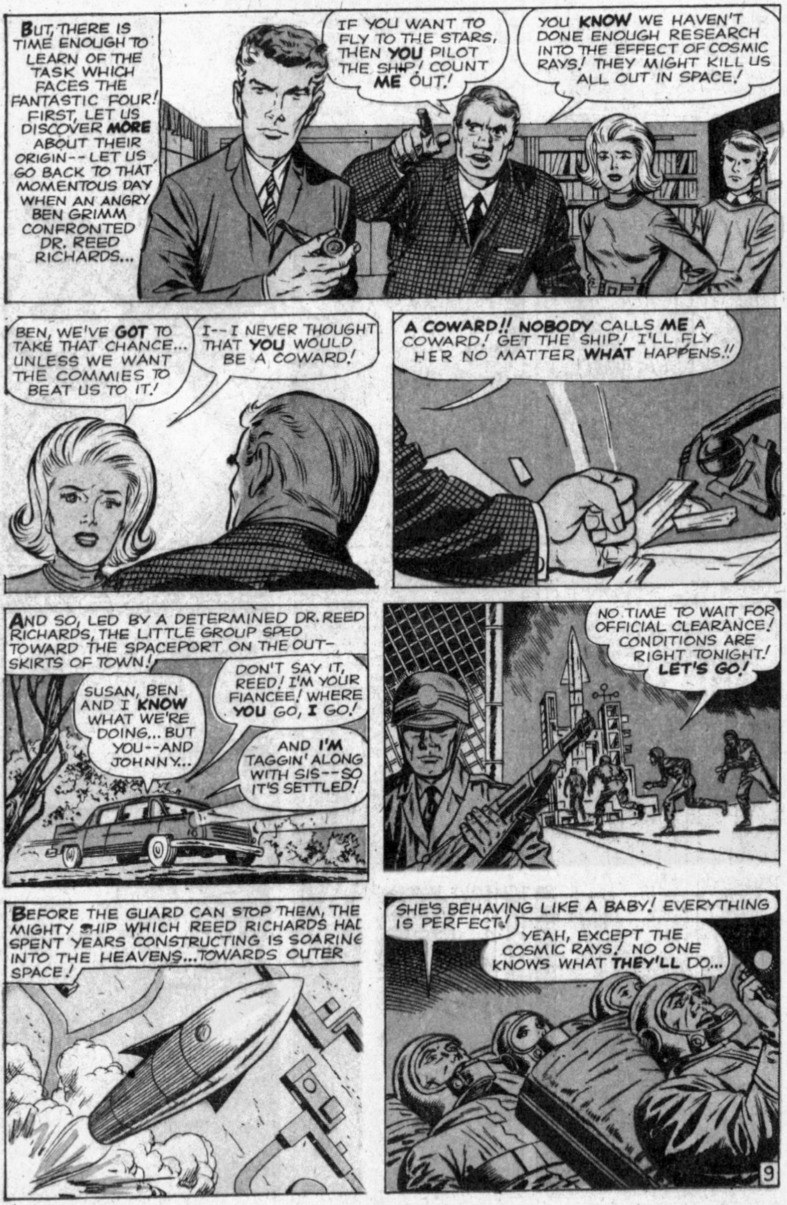

BUT, THERE IS TIME ENOUGH TO LEARN OF THE TASK WHICH FACES THE FANTASTIC FOUR! FIRST, LET US DISCOVER MORE ABOUT THEIR ORIGIN--LET US GO BACK TO THAT MOMENTOUS DAY WHEN AN ANGRY BEN GRIMM CONFRONTED DR. REED RICHARDS...
IF YOU WANT TO FLY TO THE STARS, THEN YOU PILOT THE SHIP! COUNT ME OUT!
YOU KNOW WE HAVEN'T DONE ENOUGH RESEARCH INTO THE EFFECT OF COSMIC RAYS! THEY MIGHT KILL US ALL OUT IN SPACE!
BEN, WE'VE GOT TO TAKE THAT CHANCE... UNLESS WE WANT THE COMMIES TO BEAT US TO IT!
I--I NEVER THOUGHT THAT YOU WOULD BE A COWARD!
A COWARD!! NOBODY CALLS ME A COWARD! GET THE SHIP! I'LL FLY HER NO MATTER WHAT HAPPENS!!
AND SO, LED BY A DETERMINED DR. REED RICHARDS, THE LITTLE GROUP SPED TOWARD THE SPACEPORT ON THE OUT-SKIRTS OF TOWN!
SUSAN, BEN AND I KNOW WHAT WE'RE DOING... BUT YOU--AND JOHNNY...
DON'T SAY IT, REED! I'M YOUR FIANCEE! WHERE YOU GO, I GO!
AND I'M TAGGIN' ALONG WITH SIS--SO IT'S SETTLED!
NO TIME TO WAIT FOR OFFICIAL CLEARANCE! CONDITIONS ARE RIGHT TONIGHT! LET'S GO!
BEFORE THE GUARD CAN STOP THEM, THE MIGHTY SHIP WHICH REED RICHARDS HAD SPENT YEARS CONSTRUCTING IS SOARING INTO THE HEAVENS...TOWARDS OUTER SPACE!
SHE'S BEHAVING LIKE A BABY! EVERYTHING IS PERFECT!
YEAH, EXCEPT THE COSMIC RAYS! NO ONE KNOWS WHAT THEY'LL DO...

They think Reed Richards, the pilot, is unaffected by cosmic rays, as he seems normal--
UNTIL he tries to reach for something. Then they realize his arm has STRETCHED toward the
thing he reached for. After awhile they realize Reed's body has become like RUBBER. He
can get skinny, elongated, anything that you can do with rubber. He can squeeze thru key-
holes, etc. Of course, the more stretched-out he gets, the weaker he gets-- but the point
remains that he can twist and stretch his body into almost any shape. (He can even alter
the appearance of his face to make himself look like someone else) BUT it is quite pain-
ful to do all this, so he can only maintain the strange shapes for a very short period of
time until the pain gets to be unbearable.

Finally, Ben Grimm steps out of the shadows. They all gasp-- his body has changed in the
most grotesque way of all. He's sort of shapeless-- he's become a THING. And, he's grown
more fantastically powerful than any other living thing. He is stronger than an elephant.
BUT, he is so heavy that he moves very slowly-- he's very ponderous, and those slow, ponderous movements should make him look very dramatic. He cannot alter his appearance as the
others can, so he must wear a coat with turned-up collar, sunglasses, slouch hat, and glove
when he goes out in public. But when he takes 'em off, he is a THING!

So much for who they are and how they got that way. Now, here's a gimmick I think we might
play up to advantage! Let's make The Thing the heavy- in other words, he's not really a
good guy. He's part of the Fantastic Four because they all got that way together and
they decide to remain a team, and also because he has a crush on Susan-- but actually, he
is jealous of Mr. Fantastic and dislikes Human Torch because Torch always sides with
Fantastic. Let's treat him so that reader is always afraid he will sabotage the
Fantastic Four's efforts at whatever they are doing-- he isn't interested in helping mankind the way the other three are-- he is more interested in winning Susan away from Mr.
Mr. Fantastic. (We might indicate that he feels he may return to his normal self at any
time, because none of them know how long their strange powers will last- or whether or
the effect of the cosmic rays will one day-wear off them).

Anyway, the four of them decide to form a unit-- they think it is an act of Fate
which made them as they are and they think they owe it to fate to use their powers to
help mankind. So they adopt their new names: HUMAN TORCH, MR. FANTASTIC, INVISIBLE GIRL,
and THE THING, and vow to spend their lives fighting all sorts of evil menaces which the
normal forces of the world cannot cope with. And, to keep it all from getting too goody-
goody, there is always friction between Mr. Fantastic and The Thing, with Human Torch
siding with Mr. F. Also, the other three are always afraid of The Thing getting out of
their control some day and harming mankind with his amazing strength. Occasionally also,
you might have the Thing wanting to do something for personal profit- and the other 3 try
to stop him. In other words, the Thing doesn't have the ethics that the other three have,
and consequently he will probably be the most interesting one to the reader, because he'll
always be unpredictable.

So much for the introduction--- the preceding should have covered exactly 11 pages,
consisting of 2 chapters. (Chapter one: 6 pages. Chapter 2: 5 pages)

The next two chapters, in which the Fantastic Four undertakes their first case, will also
be ten chapters for a total of 10 pages-- 5 pages to each chapter. (3,5,5.)
3   13

AND THEN THERE WERE FOUR

Above: *Fantastic Four synopsis, Stan Lee, 1961.* "We are trying,
(perhaps vainly?)," Lee wrote shortly after the issue hit newsstands, "to reach a slightly older, more sophisticated group."
Lee's treatment for the first Fantastic Four story focused on
character development rather than dialogue — that would be
added after Jack Kirby penciled the pages.

FANTASTIC FOUR No. 1

Opposite: *Interior, "The Fantastic Four"; script, Stan Lee; pencils,
Jack Kirby; inks, attributed George Klein; November 1961.*

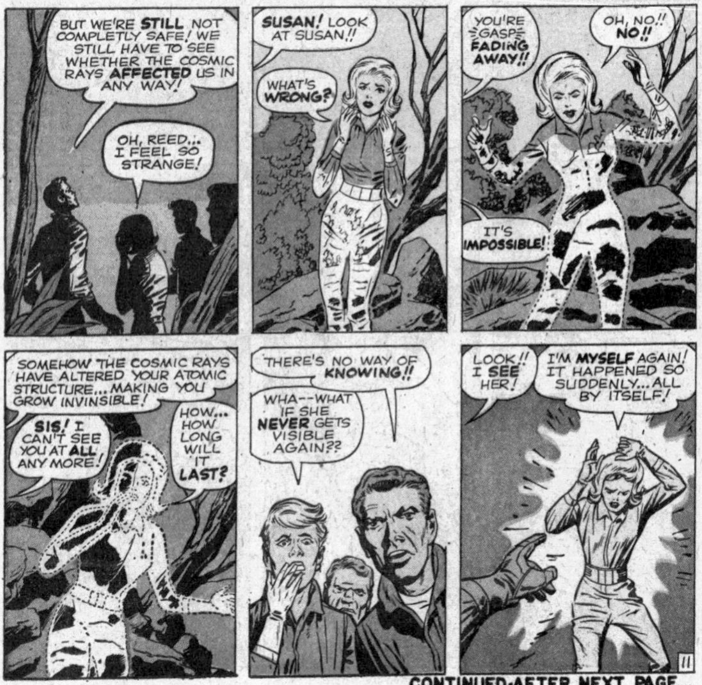
BUT WE'RE STILL NOT COMPLETLY SAFE! WE STILL HAVE TO SEE WHETHER THE COSMIC RAYS AFFECTED US IN ANY WAY!
OH, REED... I FEEL SO STRANGE!
SUSAN! LOOK AT SUSAN!!
WHAT'S WRONG?
YOU'RE -GASP- FADING AWAY!!
OH, NO!! NO!!
IT'S IMPOSSIBLE!
SOMEHOW THE COSMIC RAYS HAVE ALTERED YOUR ATOMIC STRUCTURE... MAKING YOU GROW INVINSIBLE!
SIS! I CAN'T SEE YOU AT ALL ANY MORE!
HOW... HOW LONG WILL IT LAST?
THERE'S NO WAY OF KNOWING!!
WHA--WHAT IF SHE NEVER GETS VISIBLE AGAIN??
LOOK!! I SEE HER!
I'M MYSELF AGAIN! IT HAPPENED SO SUDDENLY... ALL BY ITSELF!
11

CONTINUED AFTER NEXT PAGE...

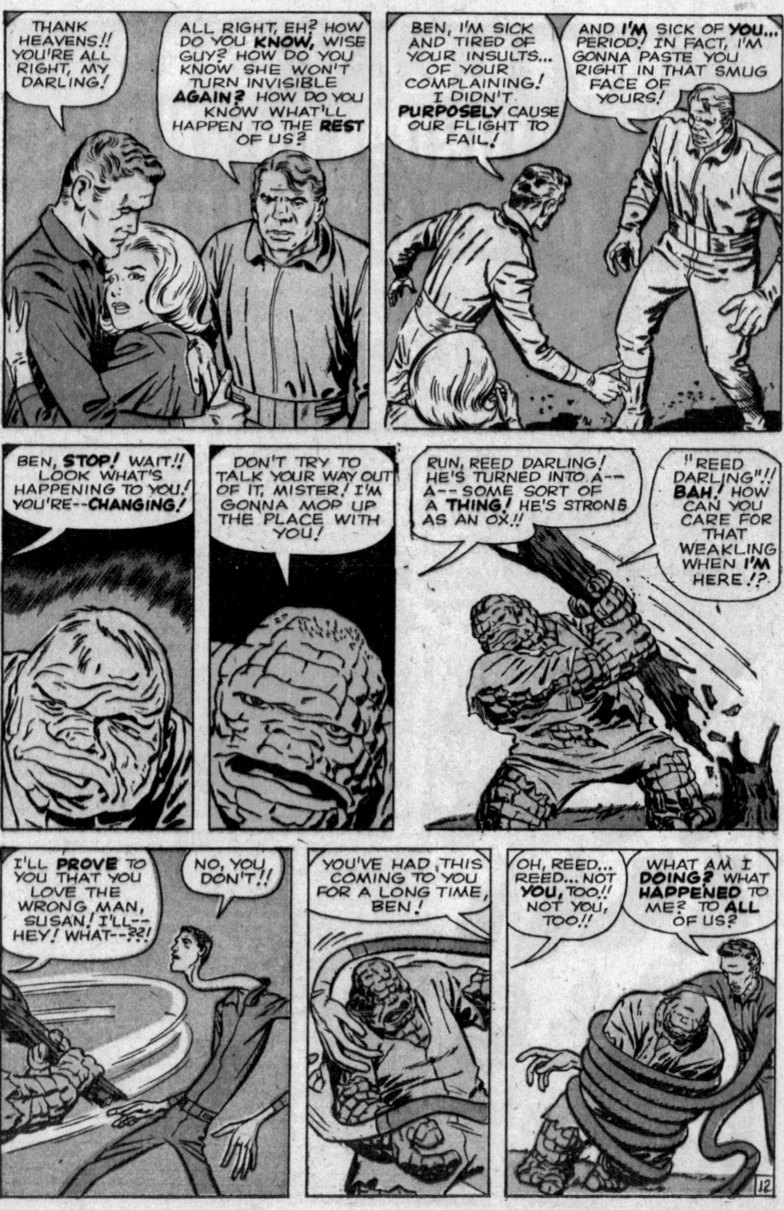
THANK HEAVENS!! YOU'RE ALL RIGHT, MY DARLING!
ALL RIGHT, EH? HOW DO YOU KNOW, WISE GUY? HOW DO YOU KNOW SHE WON'T TURN INVISIBLE AGAIN? HOW DO YOU KNOW WHAT'LL HAPPEN TO THE REST OF US?
BEN, I'M SICK AND TIRED OF YOUR INSULTS... OF YOUR COMPLAINING! I DIDN'T PURPOSELY CAUSE OUR FLIGHT TO FAIL!
AND I'M SICK OF YOU... PERIOD! IN FACT, I'M GONNA PASTE YOU RIGHT IN THAT SMUG FACE OF YOURS!
BEN, STOP! WAIT!! LOOK WHAT'S HAPPENING TO YOU! YOU'RE--CHANGING!
DON'T TRY TO TALK YOUR WAY OUT OF IT, MISTER! I'M GONNA MOP UP THE PLACE WITH YOU!
RUN, REED DARLING! HE'S TURNED INTO A-- A-- SOME SORT OF A THING! HE'S STRONG AS AN OX!!
"REED DARLING"!! BAH! HOW CAN YOU CARE FOR THAT WEAKLING WHEN I'M HERE!?
I'LL PROVE TO YOU THAT YOU LOVE THE WRONG MAN, SUSAN! I'LL-- HEY! WHAT--??!
NO, YOU DON'T!!
YOU'VE HAD THIS COMING TO YOU FOR A LONG TIME, BEN!
OH, REED... REED... NOT YOU, TOO!! NOT YOU, TOO!!
WHAT AM I DOING? WHAT HAPPENED TO ME? TO ALL OF US?
12

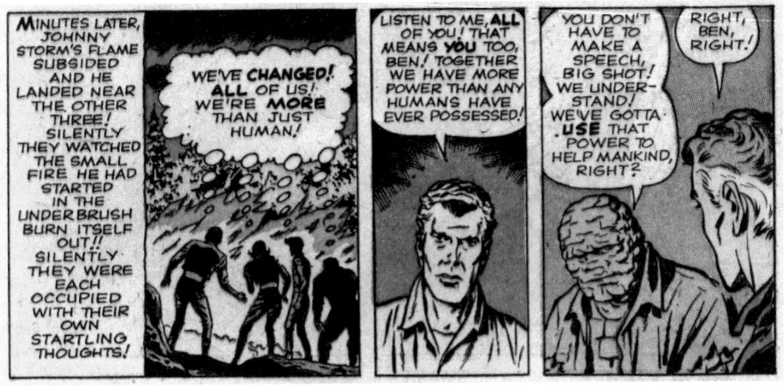
MINUTES LATER, JOHNNY STORM'S FLAME SUBSIDED AND HE LANDED NEAR THE OTHER THREE! SILENTLY THEY WATCHED THE SMALL FIRE HE HAD STARTED IN THE UNDERBRUSH BURN ITSELF OUT!! SILENTLY THEY WERE EACH OCCUPIED WITH THEIR OWN STARTLING THOUGHTS!
WE'VE CHANGED! ALL OF US! WE'RE MORE THAN JUST HUMAN!
LISTEN TO ME, ALL OF YOU! THAT MEANS YOU TOO, BEN! TOGETHER WE HAVE MORE POWER THAN ANY HUMANS HAVE EVER POSSESSED!
YOU DON'T HAVE TO MAKE A SPEECH, BIG SHOT! WE UNDERSTAND! WE'VE GOTTA USE THAT POWER TO HELP MANKIND, RIGHT?
RIGHT, BEN, RIGHT!

FANTASTIC FOUR No. 1

Opposite and above: *Interiors, "The Fantastic Four"; script, Stan Lee; pencils, Jack Kirby; inks, attributed George Klein; November 1961.* A storm bombards the four with cosmic rays, giving them super powers. The brilliant Richards gains the power to stretch his body, and takes the name Mr. Fantastic; Susan Storm gains the power to disappear, becoming the Invisible Girl; Sue's teenage brother Johnny can become a Human Torch at will (reminiscent of the 1940s character); and Ben Grimm, the pilot and Reed's brash, outspoken college buddy, transforms into a super-strong, orange monster, appropriately named the Thing.

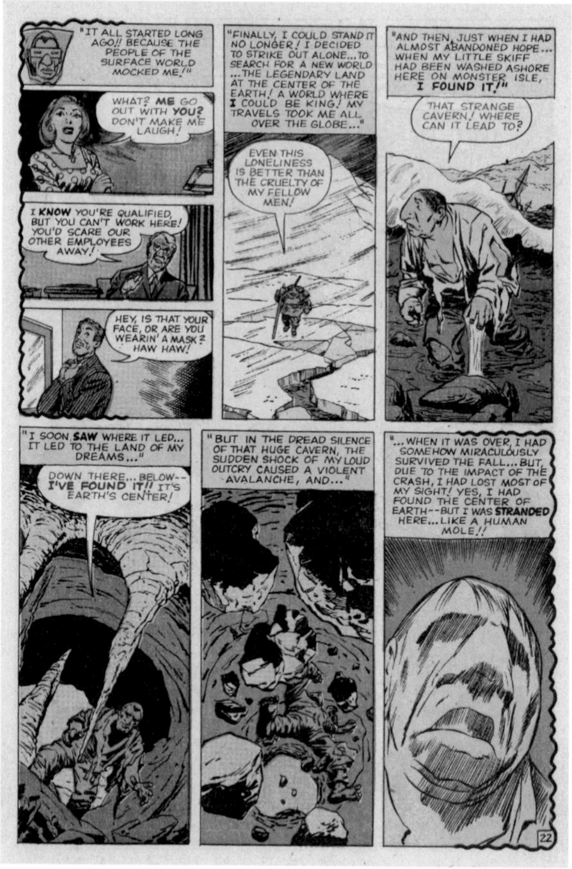
"IT ALL STARTED LONG AGO!! BECAUSE THE PEOPLE OF THE SURFACE WORLD MOCKED ME!"
WHAT? ME GO OUT WITH YOU? DON'T MAKE ME LAUGH!
I KNOW YOU'RE QUALIFIED, BUT YOU CAN'T WORK HERE! YOU'D SCARE OUR OTHER EMPLOYEES AWAY!
HEY, IS THAT YOUR FACE, OR ARE YOU WEARIN' A MASK? HAW HAW!
"FINALLY, I COULD STAND IT NO LONGER! I DECIDED TO STRIKE OUT ALONE...TO SEARCH FOR A NEW WORLD ...THE LEGENDARY LAND AT THE CENTER OF THE EARTH! A WORLD WHERE I COULD BE KING! MY TRAVELS TOOK ME ALL OVER THE GLOBE..."
EVEN THIS LONELINESS IS BETTER THAN THE CRUELTY OF MY FELLOW MEN!
"AND THEN, JUST WHEN I HAD ALMOST ABANDONED HOPE... WHEN MY LITTLE SKIFF HAD BEEN WASHED ASHORE HERE ON MONSTER ISLE, I FOUND IT!"
THAT STRANGE CAVERN! WHERE CAN IT LEAD TO?
"I SOON SAW WHERE IT LED... IT LED TO THE LAND OF MY DREAMS..."
DOWN THERE... BELOW-- I'VE FOUND IT!! IT'S EARTH'S CENTER!
"BUT IN THE DREAD SILENCE OF THAT HUGE CAVERN, THE SUDDEN SHOCK OF MY LOUD OUTCRY CAUSED A VIOLENT AVALANCHE, AND..."
"...WHEN IT WAS OVER, I HAD SOMEHOW MIRACULOUSLY SURVIVED THE FALL... BUT, DUE TO THE IMPACT OF THE CRASH, I HAD LOST MOST OF MY SIGHT! YES, I HAD FOUND THE CENTER OF EARTH--BUT I WAS STRANDED HERE... LIKE A HUMAN MOLE!!"
22

FANTASTIC FOUR No. 1

Above and opposite: *Interiors, "The Fantastic Four"; script, Stan Lee; pencils, Jack Kirby; inks, attributed George Klein; November 1961.* As Lee and Kirby begin developing their characters, the depraved, pathetic Mole Man becomes rather sympathetic. He would not be the last Marvel character to suffer as a result of his looks.

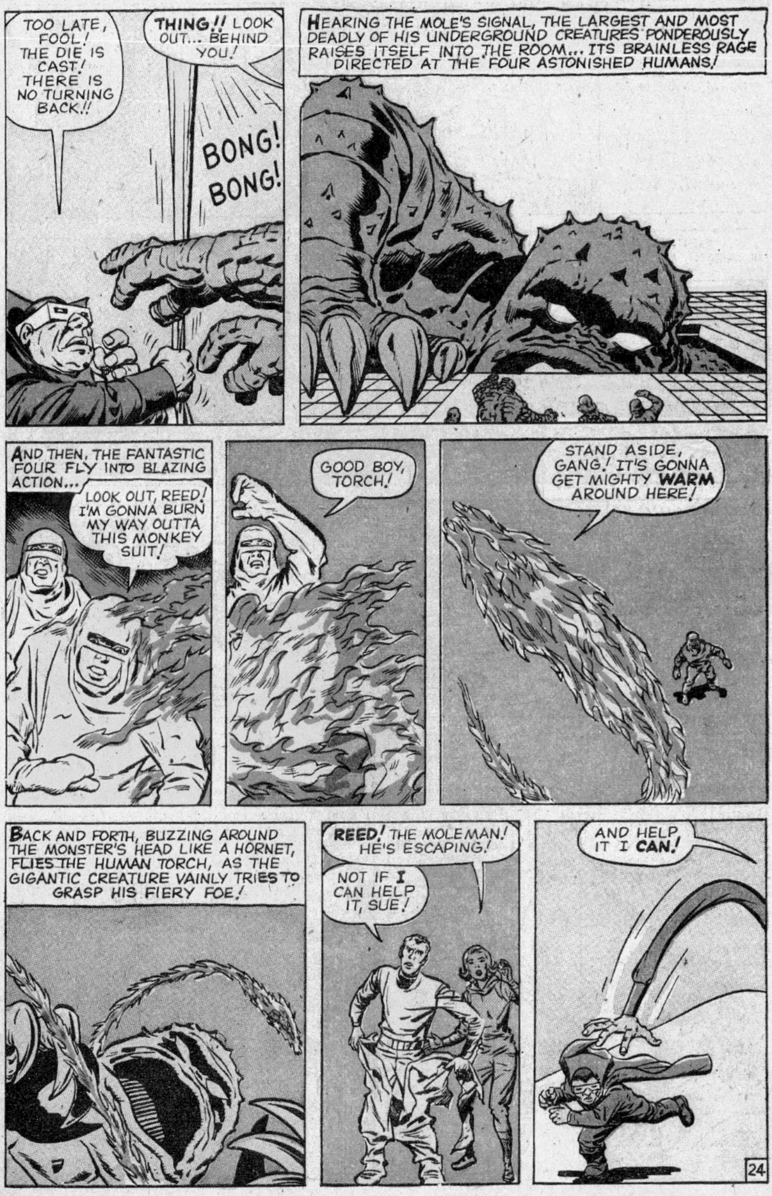

TOO LATE, FOOL! THE DIE IS CAST! THERE IS NO TURNING BACK.!!
THING!! LOOK OUT... BEHIND YOU!
BONG! BONG!
HEARING THE MOLE'S SIGNAL, THE LARGEST AND MOST DEADLY OF HIS UNDERGROUND CREATURES PONDEROUSLY RAISES ITSELF INTO THE ROOM... ITS BRAINLESS RAGE DIRECTED AT THE FOUR ASTONISHED HUMANS!
AND THEN, THE FANTASTIC FOUR FLY INTO BLAZING ACTION...
LOOK OUT, REED! I'M GONNA BURN MY WAY OUTTA THIS MONKEY SUIT!
GOOD BOY, TORCH!
STAND ASIDE, GANG! IT'S GONNA GET MIGHTY WARM AROUND HERE!
BACK AND FORTH, BUZZING AROUND THE MONSTER'S HEAD LIKE A HORNET, FLIES THE HUMAN TORCH, AS THE GIGANTIC CREATURE VAINLY TRIES TO GRASP HIS FIERY FOE!
REED! THE MOLEMAN! HE'S ESCAPING!
NOT IF I CAN HELP IT, SUE!
AND HELP IT I CAN!
24

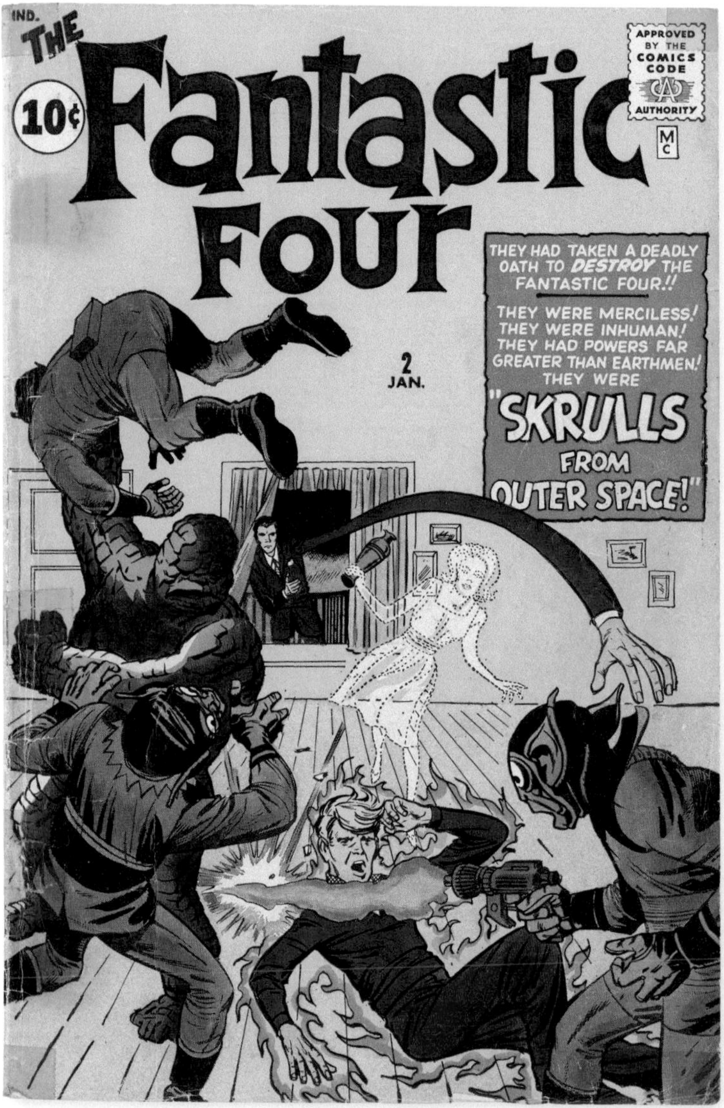
IND.
THE
Fantastic Four
10¢
APPROVED BY THE COMICS CODE AUTHORITY
MC
2
JAN.
THEY HAD TAKEN A DEADLY OATH TO DESTROY THE FANTASTIC FOUR!!
THEY WERE MERCILESS! THEY WERE INHUMAN! THEY HAD POWERS FAR GREATER THAN EARTHMEN! THEY WERE
"SKRULLS FROM OUTER SPACE!"

FANTASTIC FOUR No. 2

Opposite: *Cover; pencils, Jack Kirby; inks, George Klein; January 1962.* This issue inaugurates a successful Marvel convention—the villains impersonate the heroes. Chameleon doubles Spider-Man in his second appearance, the Space Phantom imitates everyone and everything in *The Avengers* No. 2, and the Wizard copies the Human Torch to nefarious effect in *Strange Tales* No. 102.

FANTASTIC FOUR No. 2

Below: *Interior, "The Fantastic Four Meet the Skrulls from Outer Space!"; script, Stan Lee; pencils, Jack Kirby; inks, George Klein; January 1962.* A Skrull impersonating Reed Richards resumes his original shape.

AS FOR ME, I NEEDED NO SPECIAL DEVICES! FOR IT'S AN EASY MATTER FOR ME TO ALTER MY BODY IN ANY WAY I DESIRE!
JUST AS IT IS EASY FOR ALL OF US TO DO SO!
WHICH IS WHY THE UNSUSPECTING EARTHMEN WILL NEVER KNOW THAT WE SKRULLS HAVE IMPERSONATED THEIR FAMOUS FANTASTIC FOUR!

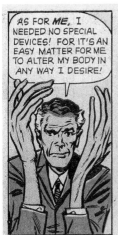

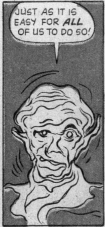

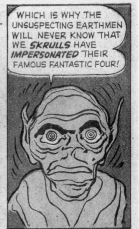

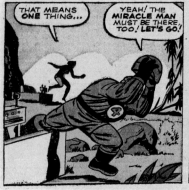

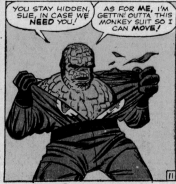

THAT MEANS ONE THING...
YEAH! THE MIRACLE MAN MUST BE THERE, TOO! LET'S GO!
YOU STAY HIDDEN, SUE, IN CASE WE NEED YOU!
AS FOR ME, I'M GETTIN' OUTTA THIS MONKEY SUIT SO I CAN MOVE!
11

FANTASTIC FOUR No. 3

Above: *Interior, "The Menace of the Miracle Man!"; script, Stan Lee; pencils, Jack Kirby; inks, Sol Brodsky; March 1962.* Continuing to break the mold of formulaic super heroes, the Fantastic Four did not have costumes in the first two issues. But fans wrote in insisting on them. However, the Thing's distinctive appearance would be covered up by a costume, so he (and Lee and Kirby) soon settled for a pair of shorts instead.

FANTASTIC FOUR No. 3

Opposite: *Cover; pencils, Jack Kirby; inks, Sol Brodsky; March 1962.* From the beginning the FF were different. Usually, super heroes gained their powers and costumes in their very first story. Meanwhile, Reed Richards, perhaps aware that his team would move to New York from Central City in the next issue, invented the Fantasti-car—the only way to get around New York in a hurry!

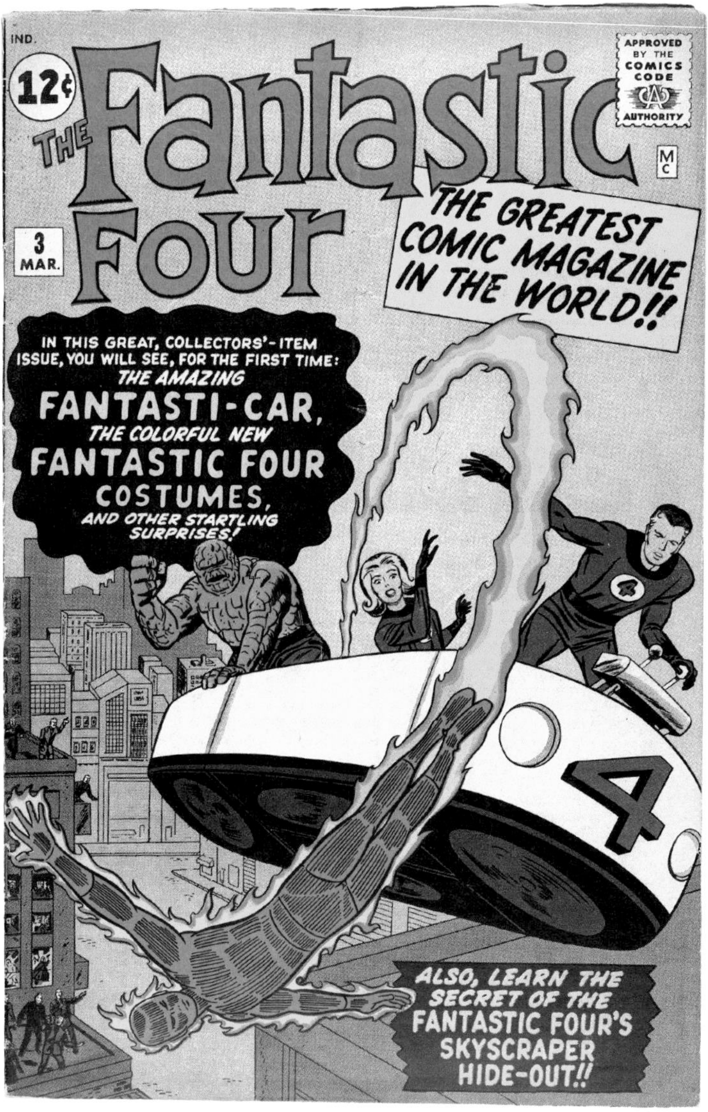
IND.
12¢
The Fantastic Four
3
MAR.
APPROVED BY THE COMICS CODE AUTHORITY
MC
THE GREATEST COMIC MAGAZINE IN THE WORLD!!
IN THIS GREAT, COLLECTORS'-ITEM ISSUE, YOU WILL SEE, FOR THE FIRST TIME: THE AMAZING FANTASTI-CAR, THE COLORFUL NEW FANTASTIC FOUR COSTUMES, AND OTHER STARTLING SURPRISES!
4
ALSO, LEARN THE SECRET OF THE FANTASTIC FOUR'S SKYSCRAPER HIDE-OUT!!

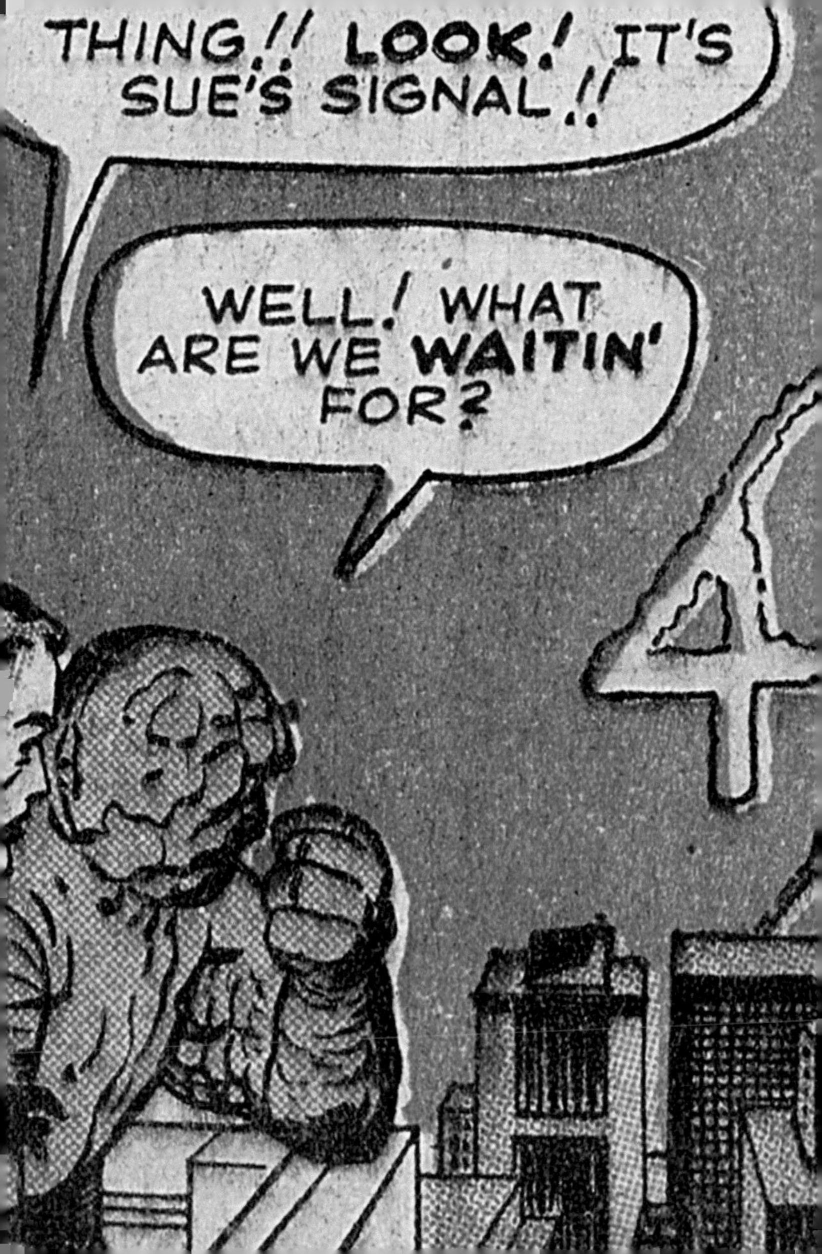
THING!! LOOK! IT'S SUE'S SIGNAL!!
WELL! WHAT ARE WE WAITIN' FOR?

FANTASTIC FOUR No. 3

Opposite and below: *Interiors, "The Menace of the Miracle Man!"; script, Stan Lee; pencils, Jack Kirby; inks, Sol Brodsky; March 1962.* The "4" symbol, a simple and iconic design by Kirby and Lee, has weathered the decades far better than the costumes that debuted in this issue. The pair had also planned on giving the FF masks, but changed their minds before the final art was published. It proved a wise decision, further differentiating the FF from the usual masked heroes who hid their identities.

FANTASTIC FOUR No. 14

Pages 34–35: *Interior, "The Sub-Mariner Strikes!"; script, Stan Lee; pencils, Jack Kirby; inks, Dick Ayers; May 1963.* Comic book artists were cinematographers, choreographers, and directors all wrapped in one. Overhead shots displayed the influence of the movie screen on avid filmgoer Jack Kirby.

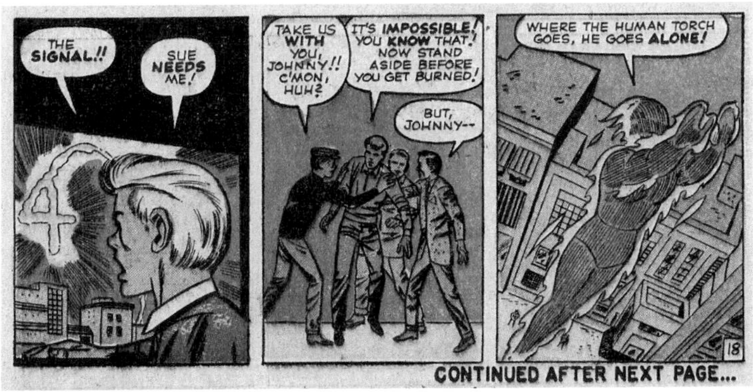
THE SIGNAL.!!
SUE NEEDS ME.!
TAKE US WITH YOU, JOHNNY!! C'MON, HUH?
IT'S IMPOSSIBLE! YOU KNOW THAT! NOW STAND ASIDE BEFORE YOU GET BURNED!
BUT, JOHNNY--
WHERE THE HUMAN TORCH GOES, HE GOES ALONE!
18
CONTINUED AFTER NEXT PAGE...

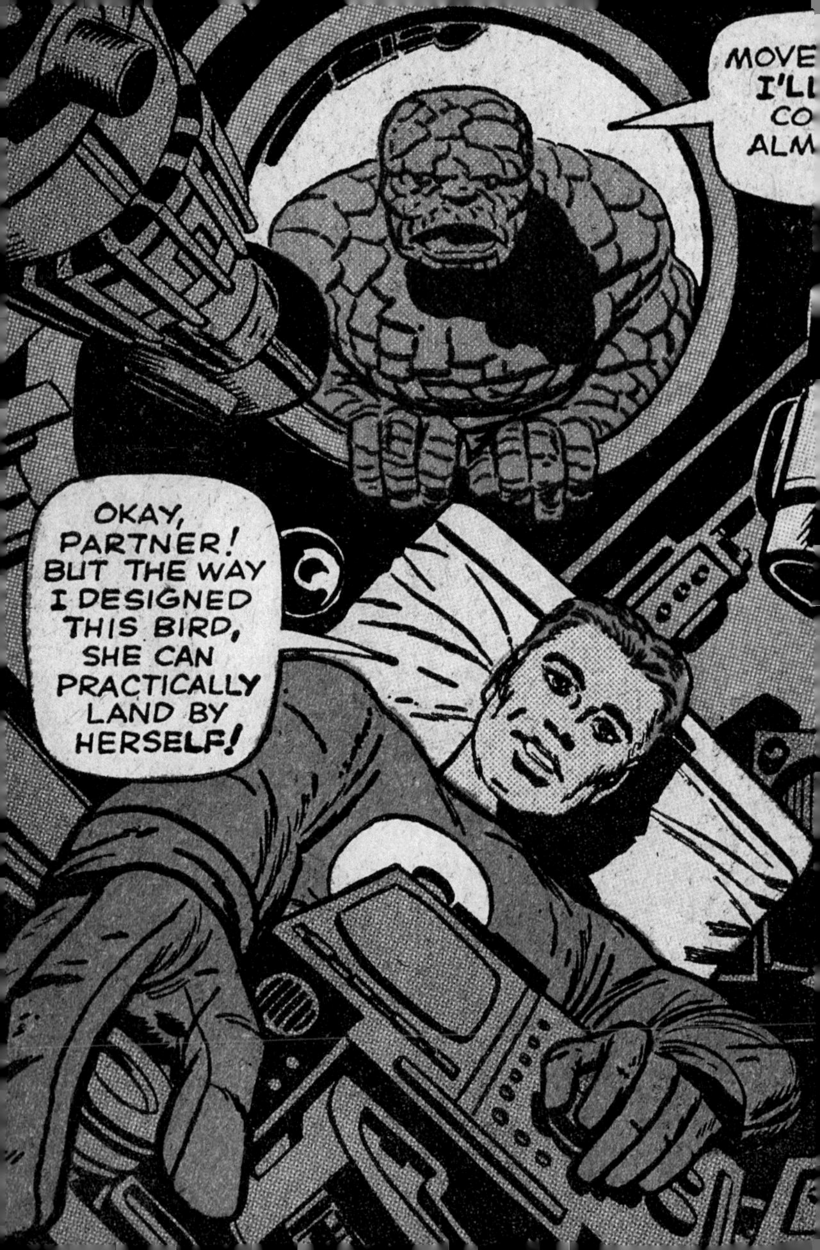
OKAY, PARTNER! BUT THE WAY I DESIGNED THIS BIRD, SHE CAN PRACTICALLY LAND BY HERSELF!

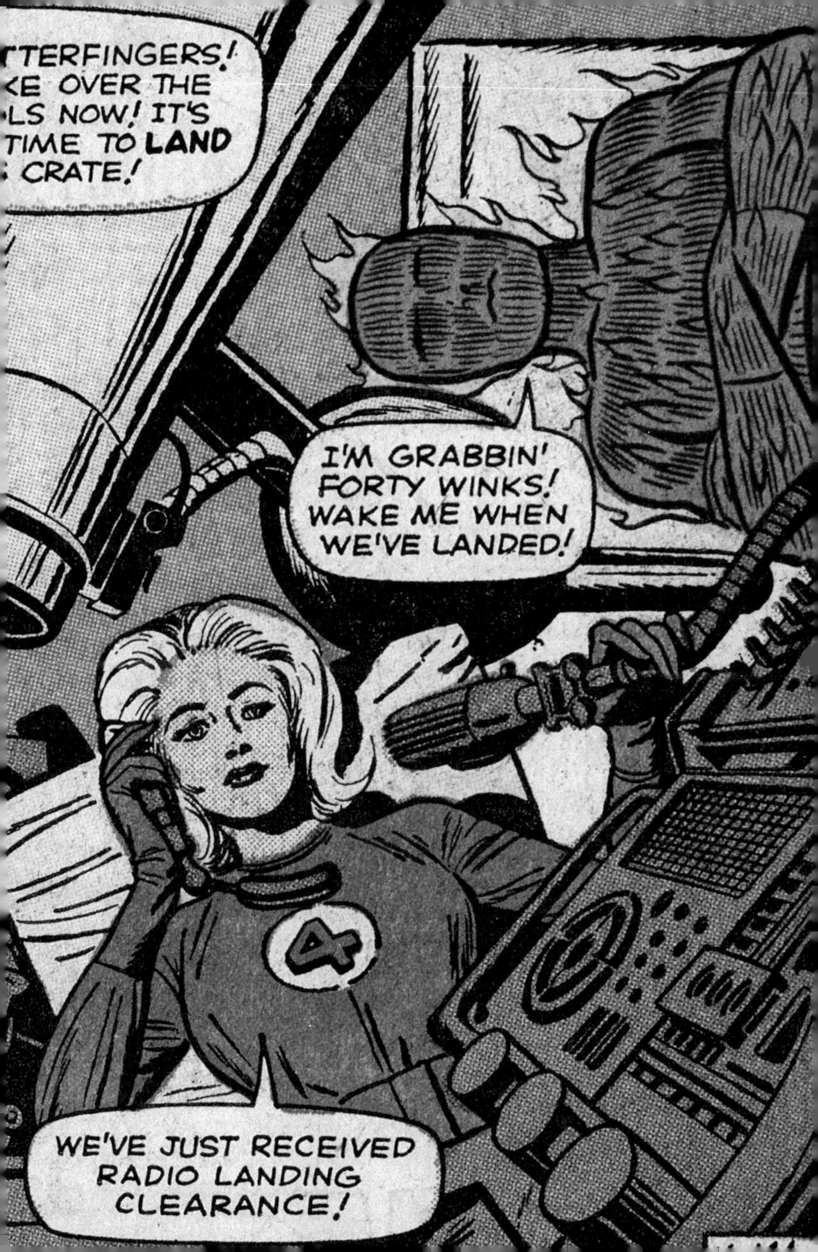
TTERFINGERS! KE OVER THE LS NOW! IT'S TIME TO **LAND** CRATE!
I'M GRABBIN' FORTY WINKS! WAKE ME WHEN WE'VE LANDED!
WE'VE JUST RECEIVED RADIO LANDING CLEARANCE!

FANTASTIC FOUR No. 4

Below: *Interior, "Enter the Sub-Mariner!"; script, Stan Lee; pencils, Jack Kirby; inks, Sol Brodsky; May 1962.* "I've got to hand it to you. It takes a lot of guts to write 'The Greatest Comic Magazine in the World' on the cover of a mag," began reader Les Blake's letter in this issue. "But, in your case, the risk paid off, because I don't think any comic reader can doubt it. The *Fantastic Four* has everything! Great art, terrific characters, and a more adult approach to the stories than any other mag I've read (except *Amazing Adult Fantasy*, which is yours, too, I understand). You are definitely starting a new trend in comics — stories about characters who act like real people, not just lily-white do-gooders who would insult the average reader's intelligence. Keep it up and I'm your fan for life!"

FANTASTIC FOUR No. 7

Opposite: *Interior, "Twenty-Four Hours Till Zero!"; script, Stan Lee; pencils, Jack Kirby; inks, Dick Ayers; October 1962.*

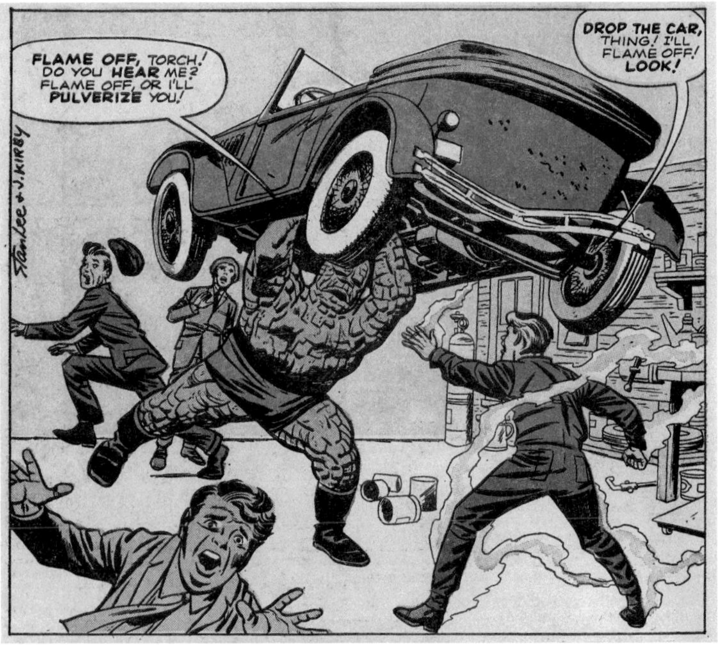
FLAME OFF, TORCH! DO YOU HEAR ME? FLAME OFF, OR I'LL PULVERIZE YOU!
DROP THE CAR, THING! I'LL FLAME OFF! LOOK!
StanLee + J.KIRBY

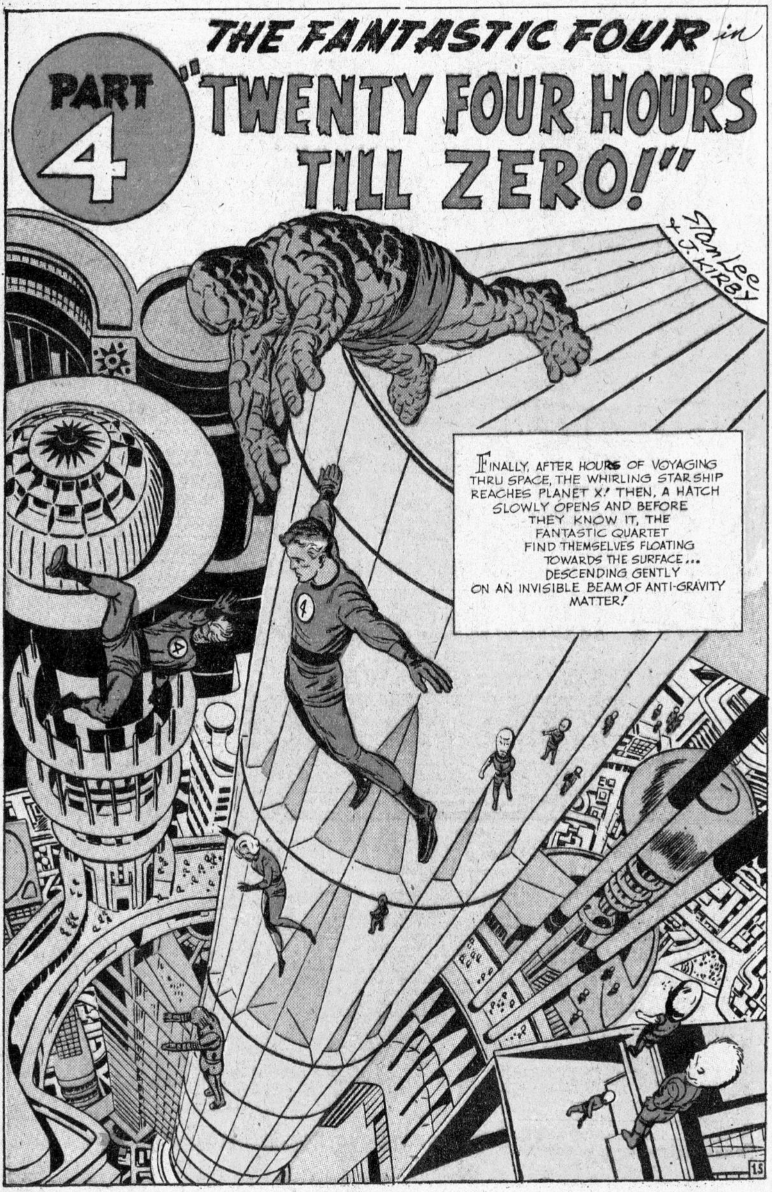
THE FANTASTIC FOUR in
PART 4
"TWENTY FOUR HOURS TILL ZERO!"
Stan Lee + J. Kirby
FINALLY, AFTER HOURS OF VOYAGING THRU SPACE, THE WHIRLING STARSHIP REACHES PLANET X! THEN, A HATCH SLOWLY OPENS AND BEFORE THEY KNOW IT, THE FANTASTIC QUARTET FIND THEMSELVES FLOATING TOWARDS THE SURFACE... DESCENDING GENTLY ON AN INVISIBLE BEAM OF ANTI-GRAVITY MATTER!
15

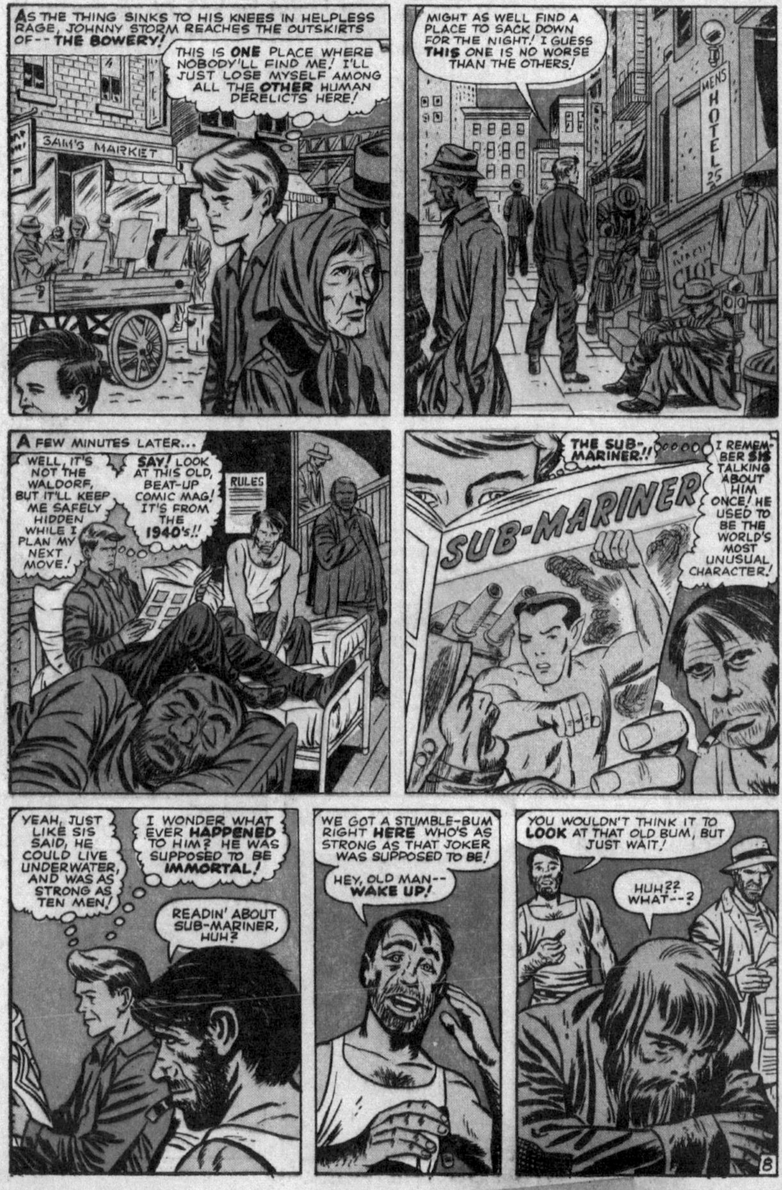
AS THE THING SINKS TO HIS KNEES IN HELPLESS RAGE, JOHNNY STORM REACHES THE OUTSKIRTS OF-- THE BOWERY!
THIS IS ONE PLACE WHERE NOBODY'LL FIND ME! I'LL JUST LOSE MYSELF AMONG ALL THE OTHER HUMAN DERELICTS HERE!
SAM'S MARKET
MIGHT AS WELL FIND A PLACE TO SACK DOWN FOR THE NIGHT! I GUESS THIS ONE IS NO WORSE THAN THE OTHERS!
MENS HOTEL 25
A FEW MINUTES LATER...
WELL, IT'S NOT THE WALDORF, BUT IT'LL KEEP ME SAFELY HIDDEN WHILE I PLAN MY NEXT MOVE!
SAY! LOOK AT THIS OLD, BEAT-UP COMIC MAG! IT'S FROM THE 1940's!!
RULES
THE SUB-MARINER!!
SUB-MARINER
I REMEMBER SIS TALKING ABOUT HIM ONCE! HE USED TO BE THE WORLD'S MOST UNUSUAL CHARACTER!
YEAH, JUST LIKE SIS SAID, HE COULD LIVE UNDERWATER, AND WAS AS STRONG AS TEN MEN!
I WONDER WHAT EVER HAPPENED TO HIM? HE WAS SUPPOSED TO BE IMMORTAL!
READIN' ABOUT SUB-MARINER, HUH?
WE GOT A STUMBLE-BUM RIGHT HERE WHO'S AS STRONG AS THAT JOKER WAS SUPPOSED TO BE!
HEY, OLD MAN-- WAKE UP!
YOU WOULDN'T THINK IT TO LOOK AT THAT OLD BUM, BUT JUST WAIT!
HUH?? WHAT--?
8

YEAH? WELL, WE'RE GONNA HELP 'IM TO FIND HIS MEMORY!!
SURE! WE'LL BEAT IT BACK INTO HIM!
WHY BOTHER? I'LL SHOW YOU AN EASIER WAY!
FIRST, WE'VE GOTTA SEE WHAT HE REALLY LOOKS LIKE!
SO LET'S GIVE 'IM A LITTLE SHAVE!
FLAME ON!
HEY! LOOK AT THAT!!
HOLY COW! IT'S THE HUMAN TORCH!
SEE HOW SIMPLE IT IS, WHEN YOU KNOW HOW?
I CAN CONTROL THE FLAME OF MY BODY TO WITHIN A HAIR'S WIDTH!
WAIT!! HIS FACE! NO--IT--CAN'T BE!!
IT IS! IT IS!! HE--HE'S THE SUB-MARINER!
10

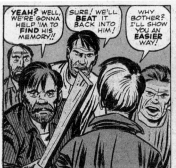

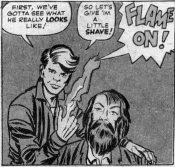

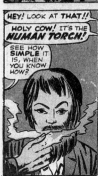

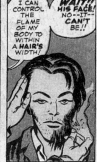

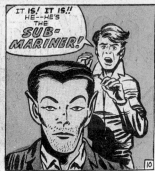

FANTASTIC FOUR No. 4

Opposite and above: *Interiors, "The Coming of Sub-Mariner!": script, Stan Lee; pencils, Jack Kirby; inks, Sol Brodsky: May 1962.* In a brilliant marketing move, Lee cast popular teenage hero Johnny Storm—the "rebooted" Human Torch—as a comics fan who learns about the Sub-Mariner from a vintage comic book! Namor's own reboot is handled with panache: The angry misfit prince, having spent years on the street in New York's Bowery, is (carefully) teased by his fellows about his super-strength before the slumming super-fan Torch recognizes him through a derelict's beard!

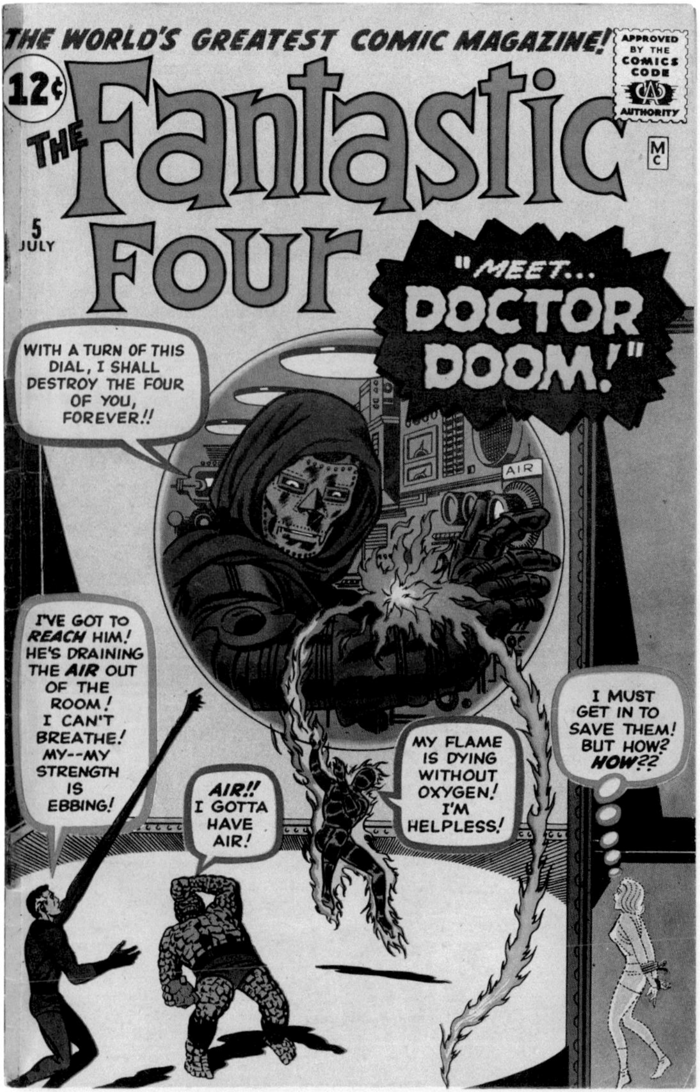
THE WORLD'S GREATEST COMIC MAGAZINE!
APPROVED BY THE COMICS CODE AUTHORITY
12¢
THE Fantastic Four
5 JULY
MC
"MEET... DOCTOR DOOM!"
WITH A TURN OF THIS DIAL, I SHALL DESTROY THE FOUR OF YOU, FOREVER!!
AIR
I'VE GOT TO REACH HIM! HE'S DRAINING THE AIR OUT OF THE ROOM! I CAN'T BREATHE! MY--MY STRENGTH IS EBBING!
AIR!! I GOTTA HAVE AIR!
MY FLAME IS DYING WITHOUT OXYGEN! I'M HELPLESS!
I MUST GET IN TO SAVE THEM! BUT HOW? HOW??

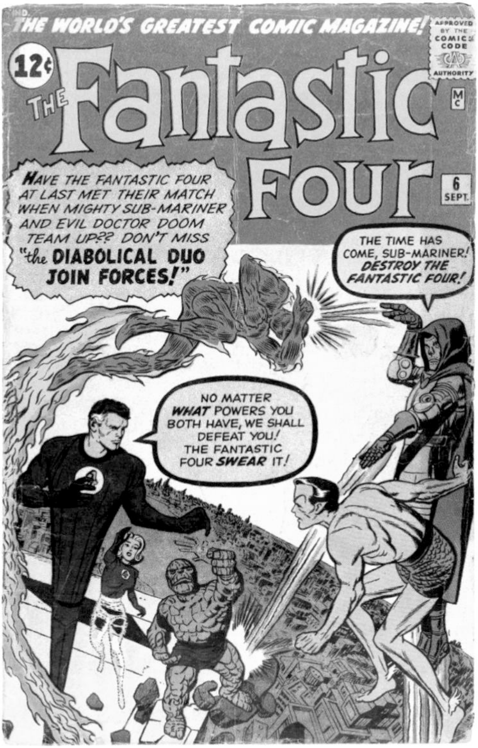
THE WORLD'S GREATEST COMIC MAGAZINE!
APPROVED BY THE COMICS CODE AUTHORITY
12¢
THE Fantastic FOUR
MC
6 SEPT.
HAVE THE FANTASTIC FOUR AT LAST MET THEIR MATCH WHEN MIGHTY SUB-MARINER AND EVIL DOCTOR DOOM TEAM UP?? DON'T MISS "the DIABOLICAL DUO JOIN FORCES!"
THE TIME HAS COME, SUB-MARINER! DESTROY THE FANTASTIC FOUR!
NO MATTER WHAT POWERS YOU BOTH HAVE, WE SHALL DEFEAT YOU! THE FANTASTIC FOUR SWEAR IT!

FANTASTIC FOUR No. 5

Opposite: *Cover; pencils, Jack Kirby; inks, Joe Sinnott; July 1962.* Dr. Doom was the FF's primary—and most popular—antagonist. Introduced in this issue, Doom was a complex, fascinating character that many see as the visual prototype of George Lucas's Darth Vader. Stan Goldberg, the staffer responsible for coloring most of Marvel's comics in the 1960s, would recall, "Jack gave them this long underwear with the letter '4' on their chest.... I made the '4' blue and kept a little area around it white, and then when the villains came in—the villains get the burnt umbers, dark greens, purples, grays, things like that—they can bounce off it."

FANTASTIC FOUR No. 6

Above: *Cover; pencils, Jack Kirby; inks, Dick Ayers; September 1962.*

IF THE FACULTY STAFF EVER LEARNS THAT YOU'VE BEEN CONDUCTING FORBIDDEN EXPERIMENTS... TRYING TO CONTACT THE NETHER WORLD...
SILENCE! JUST DO AS YOU'RE TOLD! THROW THE SWITCH!
BUT THE GYPSY GENIUS HAD MADE THE MISTAKE OF UNDERESTIMATING REED RICHARDS! FOR REED HAD BEEN RIGHT! VON DOOM'S EQUATIONS WERE A FEW DECIMALS OFF, AND SO...
WHAT WAS THAT?
IT CAME FROM VON DOOM'S DORMITORY ROOM!
DAYS LATER, THE BANDAGES FINALLY COME OFF, AND THEN...
NO! NO! I'M UGLY!!! UGLY!! WHAT HAVE I DONE TO MYSELF?? WHAT HAVE I DONE..?! MY FACE IS TOO HORRIBLE! NO OTHER EYES MUST EVER GAZE UPON IT!! I'LL HIDE FROM THE SIGHT OF MANKIND --- SOMEWHERE... SOMEHOW!!

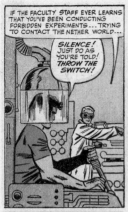

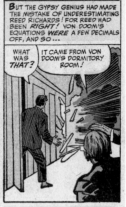

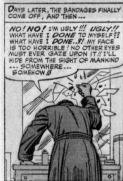

FANTASTIC FOUR ANNUAL No. 2

Above and opposite: *Interiors, "The Fantastic Origin of Dr. Doom"; script, Stan Lee; pencils, Jack Kirby; inks, Chic Stone; Summer 1964.* Unlike most comics publishers, Lee and Kirby felt no rush to tell origin stories. They took their time revealing the pasts of popular characters like Dr. Doom. What did the face behind the mask look like? Lee and Kirby each offered different interpretations: Lee maintained that Victor Von Doom had a terribly scarred face; Kirby, a decade after Doom's introduction, said it was just a small cut that Doom couldn't accept because he was a perfectionist.

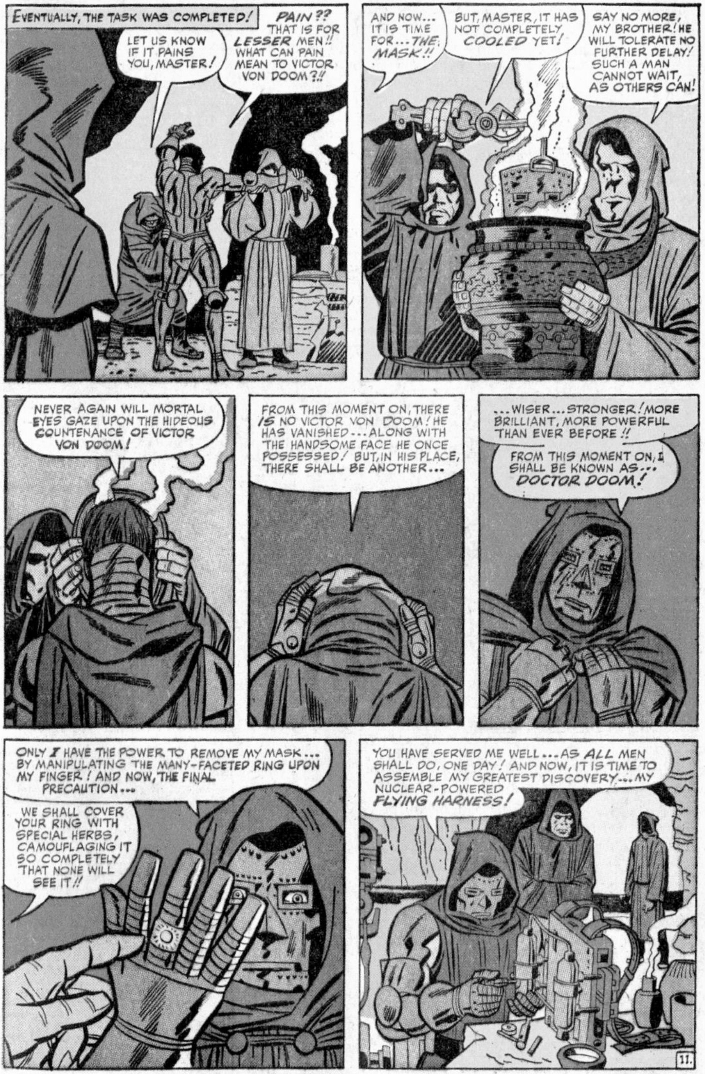

EVENTUALLY, THE TASK WAS COMPLETED!
LET US KNOW IF IT PAINS YOU, MASTER!
PAIN?? THAT IS FOR LESSER MEN!! WHAT CAN PAIN MEAN TO VICTOR VON DOOM?!!
AND NOW... IT IS TIME FOR... THE MASK!!
BUT, MASTER, IT HAS NOT COMPLETELY COOLED YET!
SAY NO MORE, MY BROTHER! HE WILL TOLERATE NO FURTHER DELAY! SUCH A MAN CANNOT WAIT, AS OTHERS CAN!
NEVER AGAIN WILL MORTAL EYES GAZE UPON THE HIDEOUS COUNTENANCE OF VICTOR VON DOOM!
FROM THIS MOMENT ON, THERE IS NO VICTOR VON DOOM! HE HAS VANISHED... ALONG WITH THE HANDSOME FACE HE ONCE POSSESSED! BUT, IN HIS PLACE, THERE SHALL BE ANOTHER...
...WISER... STRONGER! MORE BRILLIANT, MORE POWERFUL THAN EVER BEFORE!!
FROM THIS MOMENT ON, I SHALL BE KNOWN AS... DOCTOR DOOM!
ONLY I HAVE THE POWER TO REMOVE MY MASK... BY MANIPULATING THE MANY-FACETED RING UPON MY FINGER! AND NOW, THE FINAL PRECAUTION...
WE SHALL COVER YOUR RING WITH SPECIAL HERBS, CAMOUFLAGING IT SO COMPLETELY THAT NONE WILL SEE IT!!
YOU HAVE SERVED ME WELL... AS ALL MEN SHALL DO, ONE DAY! AND NOW, IT IS TIME TO ASSEMBLE MY GREATEST DISCOVERY... MY NUCLEAR-POWERED FLYING HARNESS!
11.

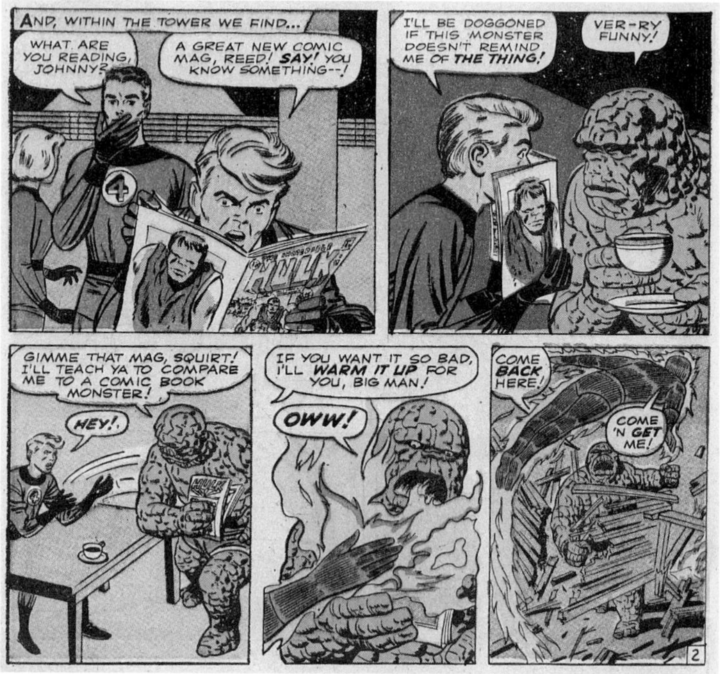
AND, WITHIN THE TOWER WE FIND...
WHAT ARE YOU READING, JOHNNY?
A GREAT NEW COMIC MAG, REED! SAY! YOU KNOW SOMETHING--!
I'LL BE DOGGONED IF THIS MONSTER DOESN'T REMIND ME OF THE THING!
VER-RY FUNNY!
GIMME THAT MAG, SQUIRT! I'LL TEACH YA TO COMPARE ME TO A COMIC BOOK MONSTER!
HEY!
IF YOU WANT IT SO BAD, I'LL WARM IT UP FOR YOU, BIG MAN!
OWW!
COME BACK HERE!
COME 'N GET ME!
2

FANTASTIC FOUR No. 5

Above and opposite: *Interiors, "Prisoners of Dr. Doom!"; script, Stan Lee; pencils, Jack Kirby; inks, Joe Sinnott; July 1962.* "Say! You know something—! I'll be doggoned if this monster doesn't remind me of the Thing!" Once again, Johnny Storm learns about a super hero by keeping up with Marvel comics. In *Strange Tales* No. 114, not too far in the future, the Torch will rediscover Captain America through a comic book as well!

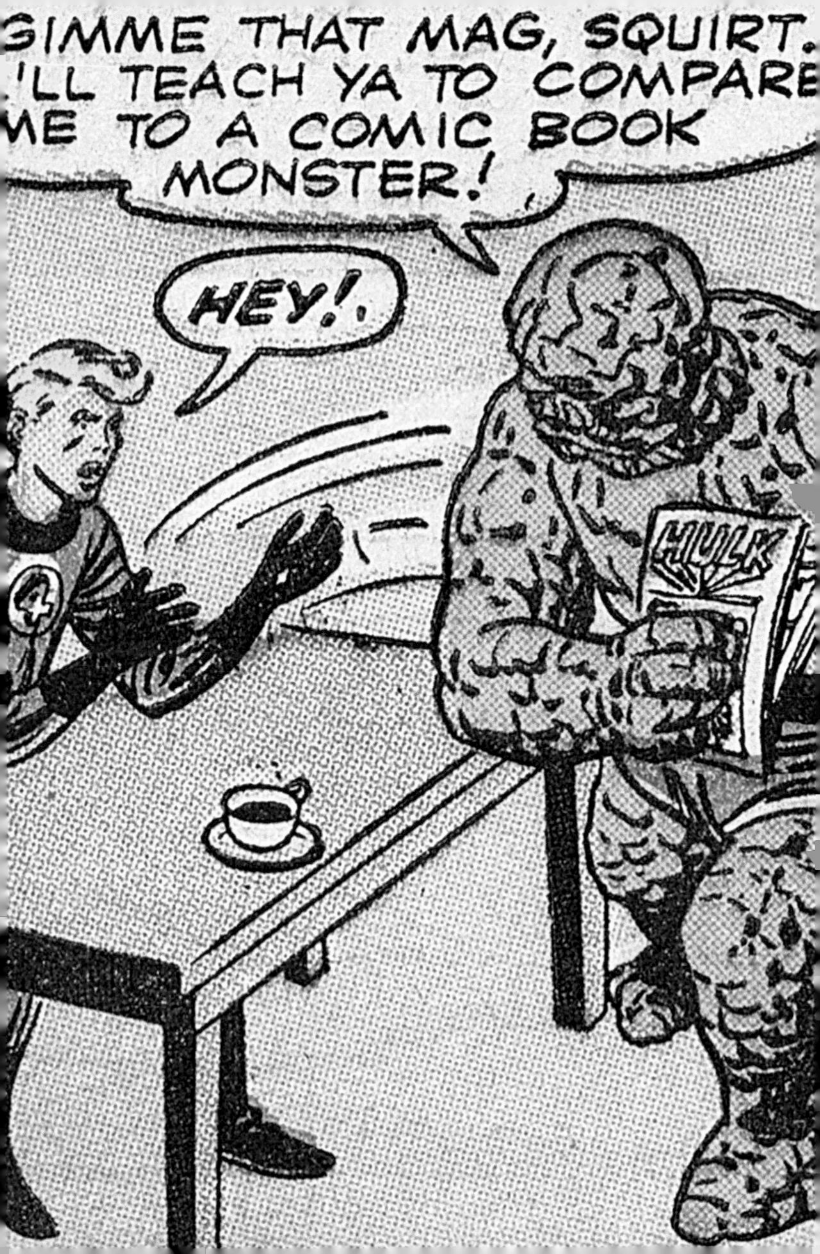
GIMME THAT MAG, SQUIRT. I'LL TEACH YA TO COMPARE ME TO A COMIC BOOK MONSTER!
HEY!
HULK

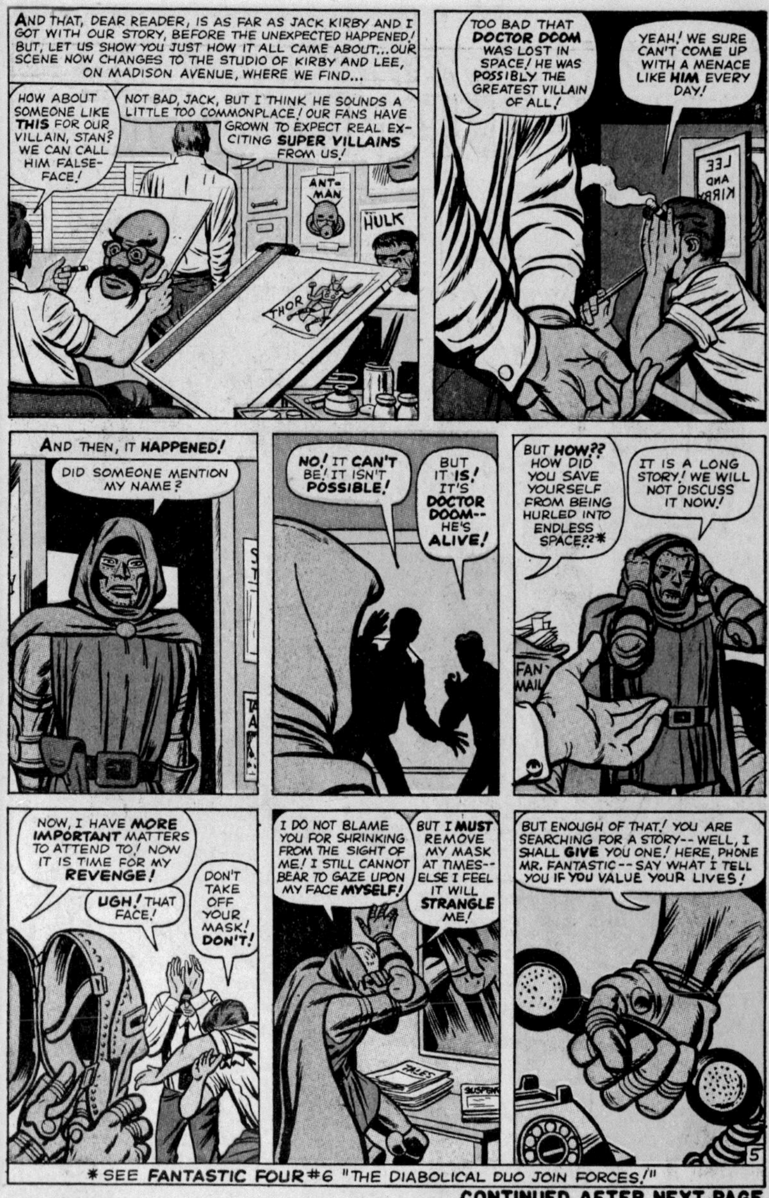
AND THAT, DEAR READER, IS AS FAR AS JACK KIRBY AND I GOT WITH OUR STORY, BEFORE THE UNEXPECTED HAPPENED! BUT, LET US SHOW YOU JUST HOW IT ALL CAME ABOUT...OUR SCENE NOW CHANGES TO THE STUDIO OF KIRBY AND LEE, ON MADISON AVENUE, WHERE WE FIND...
HOW ABOUT SOMEONE LIKE THIS FOR OUR VILLAIN, STAN? WE CAN CALL HIM FALSE-FACE!
NOT BAD, JACK, BUT I THINK HE SOUNDS A LITTLE TOO COMMONPLACE! OUR FANS HAVE GROWN TO EXPECT REAL EXCITING SUPER VILLAINS FROM US!
ANT-MAN
HULK
THOR
TOO BAD THAT DOCTOR DOOM WAS LOST IN SPACE! HE WAS POSSIBLY THE GREATEST VILLAIN OF ALL!
YEAH! WE SURE CAN'T COME UP WITH A MENACE LIKE HIM EVERY DAY!
AND THEN, IT HAPPENED!
DID SOMEONE MENTION MY NAME?
NO! IT CAN'T BE! IT ISN'T POSSIBLE!
BUT IT IS! IT'S DOCTOR DOOM-- HE'S ALIVE!
BUT HOW?? HOW DID YOU SAVE YOURSELF FROM BEING HURLED INTO ENDLESS SPACE??*
IT IS A LONG STORY! WE WILL NOT DISCUSS IT NOW!
FAN MAIL
NOW, I HAVE MORE IMPORTANT MATTERS TO ATTEND TO! NOW IT IS TIME FOR MY REVENGE!
UGH! THAT FACE!
DON'T TAKE OFF YOUR MASK! DON'T!
I DO NOT BLAME YOU FOR SHRINKING FROM THE SIGHT OF ME! I STILL CANNOT BEAR TO GAZE UPON MY FACE MYSELF!
BUT I MUST REMOVE MY MASK AT TIMES-- ELSE I FEEL IT WILL STRANGLE ME!
TALES
BUT ENOUGH OF THAT! YOU ARE SEARCHING FOR A STORY-- WELL, I SHALL GIVE YOU ONE! HERE, PHONE MR. FANTASTIC -- SAY WHAT I TELL YOU IF YOU VALUE YOUR LIVES!
5
* SEE FANTASTIC FOUR #6 "THE DIABOLICAL DUO JOIN FORCES!"

CONTINUED AFTER NEXT PAGE

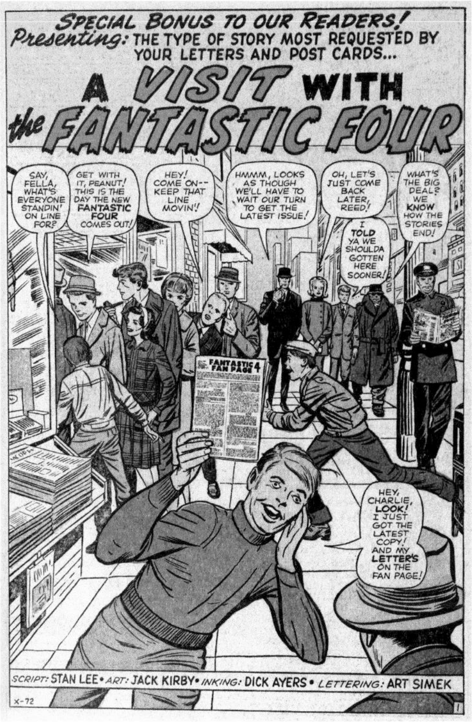
SPECIAL BONUS TO OUR READERS!
Presenting: THE TYPE OF STORY MOST REQUESTED BY YOUR LETTERS AND POST CARDS...
A VISIT WITH the FANTASTIC FOUR
SAY, FELLA, WHAT'S EVERYONE STANDIN' ON LINE FOR?
GET WITH IT, PEANUT! THIS IS THE DAY THE NEW FANTASTIC FOUR COMES OUT!
HEY! COME ON-- KEEP THAT LINE MOVIN'!
HMMM, LOOKS AS THOUGH WE'LL HAVE TO WAIT OUR TURN TO GET THE LATEST ISSUE!
OH, LET'S JUST COME BACK LATER, REED!
I TOLD YA WE SHOULDA GOTTEN HERE SOONER!
WHAT'S THE BIG DEAL? WE KNOW HOW THE STORIES END!
FANTASTIC 4 FAN PAGE
HEY, CHARLIE, LOOK! I JUST GOT THE LATEST COPY! AND MY LETTER'S ON THE FAN PAGE!
SCRIPT: STAN LEE • ART: JACK KIRBY • INKING: DICK AYERS • LETTERING: ART SIMEK
X-72

FANTASTIC FOUR No. 10

Opposite: *Interior, "The Return of Dr. Doom!"; script, Stan Lee; pencils, Jack Kirby; inks, Dick Ayers; January 1963.* In tried-and-true comic book fashion, Lee and Kirby playfully inject themselves into their own stories, something each of them had been doing since the 1940s.

FANTASTIC FOUR No. 11

Above: *Interior, "A Visit with the Fantastic Four!"; script, Stan Lee; pencils, Jack Kirby; inks, Dick Ayers; February 1963.* This story acknowledges the growing fan support for the comic while giving new readers a chance to catch up.

THE WORLD'S GREATEST COMIC MAGAZINE!
APPROVED BY THE COMICS CODE AUTHORITY
12¢
THE Fantastic Four
MC
7 OCT.
WHY DOES THE HUMAN RACE TURN AGAINST THE FANTASTIC FOUR?? ONLY "THE MASTER OF PLANET X" KNOWS THE ANSWER!!
WANTED DEAD OR ALIVE
MISTER FANTASTIC
HUMAN TORCH
THE THING
INVISIBLE GIRL
WE ESCAPED JUST IN TIME! WE CAN'T REMAIN ON EARTH ANY LONGER! WE'VE GOT TO HEAD FOR PLANET X!!
DOWN WITH THE FANTASTIC FOUR!!

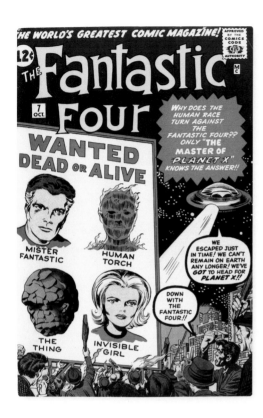

FANTASTIC FOUR No. 7

Above: *Cover; pencils and inks, Jack Kirby; October 1962.*

FANTASTIC FOUR No. 18

Opposite: *Cover; pencils, Jack Kirby; inks, Paul Reinman; September 1963.* The Skrulls, introduced in *FF* No. 2, were the first aliens in the new Marvel Universe, and unlike villains in the earlier pre-hero stories, these little green monsters were recurring antagonists. The Super-Skrull was tailor-made wish fulfillment for the era's young readers—he had *all* the FF's powers! Stan Goldberg's distinctive coloring used gradations and dark colors, helping create a unique look for Marvel on the newsstands.

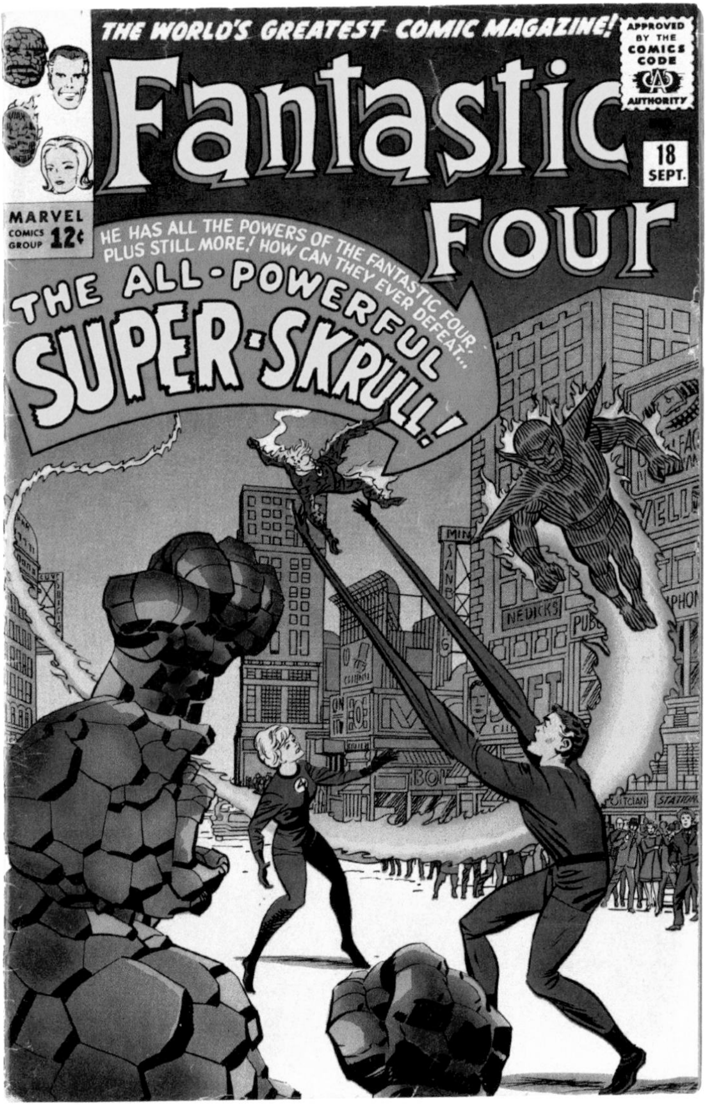
THE WORLD'S GREATEST COMIC MAGAZINE!
APPROVED BY THE COMICS CODE AUTHORITY
Fantastic Four
18 SEPT.
MARVEL COMICS GROUP 12¢
HE HAS ALL THE POWERS OF THE FANTASTIC FOUR, PLUS STILL MORE! HOW CAN THEY EVER DEFEAT...
THE ALL-POWERFUL SUPER-SKRULL!
NEDICKS

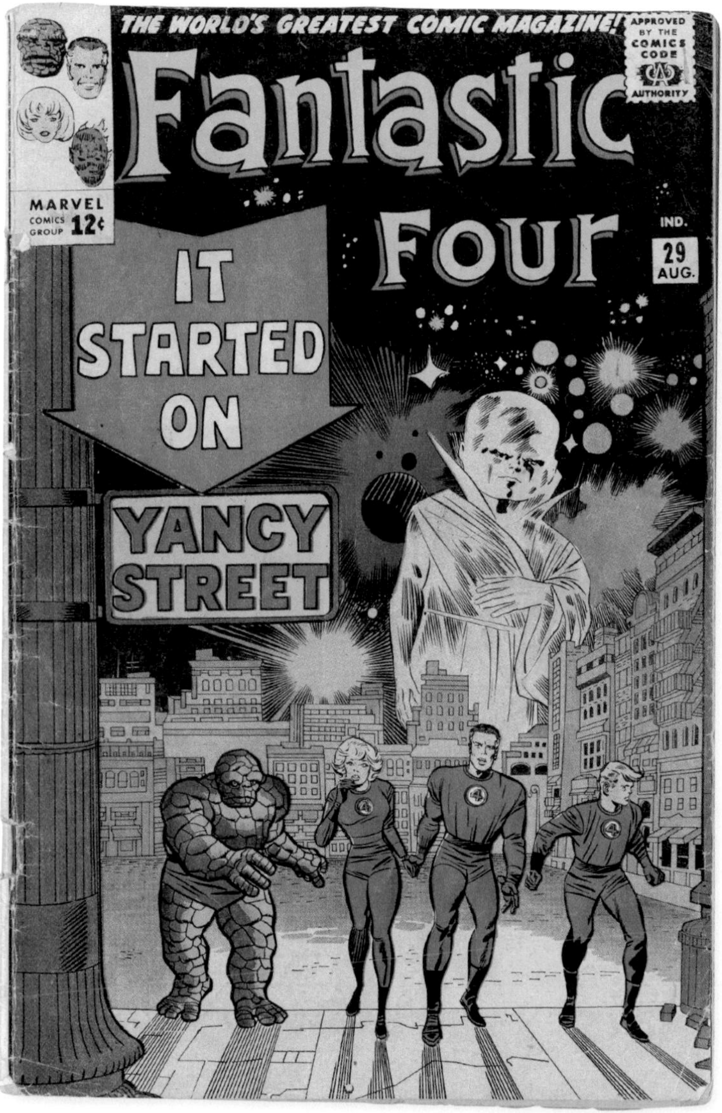
THE WORLD'S GREATEST COMIC MAGAZINE!
APPROVED BY THE COMICS CODE AUTHORITY
Fantastic Four
MARVEL COMICS GROUP 12¢
IND.
29 AUG.
IT STARTED ON
YANCY STREET

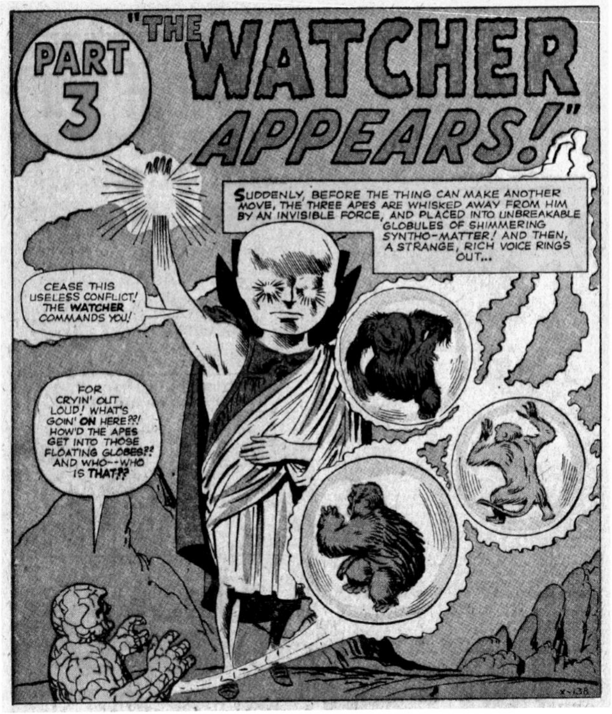
PART 3
"THE WATCHER APPEARS!"
SUDDENLY, BEFORE THE THING CAN MAKE ANOTHER MOVE, THE THREE APES ARE WHISKED AWAY FROM HIM BY AN INVISIBLE FORCE, AND PLACED INTO UNBREAKABLE GLOBULES OF SHIMMERING SYNTHO-MATTER! AND THEN, A STRANGE, RICH VOICE RINGS OUT...
CEASE THIS USELESS CONFLICT! THE WATCHER COMMANDS YOU!
FOR CRYIN' OUT LOUD! WHAT'S GOIN' ON HERE??! HOW'D THE APES GET INTO THOSE FLOATING GLOBES?? AND WHO--WHO IS THAT??

FANTASTIC FOUR No. 29

Opposite: *Cover; pencils, Jack Kirby; inks, Chic Stone; August 1964.* Many of the best *FF* covers eschewed the traditional super hero fight scenes and opted for a more subtle air of mystery…a sense of tension and the unknown. Here, the team walks through a deserted city with the Watcher looking down on them. Yancy Street was the fictional double for New York City's Delancey Street, in the heart of the Lower East Side neighborhood where Jack Kirby grew up.

FANTASTIC FOUR No. 13

Above: *Interior, "…Versus the Red Ghost and His Indescribable Super Apes!"; script, Stan Lee; pencils, Jack Kirby; inks, Steve Ditko; February 1963.* The Watcher—an incredibly powerful alien who lives on the moon and tracks all Earthly events—has pledged not to interfere. Give him time….

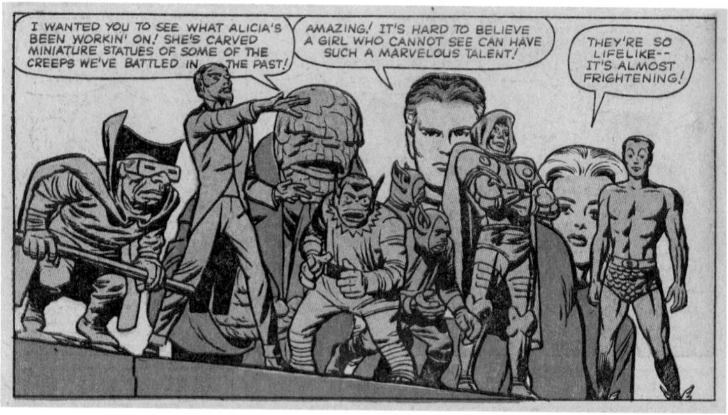
I WANTED YOU TO SEE WHAT ALICIA'S BEEN WORKIN' ON! SHE'S CARVED MINIATURE STATUES OF SOME OF THE CREEPS WE'VE BATTLED IN THE PAST!
AMAZING! IT'S HARD TO BELIEVE A GIRL WHO CANNOT SEE CAN HAVE SUCH A MARVELOUS TALENT!
THEY'RE SO LIFELIKE-- IT'S ALMOST FRIGHTENING!

FANTASTIC FOUR No. 10

Above: *Interior, "The Return of Dr. Doom!"; script, Stan Lee; pencils, Jack Kirby; inks, Dick Ayers; January 1963.* Once these "new comics" hit their groove, there was no stopping Lee and Kirby. Even the extravagant trophy rooms of Superman and Batman were brought down to earth, as blind sculptress—and Thing's love interest—Alicia Masters creates a rogues' gallery for the FF.

FANTASTIC FOUR ANNUAL No. 1

Opposite: *Interior; script, Stan Lee; pencils and inks, Jack Kirby; Summer 1963.* The Marvel Annuals, later called King-Size Specials, often contained great features including pinups, comedic stories, and insights into the characters—a reward of sorts for Marvel's increasingly dedicated fanbase. In this first *FF Annual*, Lee and Kirby unveiled the complete layout of the Baxter Building. A tantalizingly abbreviated diagram had already appeared in issue 3.

FANTASTIC FOUR No. 22

Pages 54–55: *Interior, "The Return of the Mole Man!"; script, Stan Lee; pencils, Jack Kirby; inks, George Roussos; January 1964.* Lee and company often referenced popular-culture figures and topical events, as evidenced by these two pages. Panels one and two include a caricature of Fred Gwynn as Officer Muldoon from the then-current TV comedy *Car 54, Where Are You?* The deadpan humor contrasted Marvel's world with that of its more straight-laced competitors. Marvel often poked fun at itself, too. This sendup of "abstract art" is in reality a satire of a picture drawn by Jack Kirby.

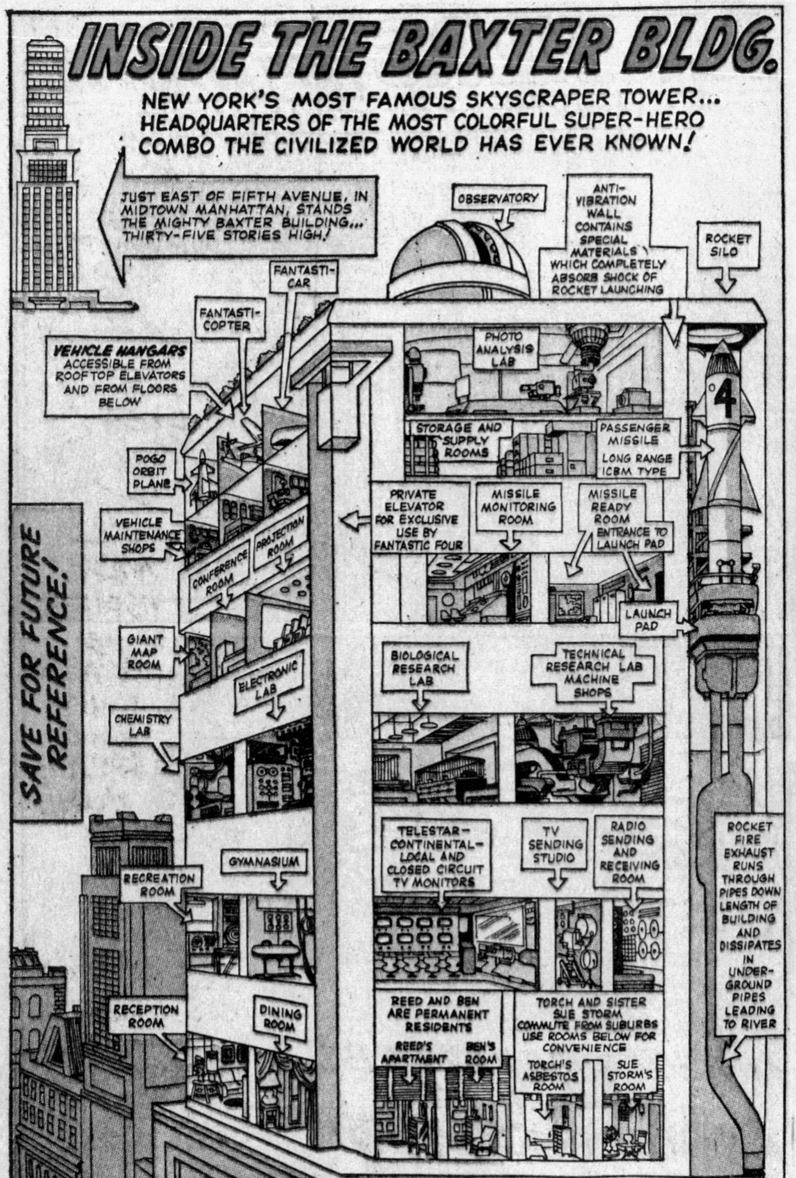
INSIDE THE BAXTER BLDG.
NEW YORK'S MOST FAMOUS SKYSCRAPER TOWER... HEADQUARTERS OF THE MOST COLORFUL SUPER-HERO COMBO THE CIVILIZED WORLD HAS EVER KNOWN!
JUST EAST OF FIFTH AVENUE, IN MIDTOWN MANHATTAN, STANDS THE MIGHTY BAXTER BUILDING... THIRTY-FIVE STORIES HIGH!
OBSERVATORY
ANTI-VIBRATION WALL CONTAINS SPECIAL MATERIALS WHICH COMPLETELY ABSORB SHOCK OF ROCKET LAUNCHING
ROCKET SILO
FANTASTI-CAR
FANTASTI-COPTER
VEHICLE HANGARS ACCESSIBLE FROM ROOFTOP ELEVATORS AND FROM FLOORS BELOW
PHOTO ANALYSIS LAB
4
STORAGE AND SUPPLY ROOMS
PASSENGER MISSILE
LONG RANGE ICBM TYPE
POGO ORBIT PLANE
PRIVATE ELEVATOR FOR EXCLUSIVE USE BY FANTASTIC FOUR
MISSILE MONITORING ROOM
MISSILE READY ROOM ENTRANCE TO LAUNCH PAD
VEHICLE MAINTENANCE SHOPS
CONFERENCE ROOM
PROJECTION ROOM
SAVE FOR FUTURE REFERENCE!
LAUNCH PAD
GIANT MAP ROOM
ELECTRONIC LAB
BIOLOGICAL RESEARCH LAB
TECHNICAL RESEARCH LAB MACHINE SHOPS
CHEMISTRY LAB
TELESTAR-CONTINENTAL-LOCAL AND CLOSED CIRCUIT TV MONITORS
TV SENDING STUDIO
RADIO SENDING AND RECEIVING ROOM
ROCKET FIRE EXHAUST RUNS THROUGH PIPES DOWN LENGTH OF BUILDING AND DISSIPATES IN UNDER-GROUND PIPES LEADING TO RIVER
GYMNASIUM
RECREATION ROOM
RECEPTION ROOM
DINING ROOM
REED AND BEN ARE PERMANENT RESIDENTS
REED'S APARTMENT
BEN'S ROOM
TORCH AND SISTER SUE STORM COMMUTE FROM SUBURBS USE ROOMS BELOW FOR CONVENIENCE
TORCH'S ASBESTOS ROOM
SUE STORM'S ROOM

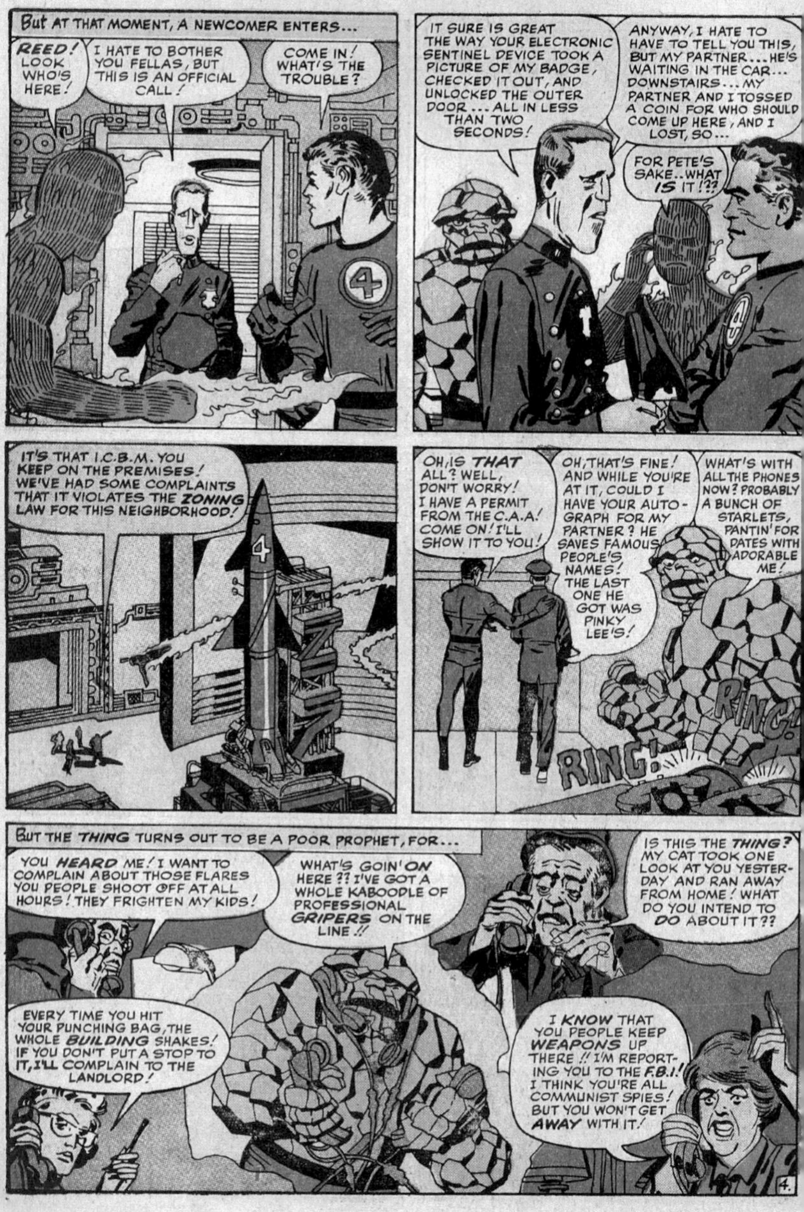
But AT THAT MOMENT, A NEWCOMER ENTERS...
REED! LOOK WHO'S HERE!
I HATE TO BOTHER YOU FELLAS, BUT THIS IS AN OFFICIAL CALL!
COME IN! WHAT'S THE TROUBLE?
IT SURE IS GREAT THE WAY YOUR ELECTRONIC SENTINEL DEVICE TOOK A PICTURE OF MY BADGE, CHECKED IT OUT, AND UNLOCKED THE OUTER DOOR ... ALL IN LESS THAN TWO SECONDS!
ANYWAY, I HATE TO HAVE TO TELL YOU THIS, BUT MY PARTNER... HE'S WAITING IN THE CAR... DOWNSTAIRS... MY PARTNER AND I TOSSED A COIN FOR WHO SHOULD COME UP HERE, AND I LOST, SO...
FOR PETE'S SAKE..WHAT IS IT!??
IT'S THAT I.C.B.M. YOU KEEP ON THE PREMISES! WE'VE HAD SOME COMPLAINTS THAT IT VIOLATES THE ZONING LAW FOR THIS NEIGHBORHOOD!
OH, IS THAT ALL? WELL, DON'T WORRY! I HAVE A PERMIT FROM THE C.A.A.! COME ON! I'LL SHOW IT TO YOU!
OH, THAT'S FINE! AND WHILE YOU'RE AT IT, COULD I HAVE YOUR AUTO-GRAPH FOR MY PARTNER? HE SAVES FAMOUS PEOPLE'S NAMES! THE LAST ONE HE GOT WAS PINKY LEE'S!
WHAT'S WITH ALL THE PHONES NOW? PROBABLY A BUNCH OF STARLETS, PANTIN' FOR DATES WITH ADORABLE ME!
RING!
RING!
BUT THE THING TURNS OUT TO BE A POOR PROPHET, FOR...
YOU HEARD ME! I WANT TO COMPLAIN ABOUT THOSE FLARES YOU PEOPLE SHOOT OFF AT ALL HOURS! THEY FRIGHTEN MY KIDS!
WHAT'S GOIN' ON HERE?? I'VE GOT A WHOLE KABOODLE OF PROFESSIONAL GRIPERS ON THE LINE!!
IS THIS THE THING? MY CAT TOOK ONE LOOK AT YOU YESTERDAY AND RAN AWAY FROM HOME! WHAT DO YOU INTEND TO DO ABOUT IT??
EVERY TIME YOU HIT YOUR PUNCHING BAG, THE WHOLE BUILDING SHAKES! IF YOU DON'T PUT A STOP TO IT, I'LL COMPLAIN TO THE LANDLORD!
I KNOW THAT YOU PEOPLE KEEP WEAPONS UP THERE!! I'M REPORTING YOU TO THE F.B.I.! I THINK YOU'RE ALL COMMUNIST SPIES! BUT YOU WON'T GET AWAY WITH IT!
4.

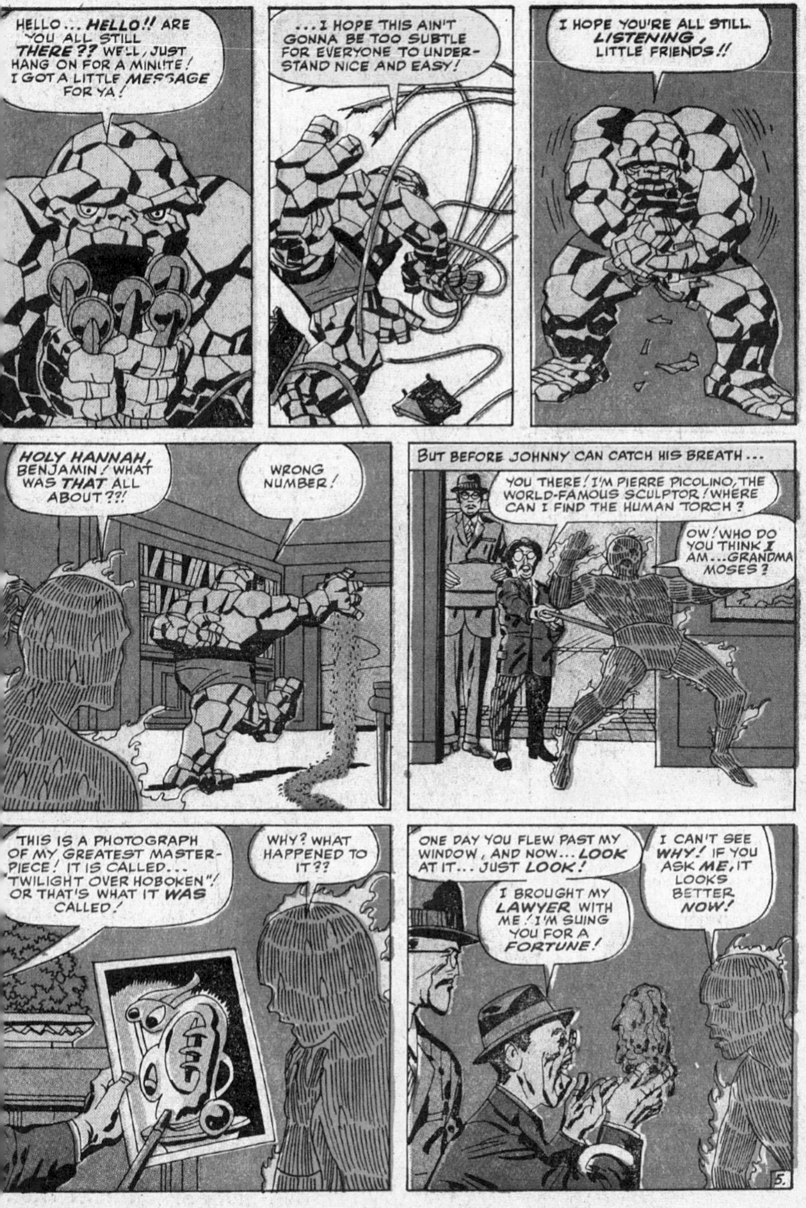
HELLO... HELLO!! ARE YOU ALL STILL THERE?? WELL, JUST HANG ON FOR A MINUTE! I GOT A LITTLE MESSAGE FOR YA!
...I HOPE THIS AIN'T GONNA BE TOO SUBTLE FOR EVERYONE TO UNDERSTAND NICE AND EASY!
I HOPE YOU'RE ALL STILL LISTENING, LITTLE FRIENDS!!
HOLY HANNAH, BENJAMIN! WHAT WAS THAT ALL ABOUT??!
WRONG NUMBER!
BUT BEFORE JOHNNY CAN CATCH HIS BREATH...
YOU THERE! I'M PIERRE PICOLINO, THE WORLD-FAMOUS SCULPTOR! WHERE CAN I FIND THE HUMAN TORCH?
OW! WHO DO YOU THINK I AM... GRANDMA MOSES?
THIS IS A PHOTOGRAPH OF MY GREATEST MASTERPIECE! IT IS CALLED... "TWILIGHT OVER HOBOKEN"! OR THAT'S WHAT IT WAS CALLED!
WHY? WHAT HAPPENED TO IT??
ONE DAY YOU FLEW PAST MY WINDOW, AND NOW... LOOK AT IT... JUST LOOK!
I BROUGHT MY LAWYER WITH ME! I'M SUING YOU FOR A FORTUNE!
I CAN'T SEE WHY! IF YOU ASK ME, IT LOOKS BETTER NOW!
5.

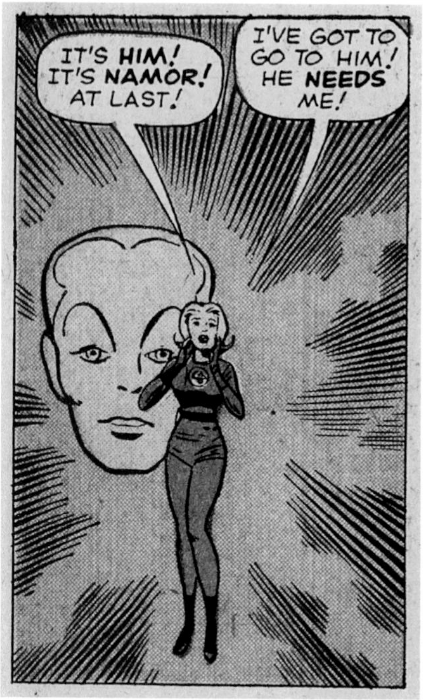
IT'S HIM! IT'S NAMOR! AT LAST!
I'VE GOT TO GO TO HIM! HE NEEDS ME!

FANTASTIC FOUR No. 14

Above: *Interior, "The Merciless Puppet Master!"; script, Stan Lee; pencils, Jack Kirby; inks, Dick Ayers; May 1963.* The Sub-Mariner quickly becomes a Marvel "supporting character," returning to the *FF* to rival Reed for Sue Storm's heart.

FANTASTIC FOUR ANNUAL No. 2

Opposite: *Interior, "The Fantastic Victory of Dr. Doom!"; script, Stan Lee; pencils, Jack Kirby; inks, Chic Stone; Summer 1964.* Jack Kirby used the comics medium to create his own iconography, which set the standard for decades to come. The simple use of "force lines" heightens the drama when Reed Richards and Dr. Doom have a showdown. Though limited by the technology of the period—and usually uncredited until January 1973 when their names were added to the credits—colorist Stan Goldberg, among other talented artists, created a vibrant palette from the very limited available colors to perfectly complement the art.

THIS MACHINE WILL PROVE ONCE AND FOR ALL...

NO NEED TO EXPLAIN, RICHARDS! I CAN DEDUCE ITS FUNCTION MOST CLEARLY! REMEMBER, I AM EVERY BIT YOUR SCIENTIFIC EQUAL!

THAT, MY IMPLACABLE ENEMY, REMAINS TO BE SEEN!

REED! NOT THE *ENCEPHALO-GUN!!* NOT *THAT!!* YOU *CAN'T!!*

STAND BACK, SUE! IT'S THE *ONLY* WAY! IF I SHOULD *LOSE*, MY DARLING, REMEMBER... I'VE LOVED YOU FROM THE FIRST! NOTHING CAN *EVER* CHANGE THAT!

FINE WORDS, RICHARDS!...FROM ONE ABOUT TO *DIE!!* WITH THIS DEVICE SET AT *FULL POWER*, THE ONE WITH THE GREATER MENTALITY WILL SEND THE OTHER TO A TIMELESS LIMBO FROM WHICH THERE IS NO RETURN! AND NOW... *BEGIN!!*

THUS COMMENCES THE MOST FANTASTIC DUEL EVER RECORDED!! TWO OF EARTH'S GREATEST GENIUSES, ONE A VALIANT IDEALIST... THE OTHER, A MERCILESS MENACE... PITTING THE POWER OF THEIR TWO *BRAINS* AGAINST EACH OTHER!

EACH ONE KNOWING THAT THE PRICE OF DEFEAT COULD BE *DEATH*... YET, EACH WELCOMING THIS FINAL OPPORTUNITY TO *PROVE* HIS OWN SUPERIORITY!!

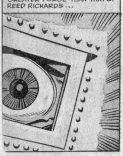

THEN, SLOWLY, INEXORABLY, THE MENTAL ENERGY GENERATED BY DOCTOR DOOM BEGINS TO SURGE INTO THE POWER UNIT WITH GREATER FORCE THAN THAT OF REED RICHARDS...

LITTLE BY LITTLE, THE AWESOME ARCH-VILLAIN SEES PANIC BEGIN TO WELL IN HIS ADVERSARY'S EYES, AS MR. FANTASTIC'S VERY FORM GROWS DIMMER AND DIMMER...

...UNTIL... *IT FADES FROM SIGHT COMPLETELY!!*

I'VE WON!! HE'S GONE! HE'S BEEN HURLED INTO LIMBO! *I AM THE VICTOR*, AS I KNEW I WAS *DESTINED* TO BE!

24.

FANTASTIC FOUR No. 30

Below: *Interior, "The Dreaded Diablo!"; script, Stan Lee; pencils, Jack Kirby; inks, Chic Stone; September 1964.* Kirby's mastery of his craft—in this case his signature use of foreshortening—created a 3-D effect that reached out and grabbed readers. No matter how impossible they were, in the hands of the King, characters like the Human Torch and the Thing looked nothing but real.

MEET THE BEATLES

Opposite: *Cover;* Strange Tales *No. 130; pencils, Jack Kirby; inks, Chic Stone; March 1965.* The Human Torch and the Thing meet the Beatles in this issue, though the Fab Four only appear in a few fleeting panels.

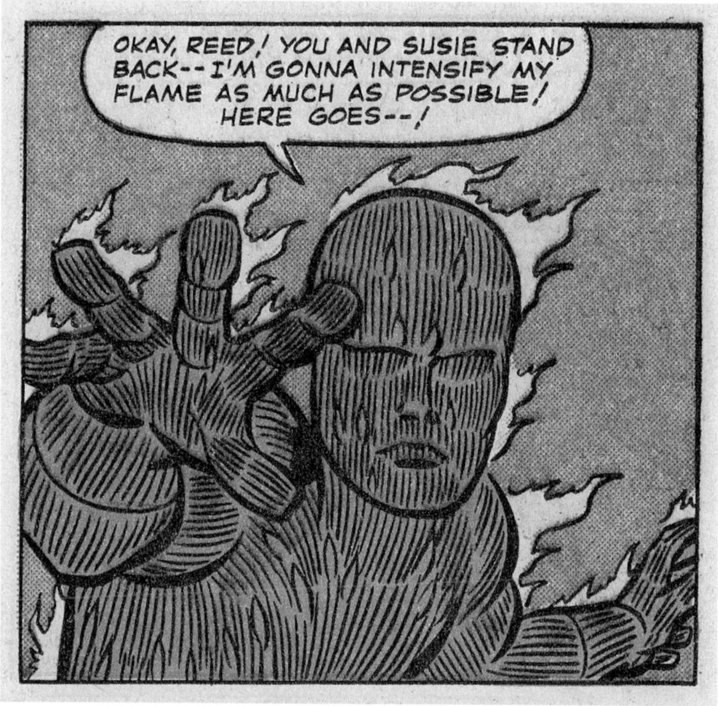
OKAY, REED! YOU AND SUSIE STAND BACK--I'M GONNA INTENSIFY MY FLAME AS MUCH AS POSSIBLE! HERE GOES--!

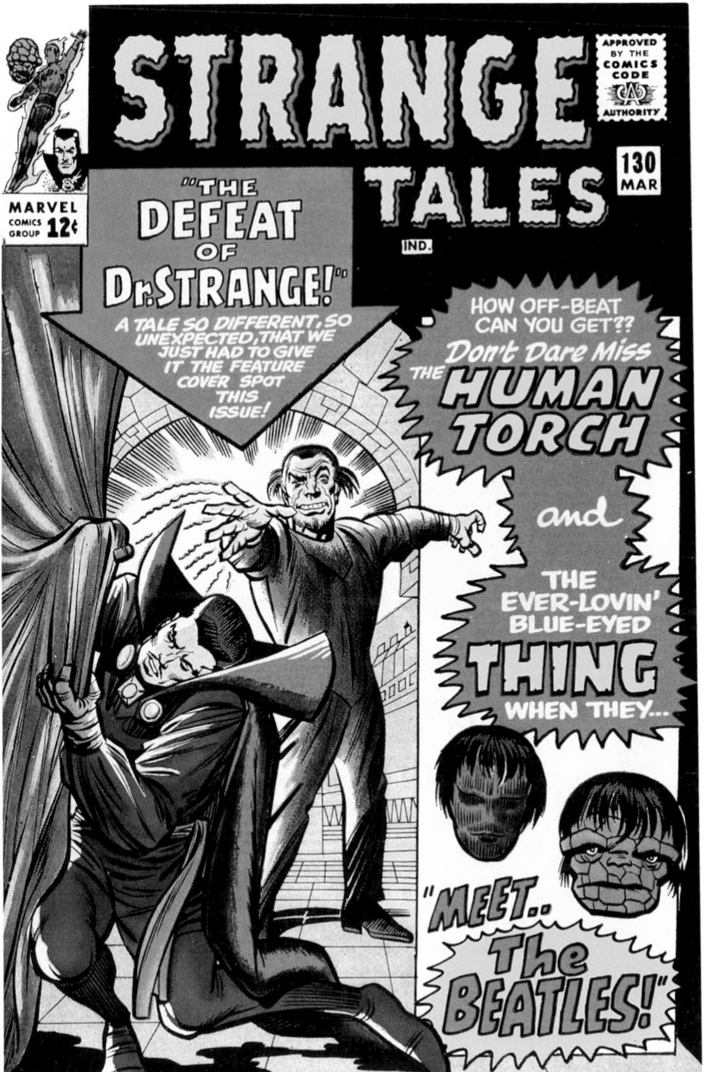
STRANGE TALES
APPROVED BY THE COMICS CODE AUTHORITY
130 MAR
MARVEL COMICS GROUP 12¢
IND.
"THE DEFEAT OF Dr. STRANGE!"
A TALE SO DIFFERENT, SO UNEXPECTED, THAT WE JUST HAD TO GIVE IT THE FEATURE COVER SPOT THIS ISSUE!
HOW OFF-BEAT CAN YOU GET??
Don't Dare Miss THE HUMAN TORCH
and
THE EVER-LOVIN' BLUE-EYED THING WHEN THEY...
"MEET.. The BEATLES!"

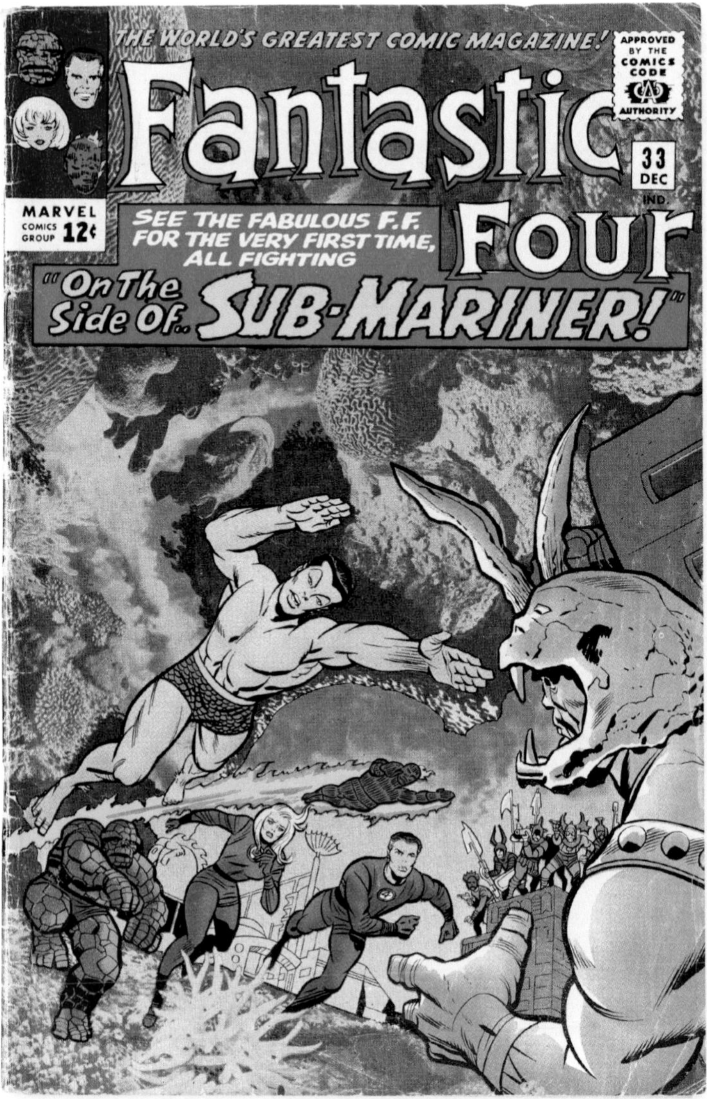
THE WORLD'S GREATEST COMIC MAGAZINE!
APPROVED BY THE COMICS CODE AUTHORITY
Fantastic Four
33 DEC
IND.
MARVEL COMICS GROUP 12¢
SEE THE FABULOUS F.F. FOR THE VERY FIRST TIME, ALL FIGHTING
"On The Side Of.. SUB-MARINER!"

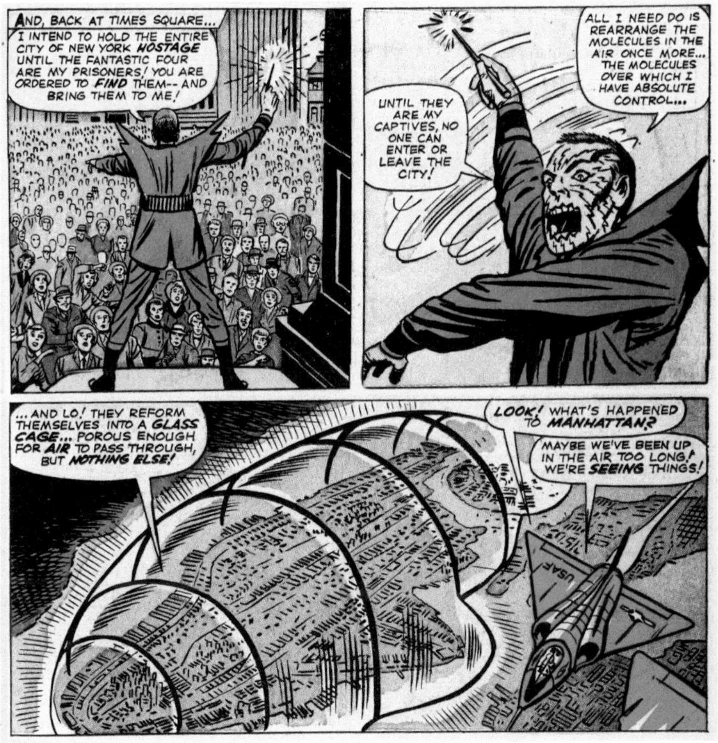
AND, BACK AT TIMES SQUARE...
I INTEND TO HOLD THE ENTIRE CITY OF NEW YORK HOSTAGE UNTIL THE FANTASTIC FOUR ARE MY PRISONERS! YOU ARE ORDERED TO FIND THEM-- AND BRING THEM TO ME!
ALL I NEED DO IS REARRANGE THE MOLECULES IN THE AIR ONCE MORE... THE MOLECULES OVER WHICH I HAVE ABSOLUTE CONTROL...
UNTIL THEY ARE MY CAPTIVES, NO ONE CAN ENTER OR LEAVE THE CITY!
... AND LO! THEY REFORM THEMSELVES INTO A GLASS CAGE... POROUS ENOUGH FOR AIR TO PASS THROUGH, BUT NOTHING ELSE!
LOOK! WHAT'S HAPPENED TO MANHATTAN?
MAYBE WE'VE BEEN UP IN THE AIR TOO LONG! WE'RE SEEING THINGS!
USAF

FANTASTIC FOUR No. 33

Opposite: *Cover; pencils, Jack Kirby; inks, Chic Stone; December 1964.* The ever-inventive Kirby often created photo collages by clipping images from magazines to use as backgrounds.

FANTASTIC FOUR No. 20

Above: *Interior, "The Mysterious Molecule Man!"; script, Stan Lee; pencils, Jack Kirby; inks, Dick Ayers; November 1963.* Setting Marvel apart from the competition, New York City takes a central role as the home base for most of its heroes beginning with *Fantastic Four* No. 4. The heroes bumping into each other in a recognizable location made Lee's alternate world that much more real to fans.

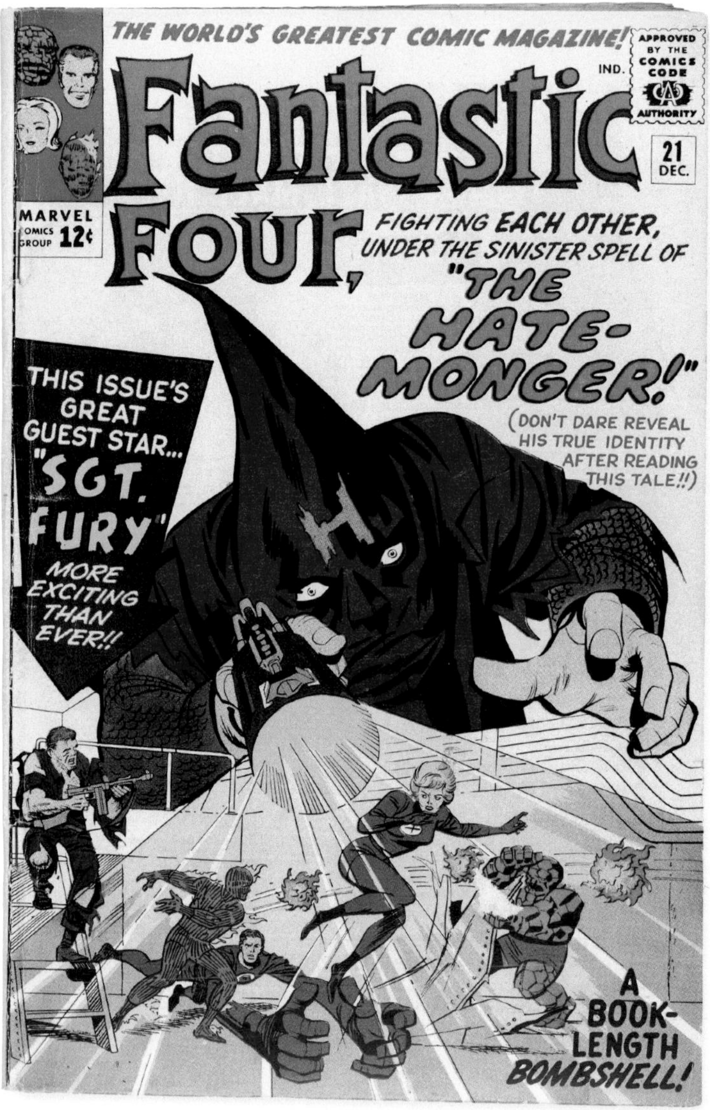
THE WORLD'S GREATEST COMIC MAGAZINE!
APPROVED BY THE COMICS CODE AUTHORITY
IND.
Fantastic Four,
21 DEC.
MARVEL COMICS GROUP 12¢
FIGHTING EACH OTHER, UNDER THE SINISTER SPELL OF "THE HATE-MONGER!"
(DON'T DARE REVEAL HIS TRUE IDENTITY AFTER READING THIS TALE!!)
THIS ISSUE'S GREAT GUEST STAR... "SGT. FURY" MORE EXCITING THAN EVER!!
A BOOK-LENGTH BOMBSHELL!

OKAY, YOU HOODED CORNBALL! GIVE RICHARDS THE ANTI-DOTE TO YOUR NERVE GAS... AND TO THE HATE RAY, BEFORE I REALLY GET MAD!
DON'T SHOOT! DON'T SHOOT!
I WILL DO AS YOU SAY!
THE C.I.A. HAS BEEN WISE TO YOU ALL ALONG, CHUM! WE KNEW WHAT YOU WERE UP TO! BUT WE COULDN'T INTERFERE IN ANOTHER NATION'S AFFAIRS! BUT WHEN YOU START MESSIN' WITH AMERICANS, THAT'S DIFFERENT!
A PITY YOU ARE TOO SQUEAMISH TO SHOOT A NOW-DEFENSELESS MAN! FOR I SHALL YET LIVE TO DESTROY YOU ALL!
SIXTY SECONDS AFTER SWALLOWING THE ANTIDOTE PILL...
NICK, YOU OL' HOUND DOG! I FEEL LIKE MYSELF AGAIN! THE HATRED IS ALL GONE!
OKAY, OKAY! QUIT SLOBBERIN' OVER ME, PAL, OR I'LL PUSH YOU UNDER THAT BLASTED MACHINE AGAIN! WE STILL GOT SOME MOPPIN' UP TO DO!
BUT, DURING THE BRIEF SECONDS THAT THEIR ATTENTION WAVERED, THE HATE-MONGER PRESSES A NEARBY BUTTON, AND...
HE TRICKED US! HE LOWERED A WALL OF BULLET-PROOF GLASS!
IT WON'T SAVE HIM FOR LONG, NICK!
18.

FANTASTIC FOUR No. 21

Opposite, above, and pages 64–65: *Cover; pencils, Jack Kirby; inks, Paul Reinman. Interiors, "The Hate-Monger!"; script, Stan Lee; pencils, Jack Kirby; inks, George Roussos. December 1963.* Ex-Sgt. Nick Fury survived the war to become a CIA agent in Marvel's 1960s. He shows up to help old buddy Reed Richards and his team against the Hate-Monger, who turns out to be... Adolf Hitler?! Fury's own book got some of the Bullpen's most memorable mail, Flo Steinberg remembers: "We got a letter to Sgt. Fury from out of somewhere, maybe Texas, saying that we were Communist pinkos because... there were different races and ethnic groups in Sgt. Fury.... He was going to come to New York and take care of us. Everybody panicked. We were all running around wondering what to do! We called the FBI. In those days, you could just call and they would respond. An FBI agent came to the office, he was really nice. He looked at the letter and said, 'Well, how many people have handled this letter?' We said, 'Oh, about 50.' Everybody had handled it! So he took the letter—after we gave him a bunch of comics—and after that, no one in the Bullpen wanted to go out to the front area where people would come into the office!"

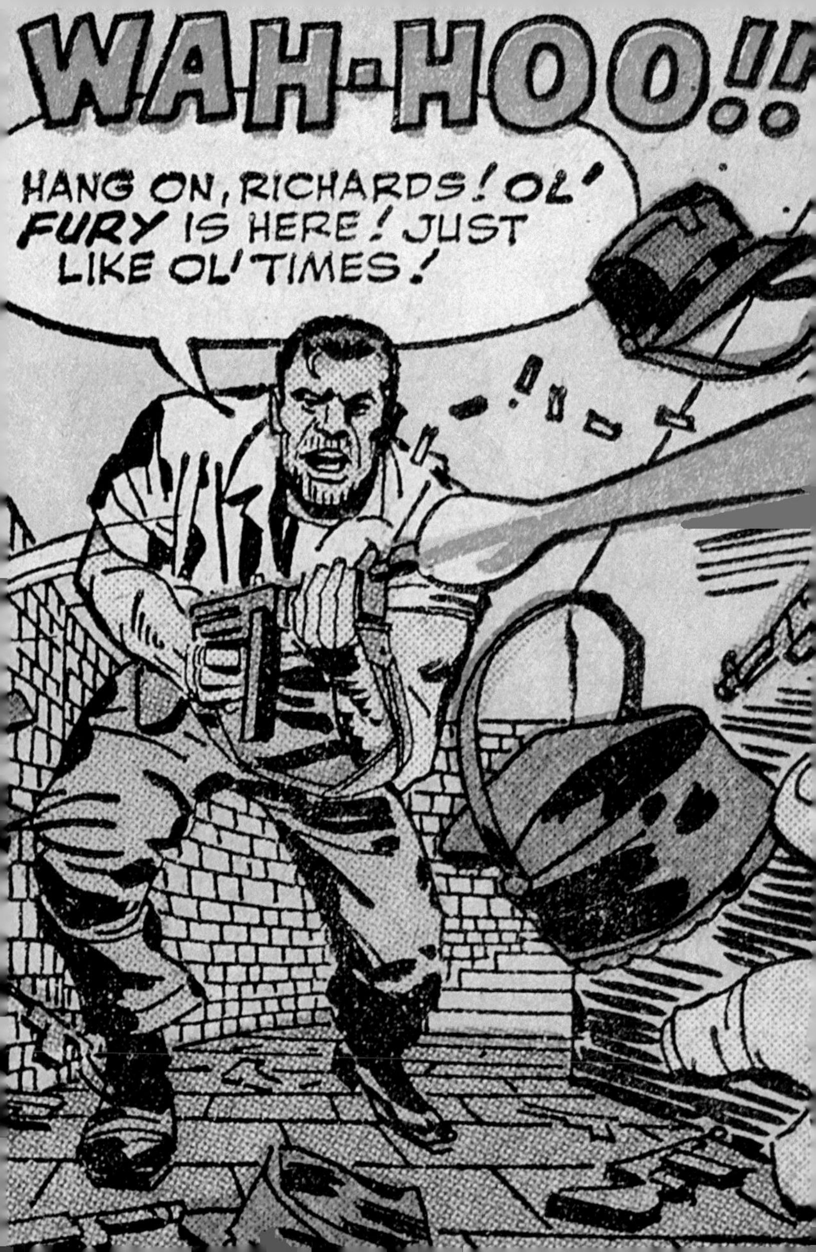
WAH-HOO!!
HANG ON, RICHARDS! OL' FURY IS HERE! JUST LIKE OL' TIMES!

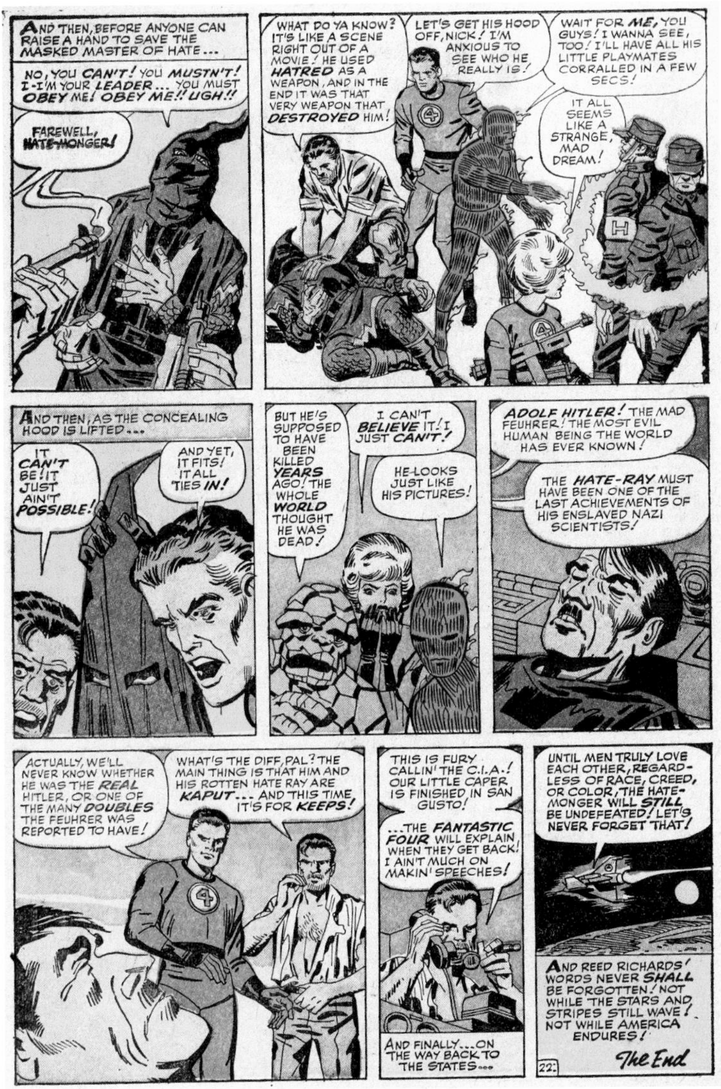

AND THEN, BEFORE ANYONE CAN RAISE A HAND TO SAVE THE MASKED MASTER OF HATE...
NO, YOU CAN'T! YOU MUSTN'T! I-I'M YOUR LEADER... YOU MUST OBEY ME! OBEY ME!! UGH!!
FAREWELL, HATE-MONGER!
WHAT DO YA KNOW? IT'S LIKE A SCENE RIGHT OUT OF A MOVIE! HE USED HATRED AS A WEAPON, AND IN THE END IT WAS THAT VERY WEAPON THAT DESTROYED HIM!
LET'S GET HIS HOOD OFF, NICK! I'M ANXIOUS TO SEE WHO HE REALLY IS!
WAIT FOR ME, YOU GUYS! I WANNA SEE, TOO! I'LL HAVE ALL HIS LITTLE PLAYMATES CORRALLED IN A FEW SECS!
IT ALL SEEMS LIKE A STRANGE, MAD DREAM!
AND THEN, AS THE CONCEALING HOOD IS LIFTED...
IT CAN'T BE! IT JUST AIN'T POSSIBLE!
AND YET, IT FITS! IT ALL TIES IN!
BUT HE'S SUPPOSED TO HAVE BEEN KILLED YEARS AGO! THE WHOLE WORLD THOUGHT HE WAS DEAD!
I CAN'T BELIEVE IT! I JUST CAN'T!
HE LOOKS JUST LIKE HIS PICTURES!
ADOLF HITLER! THE MAD FEUHRER! THE MOST EVIL HUMAN BEING THE WORLD HAS EVER KNOWN!
THE HATE-RAY MUST HAVE BEEN ONE OF THE LAST ACHIEVEMENTS OF HIS ENSLAVED NAZI SCIENTISTS!
ACTUALLY, WE'LL NEVER KNOW WHETHER HE WAS THE REAL HITLER, OR ONE OF THE MANY DOUBLES THE FEUHRER WAS REPORTED TO HAVE!
WHAT'S THE DIFF, PAL? THE MAIN THING IS THAT HIM AND HIS ROTTEN HATE RAY ARE KAPUT... AND THIS TIME IT'S FOR KEEPS!
THIS IS FURY CALLIN' THE C.I.A.! OUR LITTLE CAPER IS FINISHED IN SAN GUSTO!
...THE FANTASTIC FOUR WILL EXPLAIN WHEN THEY GET BACK! I AIN'T MUCH ON MAKIN' SPEECHES!
AND FINALLY... ON THE WAY BACK TO THE STATES...
UNTIL MEN TRULY LOVE EACH OTHER, REGARDLESS OF RACE, CREED, OR COLOR, THE HATE-MONGER WILL STILL BE UNDEFEATED! LET'S NEVER FORGET THAT!
AND REED RICHARDS' WORDS NEVER SHALL BE FORGOTTEN! NOT WHILE THE STARS AND STRIPES STILL WAVE! NOT WHILE AMERICA ENDURES!
22
The End

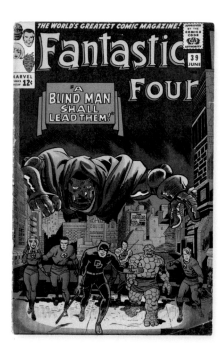

THE WORLD'S GREATEST COMIC MAGAZINE!
APPROVED BY THE COMICS CODE AUTHORITY
Fantastic
39
JUNE
MARVEL COMICS GROUP 12¢
FOUR
"A BLIND MAN SHALL LEAD THEM!"

FANTASTIC FOUR No. 39

Above: *Cover; pencils, Jack Kirby; inks, Chic Stone and Wally Wood; June 1965.* "And I will bring the blind by a way that they knew not; I will lead them in paths that they have not known." —Isaiah 42:16. Marvel's books were headed places no comic had ever been, and Stan Lee was pulling out all the stops to invite fans along.

FANTASTIC FOUR No. 39

Opposite: *Interior, "A Blind Man Shall Lead Them!"; script, Stan Lee; pencils, Jack Kirby; inks, Frank Giacoia; June 1965.* The Fantastic Four have lost their powers after being caught in an atomic blast. Here, Reed Richards tries to artificially duplicate the powers of both the Invisible Girl and the Torch. This is the start of the Marvel's two-year *annus mirabilis,* arguably the best years in comics history. The *FF* alone brought the world the Inhumans, the Silver Surfer, Galactus, and the Black Panther. Read on!

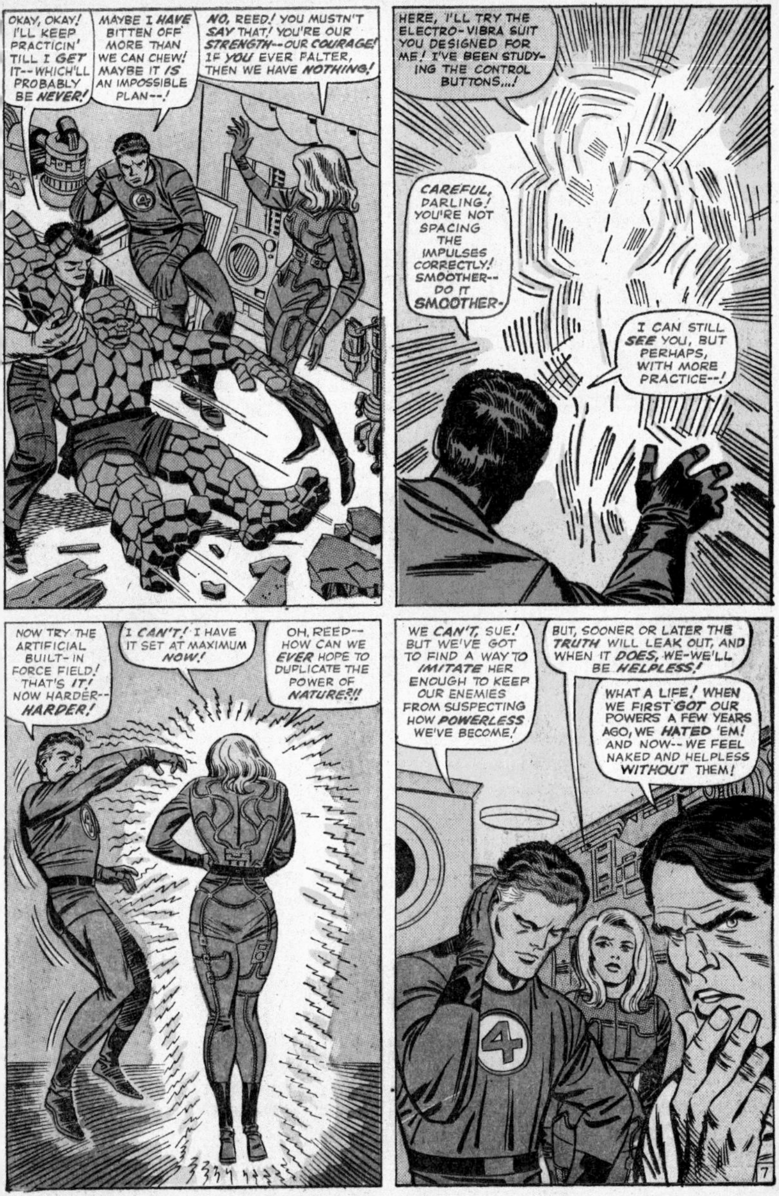
OKAY, OKAY! I'LL KEEP PRACTICIN' TILL I GET IT--WHICH'LL PROBABLY BE NEVER!
MAYBE I HAVE BITTEN OFF MORE THAN WE CAN CHEW! MAYBE IT IS AN IMPOSSIBLE PLAN--!
NO, REED! YOU MUSTN'T SAY THAT! YOU'RE OUR STRENGTH--OUR COURAGE! IF YOU EVER FALTER, THEN WE HAVE NOTHING!
HERE, I'LL TRY THE ELECTRO-VIBRA SUIT YOU DESIGNED FOR ME! I'VE BEEN STUDYING THE CONTROL BUTTONS...!
CAREFUL, DARLING! YOU'RE NOT SPACING THE IMPULSES CORRECTLY! SMOOTHER-- DO IT SMOOTHER-
I CAN STILL SEE YOU, BUT PERHAPS, WITH MORE PRACTICE--!
NOW TRY THE ARTIFICIAL BUILT-IN FORCE FIELD! THAT'S IT! NOW HARDER-- HARDER!
I CAN'T! I HAVE IT SET AT MAXIMUM NOW!
OH, REED-- HOW CAN WE EVER HOPE TO DUPLICATE THE POWER OF NATURE?!!
WE CAN'T, SUE! BUT WE'VE GOT TO FIND A WAY TO IMITATE HER ENOUGH TO KEEP OUR ENEMIES FROM SUSPECTING HOW POWERLESS WE'VE BECOME!
BUT, SOONER OR LATER THE TRUTH WILL LEAK OUT, AND WHEN IT DOES, WE-WE'LL BE HELPLESS!
WHAT A LIFE! WHEN WE FIRST GOT OUR POWERS A FEW YEARS AGO, WE HATED 'EM! AND NOW-- WE FEEL NAKED AND HELPLESS WITHOUT THEM!
7

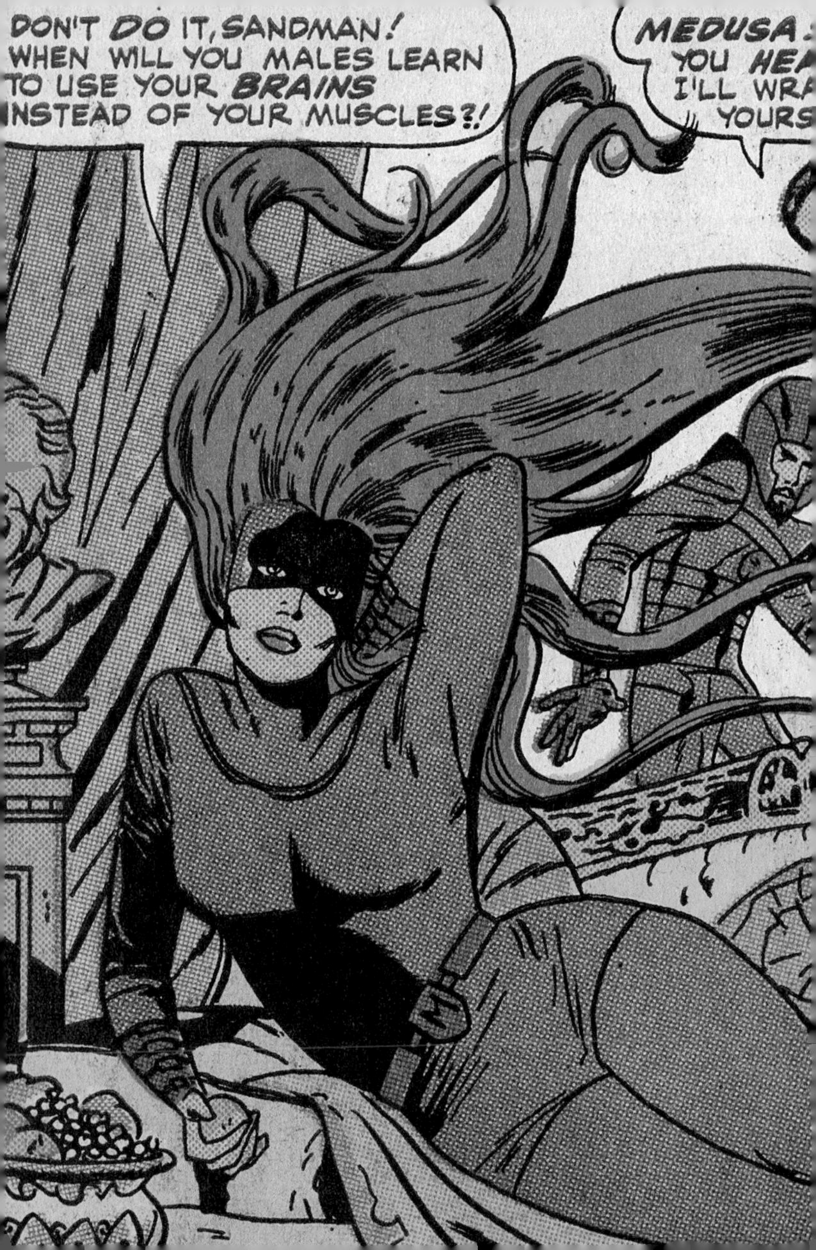
DON'T DO IT, SANDMAN! WHEN WILL YOU MALES LEARN TO USE YOUR BRAINS INSTEAD OF YOUR MUSCLES?!
MEDUSA YOU HEA I'LL WRA YOURS

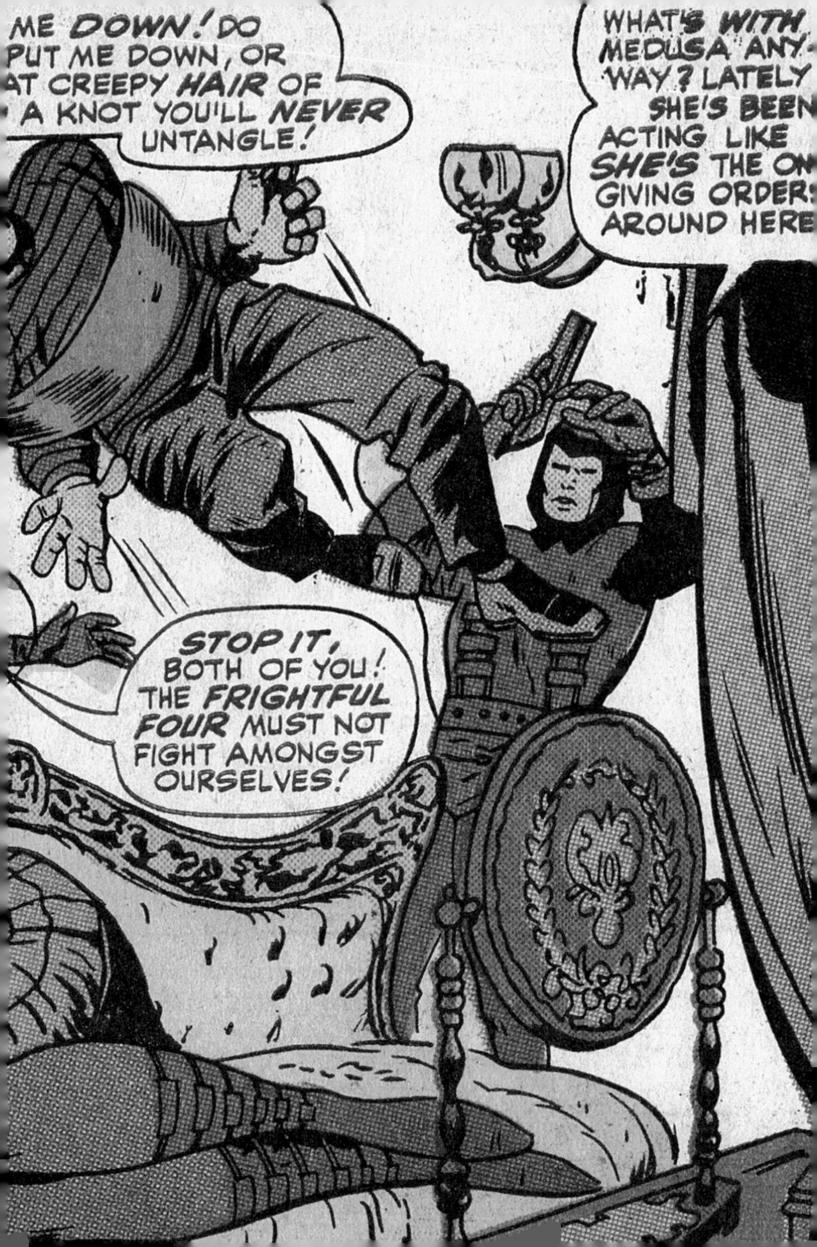
ME DOWN! DO PUT ME DOWN, OR AT CREEPY HAIR OF A KNOT YOU'LL NEVER UNTANGLE!
WHAT'S WITH MEDUSA ANYWAY? LATELY SHE'S BEEN ACTING LIKE SHE'S THE ON GIVING ORDERS AROUND HERE
STOP IT, BOTH OF YOU! THE FRIGHTFUL FOUR MUST NOT FIGHT AMONGST OURSELVES!

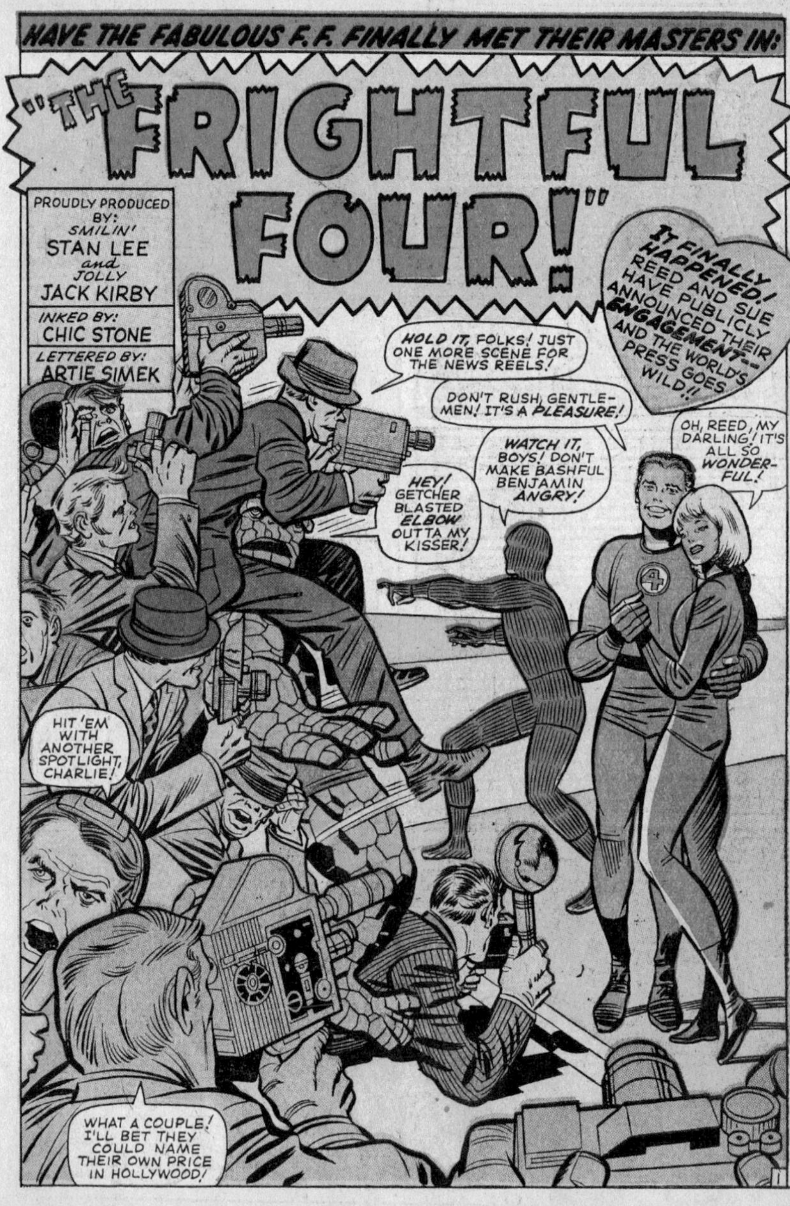
HAVE THE FABULOUS F.F. FINALLY MET THEIR MASTERS IN:
"THE FRIGHTFUL FOUR!"
PROUDLY PRODUCED BY: SMILIN' STAN LEE and JOLLY JACK KIRBY
INKED BY: CHIC STONE
LETTERED BY: ARTIE SIMEK
IT FINALLY HAPPENED! REED AND SUE HAVE PUBLICLY ANNOUNCED THEIR ENGAGEMENT-- AND THE WORLD'S PRESS GOES WILD!!
HOLD IT, FOLKS! JUST ONE MORE SCENE FOR THE NEWS REELS!
DON'T RUSH, GENTLE-MEN! IT'S A PLEASURE!
OH, REED, MY DARLING! IT'S ALL SO WONDER-FUL!
WATCH IT, BOYS! DON'T MAKE BASHFUL BENJAMIN ANGRY!
HEY! GETCHER BLASTED ELBOW OUTTA MY KISSER!
HIT 'EM WITH ANOTHER SPOTLIGHT, CHARLIE!
WHAT A COUPLE! I'LL BET THEY COULD NAME THEIR OWN PRICE IN HOLLYWOOD!
1

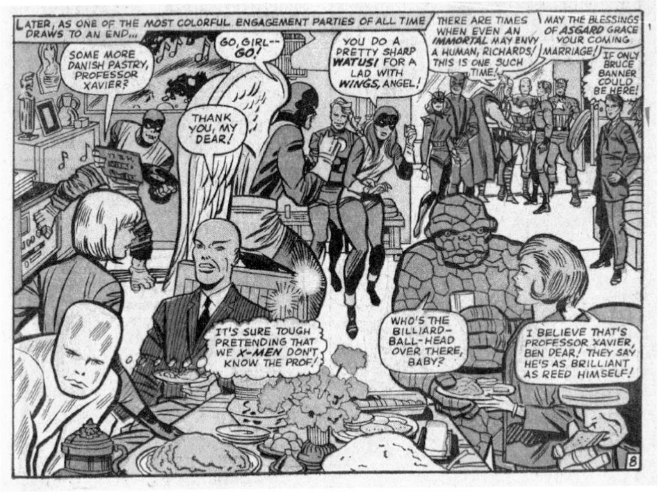
LATER, AS ONE OF THE MOST COLORFUL ENGAGEMENT PARTIES OF ALL TIME DRAWS TO AN END...
SOME MORE DANISH PASTRY, PROFESSOR XAVIER?
GO, GIRL-- GO!
YOU DO A PRETTY SHARP WATUSI FOR A LAD WITH WINGS, ANGEL!
THANK YOU, MY DEAR!
THERE ARE TIMES WHEN EVEN AN IMMORTAL MAY ENVY A HUMAN, RICHARDS! THIS IS ONE SUCH TIME!
MAY THE BLESSINGS OF ASGARD GRACE YOUR COMING MARRIAGE!
IF ONLY BRUCE BANNER COULD BE HERE!
IT'S SURE TOUGH PRETENDING THAT WE X-MEN DON'T KNOW THE PROF!
WHO'S THE BILLIARD-BALL-HEAD OVER THERE, BABY?
I BELIEVE THAT'S PROFESSOR XAVIER, BEN DEAR! THEY SAY HE'S AS BRILLIANT AS REED HIMSELF!
8

FANTASTIC FOUR No. 36

Pages 68–69: *Interior, "The Frightful Four!"; script, Stan Lee; pencils, Jack Kirby; inks, Chic Stone. March 1965.* Marvel's villains usually played fair against their heroic counterparts. Hence we got the Frightful Four, and not the Frightful Six, and they always had an equal number of women as well. Medusa filled the Wizard's quota, despite the reservations of Sandman and Paste-Pot Pete. Madame Medusa started out as a criminal, but her character would soon evolve and she would become part of a larger storyline. A powerful female as dangerous as the male members of the Frightful Four was a rarity in the early 1960s. Even more surprising was how, even under the watchful eye of the Comics Code Authority, Jack Kirby was able to imbue Medusa (posed like an Ingres odalisque, or Manet's *Olympia*) with an air of sensuality.

FANTASTIC FOUR No. 36

Opposite and above: *Interiors, "The Frightful Four!"; script, Stan Lee; pencils, Jack Kirby; inks, Chic Stone; March 1965.* Unlike most other heroes in the Marvel Universe, the Fantastic Four were adored by the public and treated as Hollywood royalty or rock stars, so the announcement of an engagement between Reed and Sue would naturally bring out the paparazzi. When the Elongated Man at DC got married, it was "off camera" and between issues. Here, everyone celebrates and it brings the Marvel Universe closer.

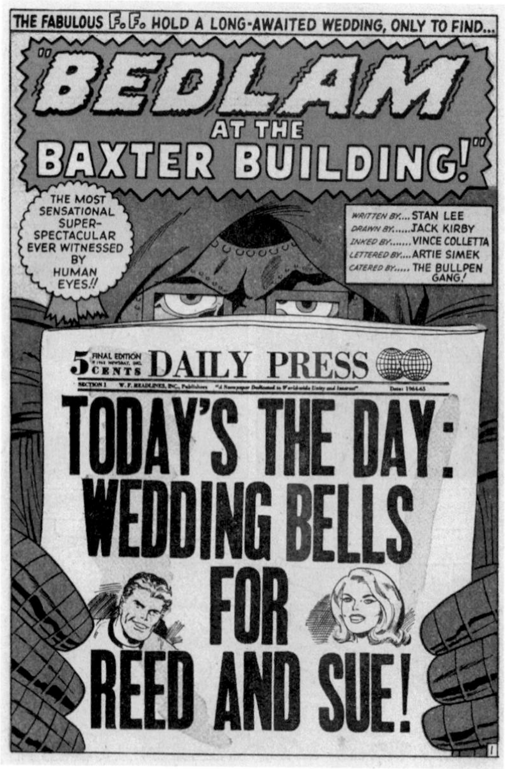
THE FABULOUS F.F. HOLD A LONG-AWAITED WEDDING, ONLY TO FIND...
"BEDLAM AT THE BAXTER BUILDING!"
THE MOST SENSATIONAL SUPER-SPECTACULAR EVER WITNESSED BY HUMAN EYES!!
WRITTEN BY....STAN LEE
DRAWN BY......JACK KIRBY
INKED BY.......VINCE COLLETTA
LETTERED BY....ARTIE SIMEK
CATERED BY..... THE BULLPEN GANG!
5 CENTS FINAL EDITION
DAILY PRESS
TODAY'S THE DAY: WEDDING BELLS FOR REED AND SUE!
1

FANTASTIC FOUR ANNUAL No. 3

Above and opposite: *Interiors, "Battle of the Baxter Building!"; script, Stan Lee; pencils, Jack Kirby; inks, Vince Colletta; 1965.* "The standard sound bite that Stan used to say back in those days, because he was talking to newspapers and they wanted sound bites, was that it was 'heroes with hang-ups, heroes with problems,'" Jim Shooter said at Stan Lee's "roast" in 1995. "But the fact is, it was a lot more than that. It was heroes with lives that we could identify with. And that was revolutionary." Virtually every Marvel hero and villain (and even Patsy Walker and Hedy Wolfe) show up for the wedding of Sue and Reed. Lee and Kirby also show up, but are blocked at the entrance by S.H.I.E.L.D. agents.

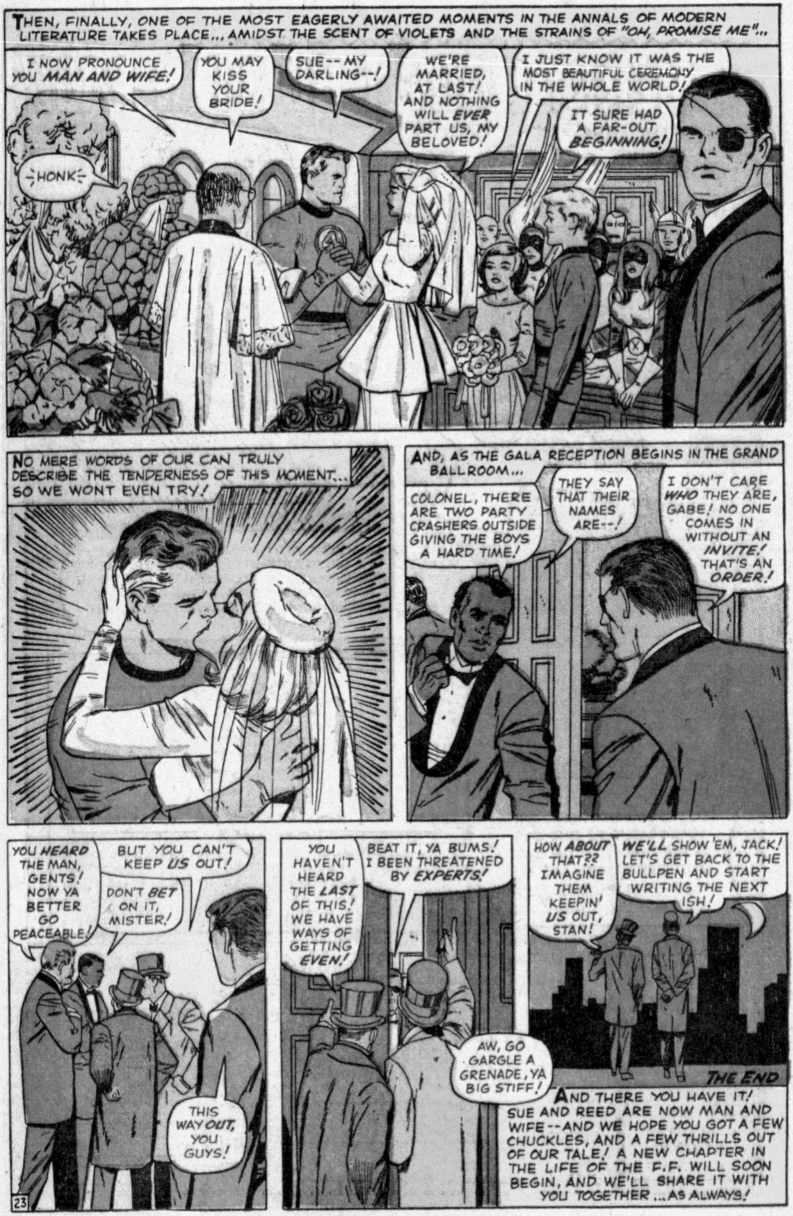
THEN, FINALLY, ONE OF THE MOST EAGERLY AWAITED MOMENTS IN THE ANNALS OF MODERN LITERATURE TAKES PLACE... AMIDST THE SCENT OF VIOLETS AND THE STRAINS OF "OH, PROMISE ME"...
I NOW PRONOUNCE YOU MAN AND WIFE!
YOU MAY KISS YOUR BRIDE!
SUE-- MY DARLING--!
WE'RE MARRIED, AT LAST! AND NOTHING WILL EVER PART US, MY BELOVED!
I JUST KNOW IT WAS THE MOST BEAUTIFUL CEREMONY IN THE WHOLE WORLD!
IT SURE HAD A FAR-OUT BEGINNING!
-HONK-
NO MERE WORDS OF OUR CAN TRULY DESCRIBE THE TENDERNESS OF THIS MOMENT... SO WE WONT EVEN TRY!
AND, AS THE GALA RECEPTION BEGINS IN THE GRAND BALLROOM...
COLONEL, THERE ARE TWO PARTY CRASHERS OUTSIDE GIVING THE BOYS A HARD TIME!
THEY SAY THAT THEIR NAMES ARE--!
I DON'T CARE WHO THEY ARE, GABE! NO ONE COMES IN WITHOUT AN INVITE! THAT'S AN ORDER!
YOU HEARD THE MAN, GENTS! NOW YA BETTER GO PEACEABLE!
BUT YOU CAN'T KEEP US OUT!
DON'T BET ON IT, MISTER!
THIS WAY OUT, YOU GUYS!
23
YOU HAVEN'T HEARD THE LAST OF THIS! WE HAVE WAYS OF GETTING EVEN!
BEAT IT, YA BUMS! I BEEN THREATENED BY EXPERTS!
AW, GO GARGLE A GRENADE, YA BIG STIFF!
HOW ABOUT THAT?? IMAGINE THEM KEEPIN' US OUT, STAN!
WE'LL SHOW 'EM, JACK! LET'S GET BACK TO THE BULLPEN AND START WRITING THE NEXT ISH!
THE END
AND THERE YOU HAVE IT! SUE AND REED ARE NOW MAN AND WIFE--AND WE HOPE YOU GOT A FEW CHUCKLES, AND A FEW THRILLS OUT OF OUR TALE! A NEW CHAPTER IN THE LIFE OF THE F.F. WILL SOON BEGIN, AND WE'LL SHARE IT WITH YOU TOGETHER... AS ALWAYS!

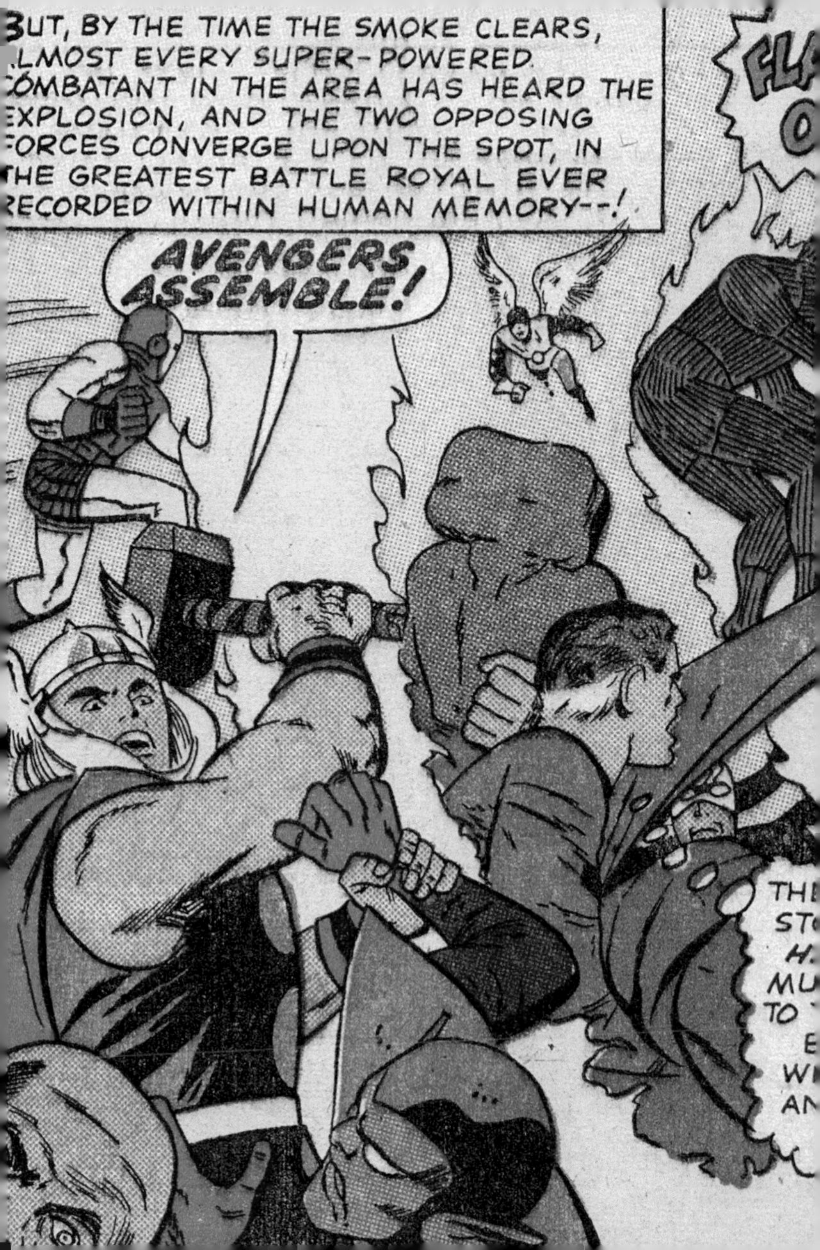
BUT, BY THE TIME THE SMOKE CLEARS, ALMOST EVERY SUPER-POWERED COMBATANT IN THE AREA HAS HEARD THE EXPLOSION, AND THE TWO OPPOSING FORCES CONVERGE UPON THE SPOT, IN THE GREATEST BATTLE ROYAL EVER RECORDED WITHIN HUMAN MEMORY--!
AVENGERS ASSEMBLE!

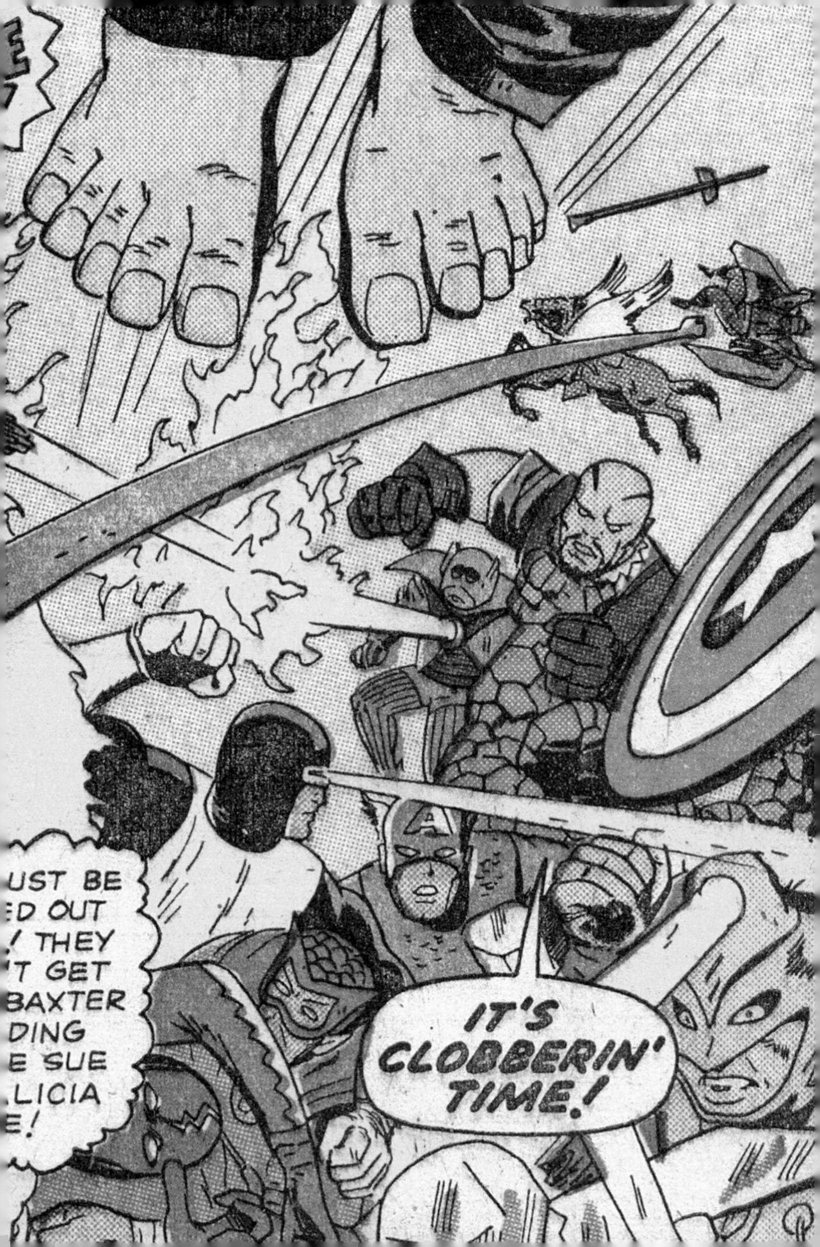

UST BE
ED OUT
! THEY
'T GET
BAXTER
DING
E SUE
LICIA
E!
IT'S CLOBBERIN' TIME!

FANTASTIC FOUR ANNUAL No. 3

Pages 74–75: *Interior, "Bedlam at the Baxter Building!"; script, Stan Lee; pencils, Jack Kirby; inks, Vince Colletta; November 1965.* The fabulous FF hold the long-awaited wedding of Reed and Sue, an event celebrated by the appearance of almost every major Marvel character — except the fugitive Hulk, who wasn't much for leaving his forwarding address!

THE MAN AND THE KING

Above: *Photograph, Stan Lee and Jack Kirby, 1966.*

FANTASTIC FOUR No. 26

Opposite: *Cover; pencils, Jack Kirby; inks, Sol Brodsky; May 1964.* Chaos, confusion, and continuity! The Marvel Universe of crossovers, epic battles, and heroes intermingling grew exponentially in the years ahead, and Stan Lee had a field day coordinating everything. Midtown Manhattan miraculously survived these clashes apparently unscathed! Stan Lee sums up the success of Marvel's first wave of super hero titles in a response about Marvel's best sellers for *Crusader* fanzine's winter 1964–65 issue: "Well, of course, *Fantastic Four*, but *Spider-Man*, *Sgt. Fury*, and *Avengers* are all big hits… AND, all of a sudden, *Thor* is becoming a big hit. But it's a funny thing, because all of a sudden *Suspense* and *Astonish* are becoming big because we have added Hulk and Captain America. And *X-Men*! *X-Men* is really selling, so… we really don't have a bad seller! It's just great!"

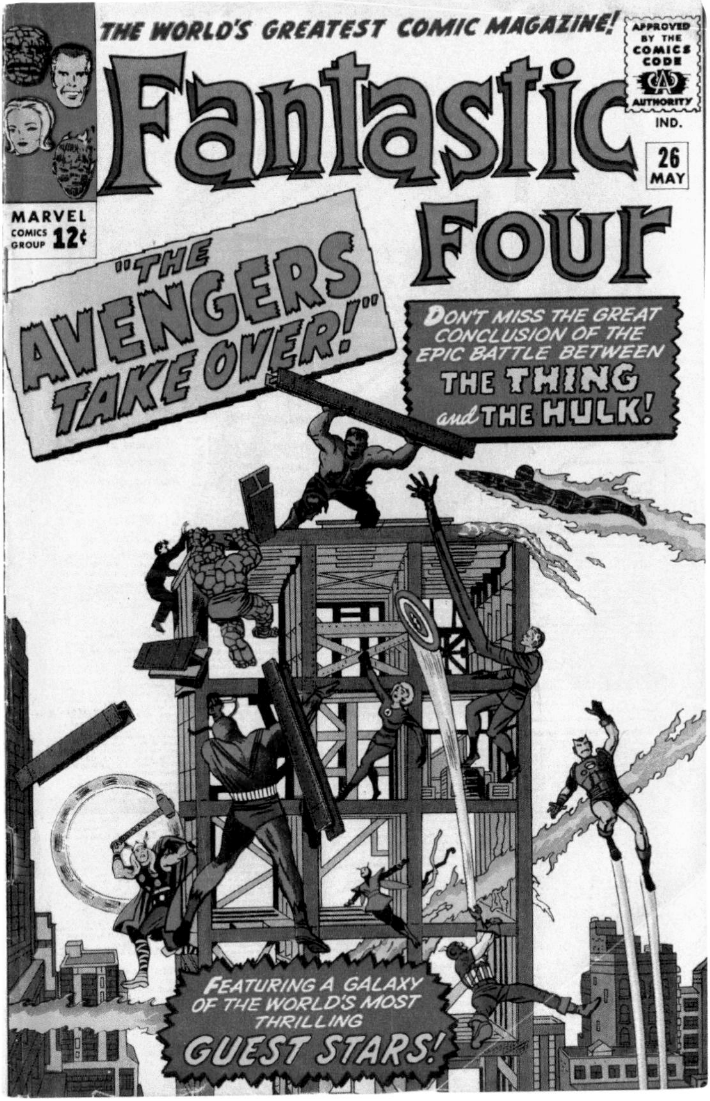
THE WORLD'S GREATEST COMIC MAGAZINE!
APPROVED BY THE COMICS CODE AUTHORITY
Fantastic Four
IND.
26 MAY
MARVEL COMICS GROUP 12¢
"THE AVENGERS TAKE OVER!"
DON'T MISS THE GREAT CONCLUSION OF THE EPIC BATTLE BETWEEN THE THING and THE HULK!
FEATURING A GALAXY OF THE WORLD'S MOST THRILLING GUEST STARS!

WELCOME TO THE ANCIENT AND HONORABLE ORDER OF

The Merry Marvel Marching Society

THE MARVEL AGE OF COMICS
E PLURIBUS MARVEL
"NUFF SAID!"

Congratulations, favored one!

...For having the wisdom and wit to become a Merry Marvel Marcher!

Your name has been ceremoniously entered in our log book, and your dollar has been avariciously deposited in our treasury!

From this day forth, you will stand a little straighter, speak a little wiser, and walk a little prouder. You've made the scene! You're in! You've joined the winning team!

But, with such triumph comes responsibility. You must use your valued membership privileges judiciously. You must be true to the Marvel Code of Ethics: Be not arrogant towards those who have shunned our ranks, for they know not what they're missing. Be not hostile towards unbelievers who march with others, for they're more to be pitied than scorned. Be not intolerant of Marvel-defamers, for they too shall someday see the light. And, above all, be not forgetful that you have become our bullpen buddy. Henceforth, you shall never march alone!

Thus, we welcome you to the fold with this sagacious admonition—FACE FRONT! You're one of us now!

'Nuff said!

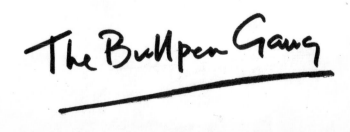

The Bullpen Gang

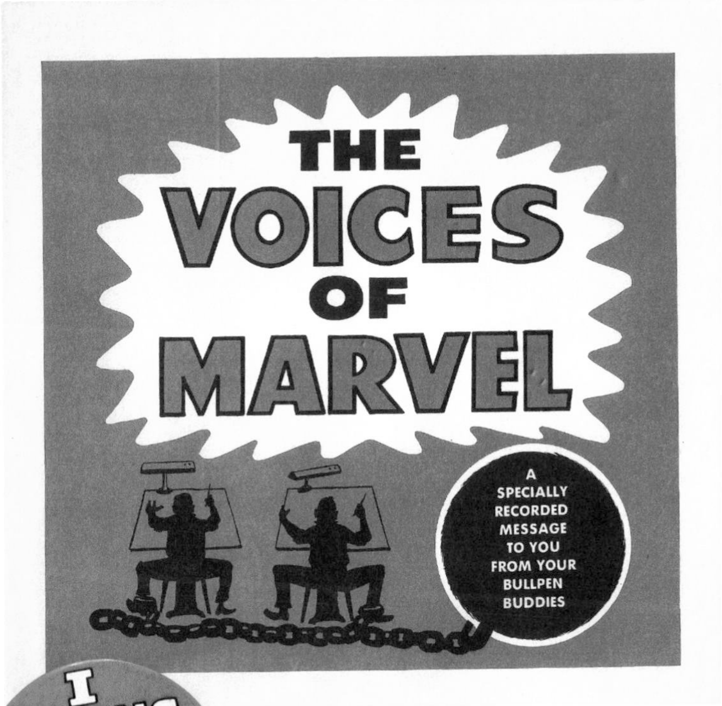
THE
VOICES
OF
MARVEL
A SPECIALLY RECORDED MESSAGE TO YOU FROM YOUR BULLPEN BUDDIES

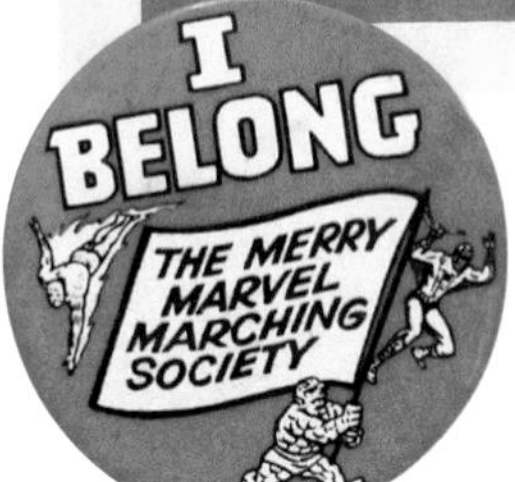
I BELONG
THE MERRY MARVEL MARCHING SOCIETY

YOU'RE ONE OF US NOW

Opposite and above: *Membership welcome package, Merry Marvel Marching Society (M.M.M.S.), 1964.* Flo Steinberg recalled the fan club's beginnings in a 2002 interview: "Bags and bags of mail would come and we would have to open them up and—this was before computers—we had to write down everybody's name and make labels for each one, and pull out all these hundreds of dollar bills. We were throwing them at each other there were so many! It was amazing." For their buck, fans who joined would receive a welcome letter, membership card, scratch pad, sticker, pinback button, membership certificate, and a $33\frac{1}{3}$ rpm record, *The Voices of Marvel.*

THE MERRY MARVEL MESSENGER

"FACE FRONT, MARVELITES"

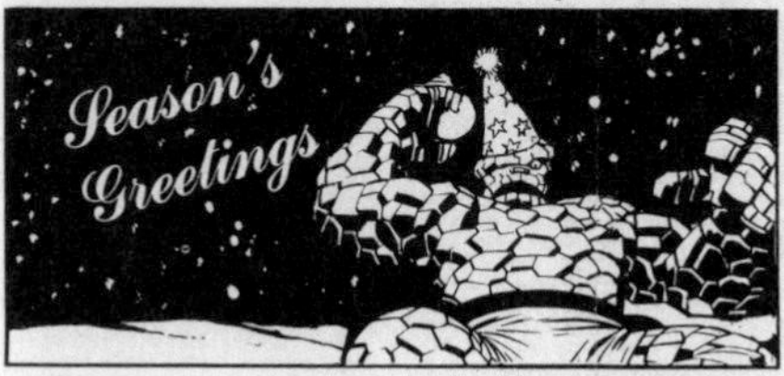
Season's Greetings

INTRODUCING: OUR NEWEST BULLPEN BOMBSHELL!

Hang loose, frantic ones – and feast your eyes on the latest labor of love from your blushin' Bullpen!

We've been promising all of you a regularly-published newsletter for a long time now–and, like the man said, here it is!

After many long hours of sleepless brain-searching, we decided that the best way to print news is in – wouldja believe a newspaper? So, we've created the Merry Marvel Messenger for MMMS members only–to keep you clued-in on all the latest happenings in and around the Marvel Madhouse!

And, that's not all. We're gonna give all you madcap marchers a chance to tell us–and all the rest of Marveldom–what's cooking with your local chapters! You send us the news, and we'll do our best to print it–right on the pages of this, your exclusive club bulletin! But, we'll tell you how to go about sending in your nutty news elsewhere in this frantic first ish!

Now, in addition to telling you what's cooking in the Bullpen, we're also gonna toss in some crazy contests, frenzied features about all the Marvel Maniacs and a gob of other goodies too numerous to mention right now! And, if any of you have ideas of things you'd like to see in the Marvel Messenger–don't hesitate, let us hear about it! Got it? Got it!

So, before you get so excited about jotting down all of your scintillatin' suggestions that you forget to read the rest of the paper, we're gonna cool it–and just tell ya to feast your eyes and enjoy! After all, we did all'a this just for you, tiger! ★ ★ ★

BLASTS AND BRAVOS ON TV SUPER-HEROES

Response to our bombastic boob-tube venture have been so overwhelming the past few weeks that the Post Office is threatening to make Irv Forbush help them deliver all of your letters!

But, at least we know that somebody out there must be tuning us in – 'cause Smilin Stan hasn't been able to dig his way through last week's mail! And, by now, the letters are piled up so high in front of his door that it looks like he may be confined to his office for eternity!

Just before we went to press, though, he did send up a smoke signal to let us know that a majority of you frantic fanatics think the show is a gas. Of course, on the other hand – a lot of you have spotted a few fumblin' flaws in the show, and you should see how many *we* found, ourselves!

Just like many of you, your brain-bustin' Bullpen realizes that the animation isn't up to Walt Disney, yet–and one or two of your respective hosts may be playing up a bit much to the bubble-gum brigade–but just wait till next season! All in all, we think old Wing-Head, Fish-Face, Green Skin, Goldilocks, and Shell-Head come off pretty well in videoville!

And we're mighty glad that enough of you agree with us to make Marvel Super-Heroes a top-rated show in its time-slot in most areas of the country! ★ ★ ★

WE NEED HELP, O, TRUE BELIEVER

Clutch your MMMS membership button to your bosom – keep calm, and, above all, don't fool with your cool! 'Cause this is your chance to become an important part of our glitzy little group!

Starting right now, pussycat, the MMMS needs you! No, not as a member! If you're reading this, we've already got you hawgtied! What we need from you is news! We want you to write and tell us what's going on among the rank and file of your own cavortin' chapters!

Get the picture? Good! Now, all you have to do is send your reports to Marvel Comics Group, News Dept., 625 Madison Avenue, New York, N. Y. 10022! We'll print the best of your batty bulletins in each future issue along with the name, address and MMMS number of the reporters who submitted them.

Ready? Then rush to your typewriters and get with it! After all, we can't print the news until you've made it!

And, in case your chapter hasn't made any news lately (and we shudder at the thought), we might suggest a few worthwhile projects! You might take a green-skinned monster to the cafeteria for lunch–or you might arrange for one of your classmates to be bitten by a radio-active spider! But, if neither of those ideas grab you, why not march on city hall in your Thing and Hulk sweat shirts. (Marvel T-shirts should be permissible dress for those few Marvelites who are still dwelling in the last century and haven't ordered their sweat shirts yet!) ★ ★ ★

MERRY MARVEL MESSENGER

Above: *Newsletter; pencils, Jack Kirby; inks, Joe Sinnott; 1966.* While Superman fans were still decoding messages that were a plug for DC comics, Marvel began sending M.M.M.S. members this newsletter, the forerunner of *Marvelmania* magazine.

FANTASTIC FOUR No. 39

Opposite: *Original interior art; pencils and collage, Jack Kirby; inks, attributed Carl Hubbell; June 1965.*

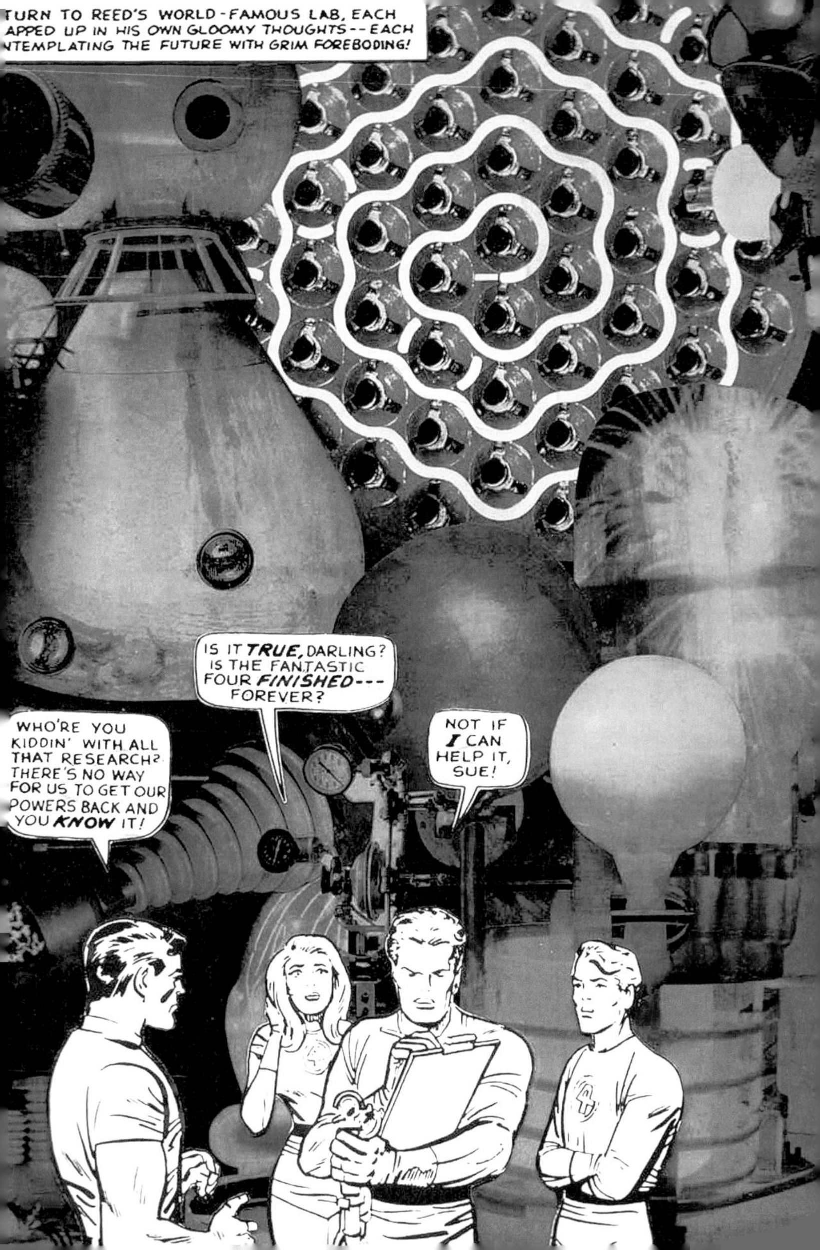

TURN TO REED'S WORLD-FAMOUS LAB, EACH
APPED UP IN HIS OWN GLOOMY THOUGHTS--EACH
NTEMPLATING THE FUTURE WITH GRIM FOREBODING!
IS IT TRUE, DARLING? IS THE FANTASTIC FOUR FINISHED--- FOREVER?
WHO'RE YOU KIDDIN' WITH ALL THAT RESEARCH? THERE'S NO WAY FOR US TO GET OUR POWERS BACK AND YOU KNOW IT!
NOT IF I CAN HELP IT, SUE!

FANTASTIC FOUR No. 37

Opposite: *Original interior art, "Behold! A Distant Star!"; script,
Stan Lee; pencils, Jack Kirby; inks, Chic Stone; April 1964.* Chic
Stone was Kirby's primary inker ca.1964–65, giving the early
Marvel line a cohesive look. Stone's bold, solid blacks were a
perfect fit, adding weight and dimension to Kirby's pencils.
Stone was a comics veteran dating as far back as 1939, drawing for outfits such as Fawcett, Lev Gleason, and Timely, and
he found satisfaction in being Kirby's primary inker, calling
the King's pencils "magnificent."

FANTASTIC FOUR No. 50

Pages 84–85: *Interior, "The Startling Saga of the Silver Surfer!";
script, Stan Lee; pencils, Jack Kirby; inks, Joe Sinnott; May 1966.*
"One other thing I think we've innovated that has been pretty
successful is overlapping characters and books," Stan Lee
told WBAI Radio in 1967. "In fact, all our books are one big
continued story. And in the mail we received from so many
college kids, they now refer to those books. They'll say, 'By
the way, regarding your "Galactus Trilogy"...' And, you know,
they're referring to this as though it's *The Rise and Fall
of the Roman Empire*, which I love! This is wonderful! It
means we're really reaching them."

FANTASTIC FOUR 36 APR 6 1/4 x 9 1/4 · No SPS 1.

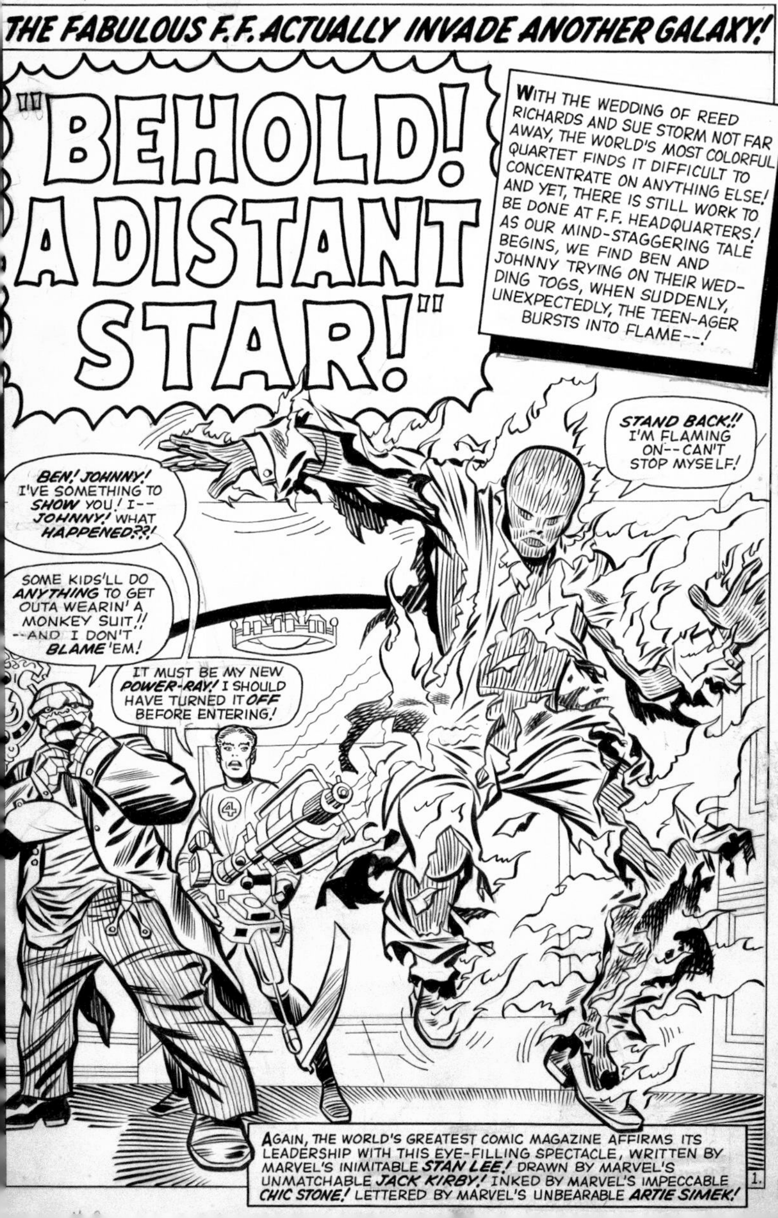
THE FABULOUS F.F. ACTUALLY INVADE ANOTHER GALAXY!
"BEHOLD! A DISTANT STAR!"
WITH THE WEDDING OF REED RICHARDS AND SUE STORM NOT FAR AWAY, THE WORLD'S MOST COLORFUL QUARTET FINDS IT DIFFICULT TO CONCENTRATE ON ANYTHING ELSE! AND YET, THERE IS STILL WORK TO BE DONE AT F.F. HEADQUARTERS! AS OUR MIND-STAGGERING TALE BEGINS, WE FIND BEN AND JOHNNY TRYING ON THEIR WEDDING TOGS, WHEN SUDDENLY, UNEXPECTEDLY, THE TEEN-AGER BURSTS INTO FLAME--!
BEN! JOHNNY! I'VE SOMETHING TO SHOW YOU! I-- JOHNNY! WHAT HAPPENED??!
STAND BACK!! I'M FLAMING ON--CAN'T STOP MYSELF!
SOME KIDS'LL DO ANYTHING TO GET OUTA WEARIN' A MONKEY SUIT!! --AND I DON'T BLAME 'EM!
IT MUST BE MY NEW POWER-RAY! I SHOULD HAVE TURNED IT OFF BEFORE ENTERING!
AGAIN, THE WORLD'S GREATEST COMIC MAGAZINE AFFIRMS ITS LEADERSHIP WITH THIS EYE-FILLING SPECTACLE, WRITTEN BY MARVEL'S INIMITABLE STAN LEE! DRAWN BY MARVEL'S UNMATCHABLE JACK KIRBY! INKED BY MARVEL'S IMPECCABLE CHIC STONE! LETTERED BY MARVEL'S UNBEARABLE ARTIE SIMEK!
1.

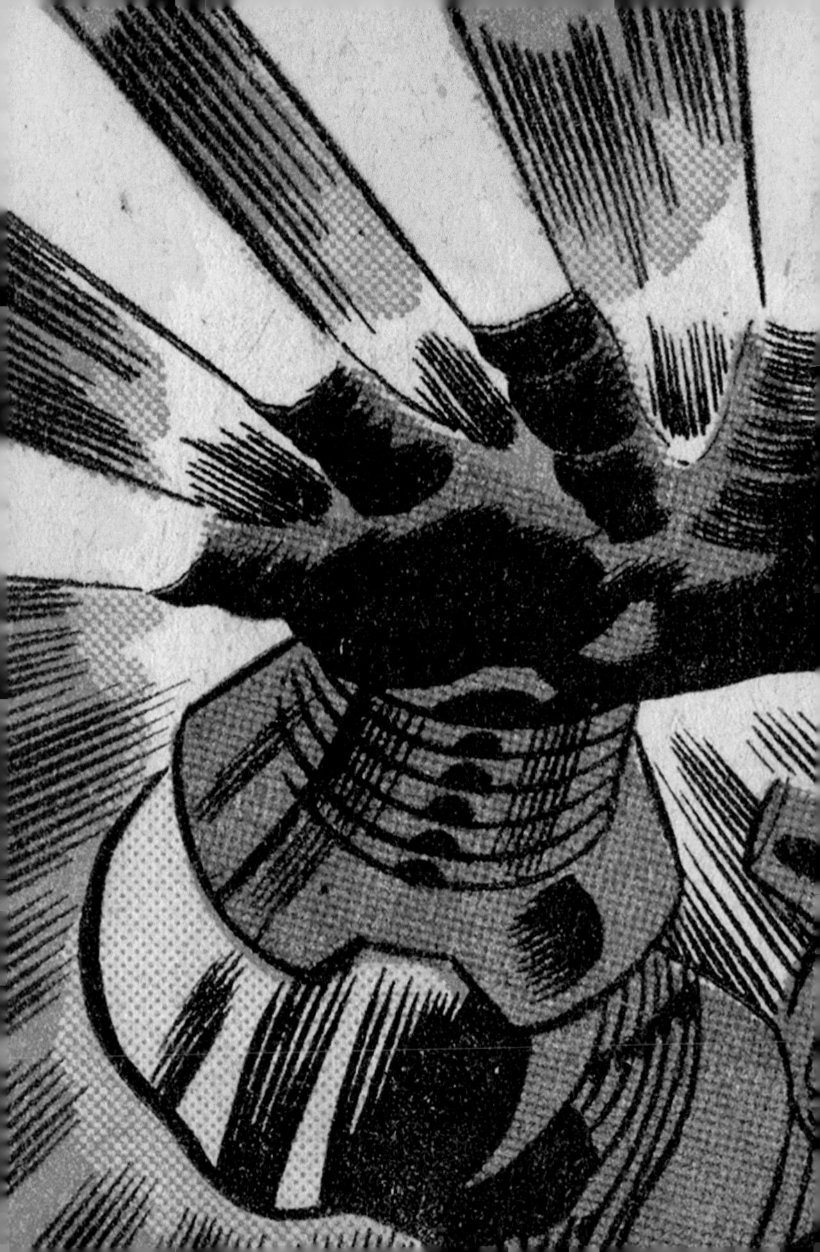

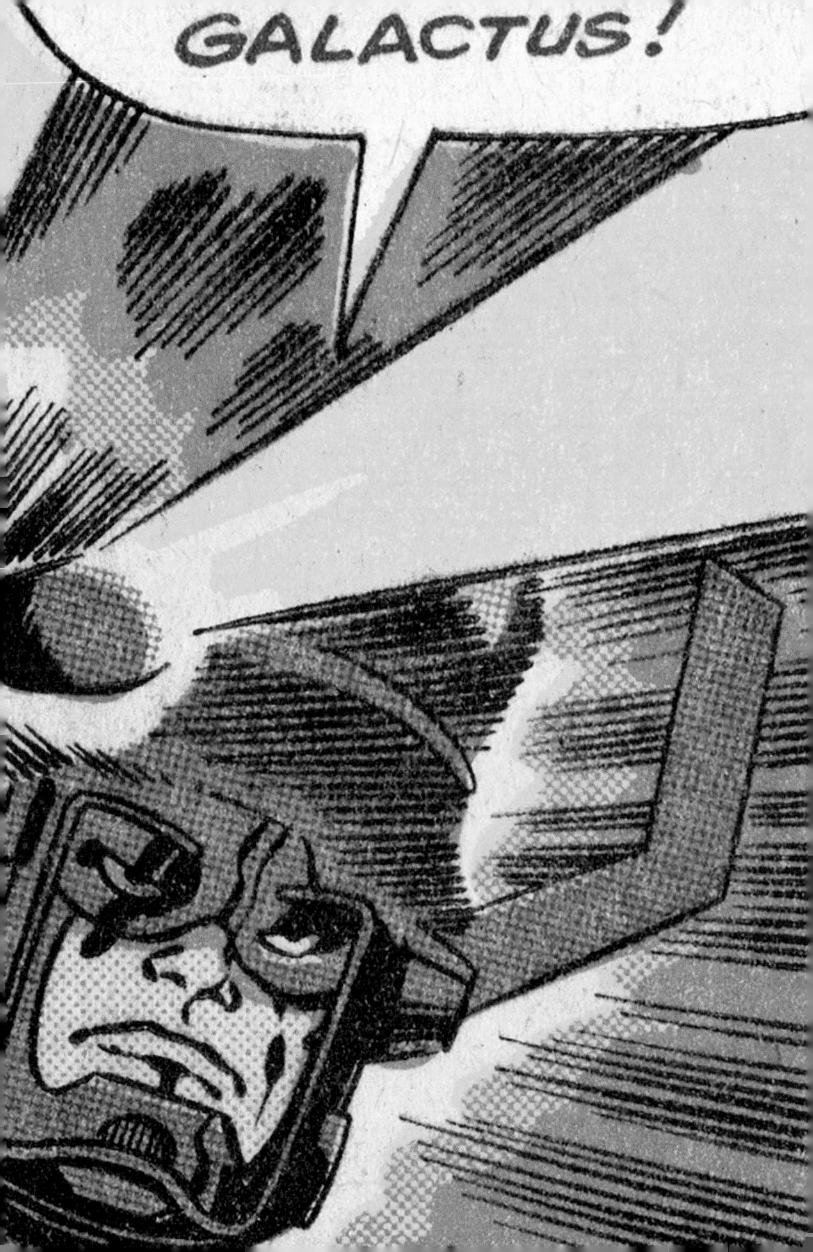
GALACTUS!

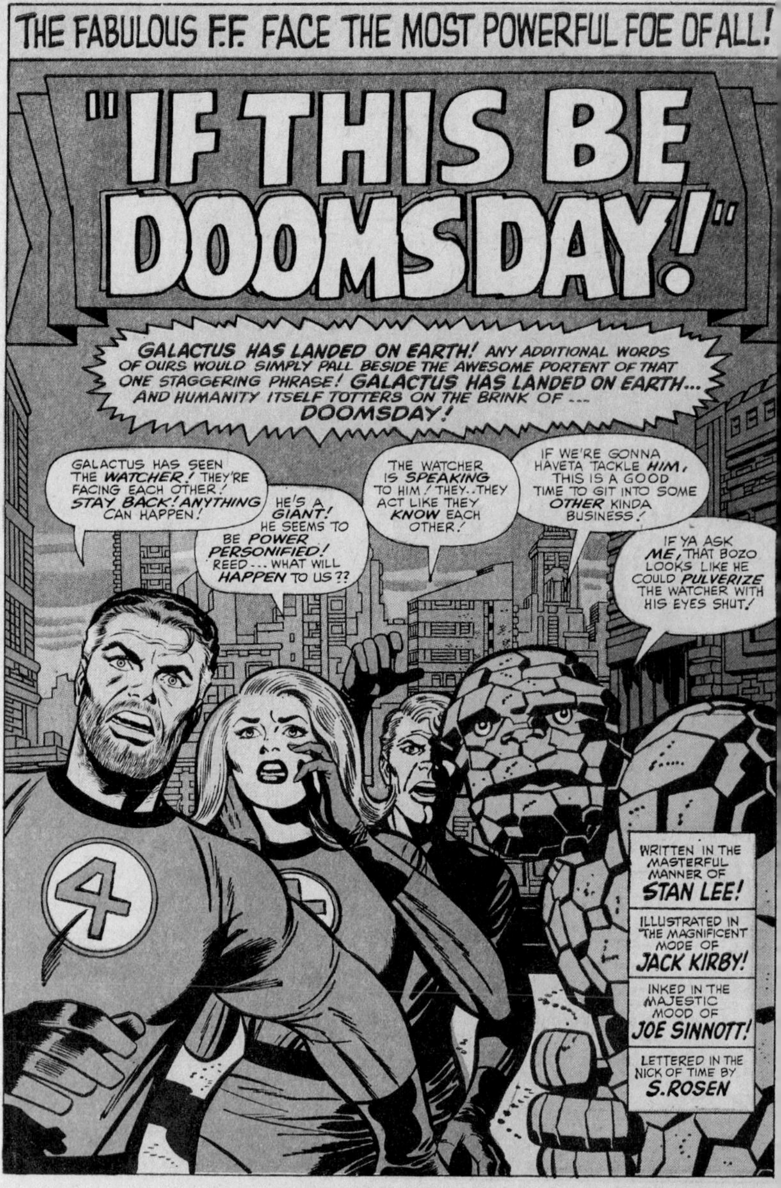
THE FABULOUS F.F. FACE THE MOST POWERFUL FOE OF ALL!
"IF THIS BE DOOMSDAY!"
GALACTUS HAS LANDED ON EARTH! ANY ADDITIONAL WORDS OF OURS WOULD SIMPLY PALL BESIDE THE AWESOME PORTENT OF THAT ONE STAGGERING PHRASE! GALACTUS HAS LANDED ON EARTH... AND HUMANITY ITSELF TOTTERS ON THE BRINK OF --- DOOMSDAY!
GALACTUS HAS SEEN THE WATCHER! THEY'RE FACING EACH OTHER! STAY BACK! ANYTHING CAN HAPPEN!
HE'S A GIANT! HE SEEMS TO BE POWER PERSONIFIED! REED--- WHAT WILL HAPPEN TO US??
THE WATCHER IS SPEAKING TO HIM! THEY..THEY ACT LIKE THEY KNOW EACH OTHER!
IF WE'RE GONNA HAVETA TACKLE HIM, THIS IS A GOOD TIME TO GIT INTO SOME OTHER KINDA BUSINESS!
IF YA ASK ME, THAT BOZO LOOKS LIKE HE COULD PULVERIZE THE WATCHER WITH HIS EYES SHUT!
WRITTEN IN THE MASTERFUL MANNER OF STAN LEE!
ILLUSTRATED IN THE MAGNIFICENT MODE OF JACK KIRBY!
INKED IN THE MAJESTIC MOOD OF JOE SINNOTT!
LETTERED IN THE NICK OF TIME BY S. ROSEN

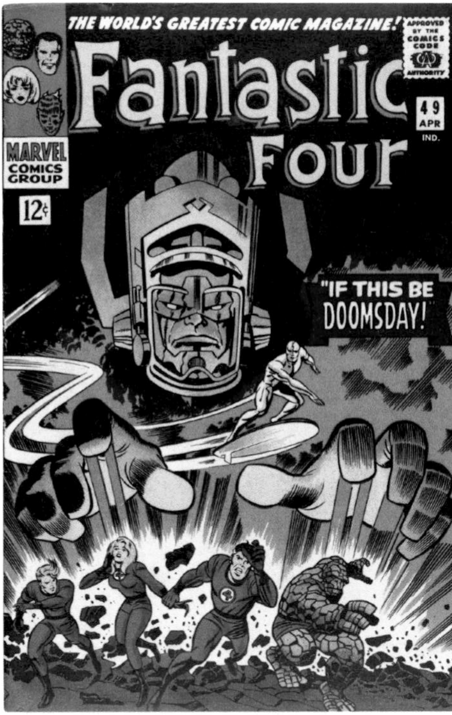
THE WORLD'S GREATEST COMIC MAGAZINE!
APPROVED BY THE COMICS CODE AUTHORITY
Fantastic Four
49 APR
IND.
MARVEL COMICS GROUP
12¢
"IF THIS BE DOOMSDAY!"

FANTASTIC FOUR No. 49

Opposite: *Interior, "If This Be Doomsday!"; script, Stan Lee; pencils, Jack Kirby; inks, Joe Sinnott; April 1966.* In part two of comics' most famous trilogy, Galactus and his herald, the Silver Surfer, have landed on Earth. The looks of fear and terror are so well defined on the faces of the Four that even the staunchest fans wonder how they will defend this planet.

FANTASTIC FOUR No. 49

Above: *Cover; pencils, Jack Kirby; inks, Joe Sinnott; April 1966.* "Galactus was God, and I was looking for God. When I first came up with Galactus, I was very awed by him. I didn't know what to do with the character. Everybody talks about God, but what the heck does he look like? Well, he's supposed to be awesome, and Galactus is awesome to me." —Jack Kirby

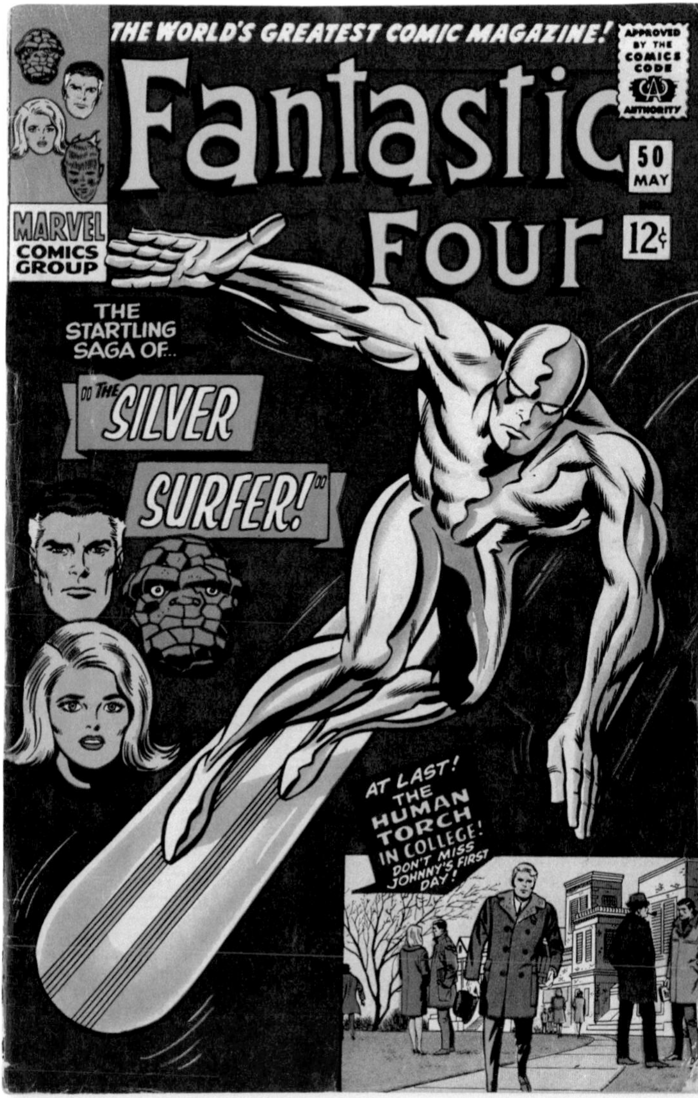
THE WORLD'S GREATEST COMIC MAGAZINE!
APPROVED BY THE COMICS CODE AUTHORITY
Fantastic Four
50 MAY
12¢
MARVEL COMICS GROUP
THE STARTLING SAGA OF..
"THE SILVER SURFER!"
AT LAST! THE HUMAN TORCH IN COLLEGE! DON'T MISS JOHNNY'S FIRST DAY!

ON AND ON HE SOARS, DODGING METEORS--SKIRTING AROUND ASTEROIDS--ROCKETING FROM PLANET TO PLANET--WITH ENTIRE *GALAXIES* AS HIS PORTS OF CALL-- WITH THE KNOWN *UNIVERSE* ITSELF AS HIS HIGHWAY--!

FANTASTIC FOUR No. 50

Opposite: *Cover; pencils, Jack Kirby; inks, Joe Sinnott; May 1966.* "And somewhere in the deep vastness of outer space, an incredible figure hurtles thru the Cosmos! A being whom we shall call the Silver Surfer, for want of a better name!" This story is not just the development of the Surfer and his discovery of his humanity. It is also about the maturation of Johnny Storm as he enters college — as will Peter Parker and the X-Men in their own magazines.

FANTASTIC FOUR No. 48

Above: *Interior, "The Coming of Galactus!"; script, Stan Lee; pencils, Jack Kirby; inks, Joe Sinnott; March 1966.* After their adventure with the Inhumans, life goes on and the Silver Surfer searches through space. Kirby gave him form and Lee gave him substance, but no one gave him pants. The Surfer is, at first, a blank slate.

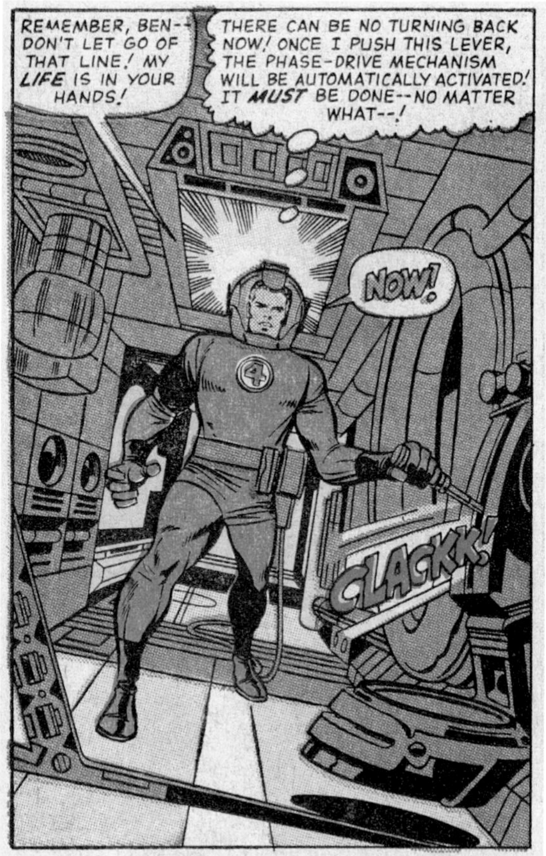
REMEMBER, BEN--
DON'T LET GO OF
THAT LINE! MY
LIFE IS IN YOUR
HANDS!
THERE CAN BE NO TURNING BACK
NOW! ONCE I PUSH THIS LEVER,
THE PHASE-DRIVE MECHANISM
WILL BE AUTOMATICALLY ACTIVATED!
IT MUST BE DONE--NO MATTER
WHAT--!
NOW!
CLACKK!

FANTASTIC FOUR No. 51

Above and opposite: *Interiors, "This Man, This Monster!"; script, Stan Lee; pencils, Jack Kirby; inks, Joe Sinnott; June 1966.* How did Lee, Kirby, and Sinnott follow the Inhumans saga and the Galactus trilogy? With a personal story of redemption, full of emotion and suspense in what many believe to be the greatest single story of the Marvel Age.

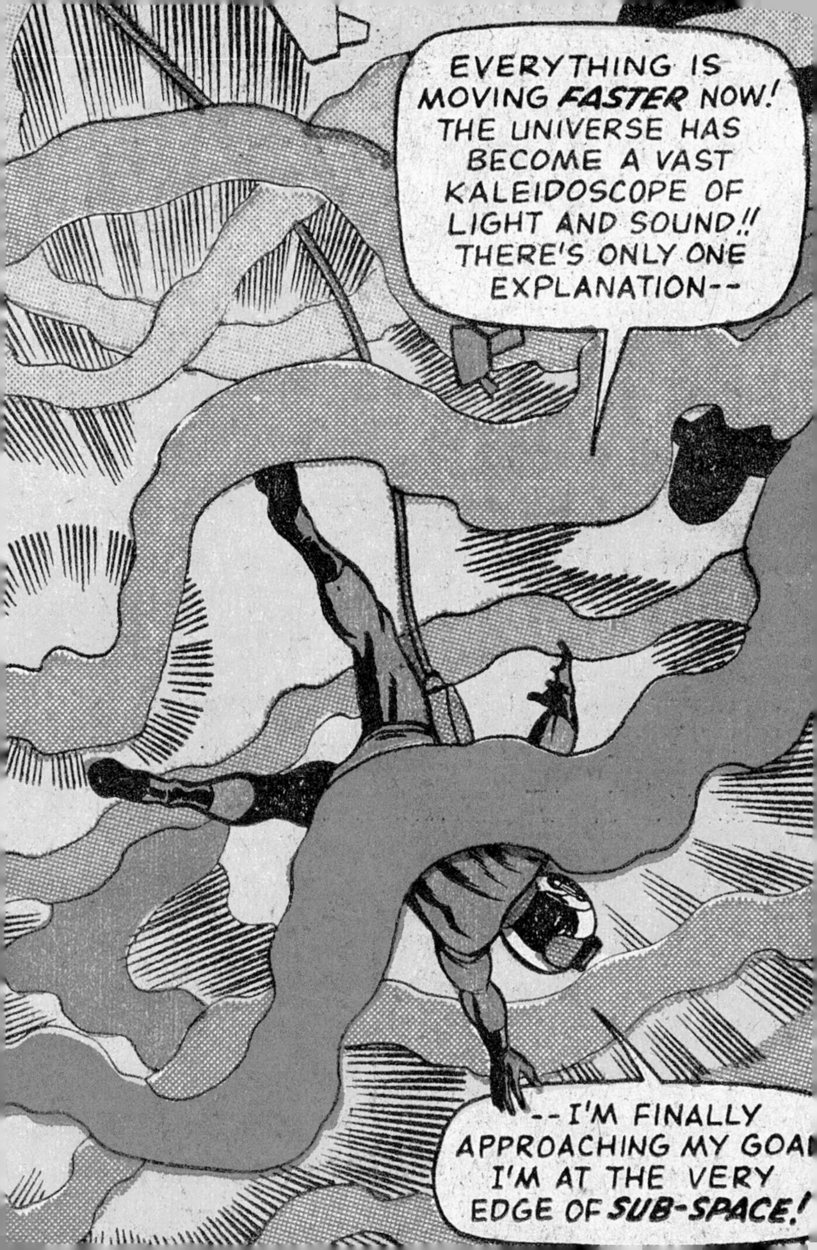
EVERYTHING IS MOVING FASTER NOW! THE UNIVERSE HAS BECOME A VAST KALEIDOSCOPE OF LIGHT AND SOUND!! THERE'S ONLY ONE EXPLANATION--
--I'M FINALLY APPROACHING MY GOA I'M AT THE VERY EDGE OF SUB-SPACE!

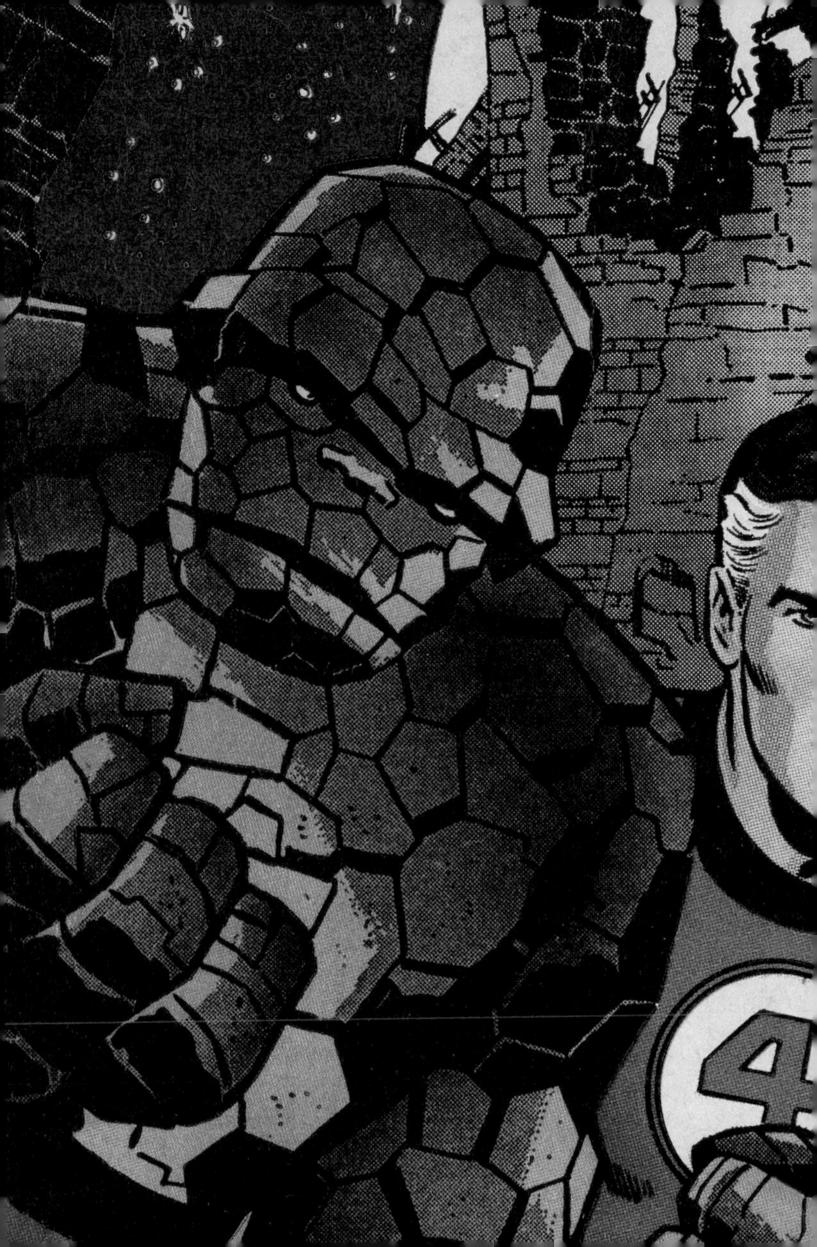

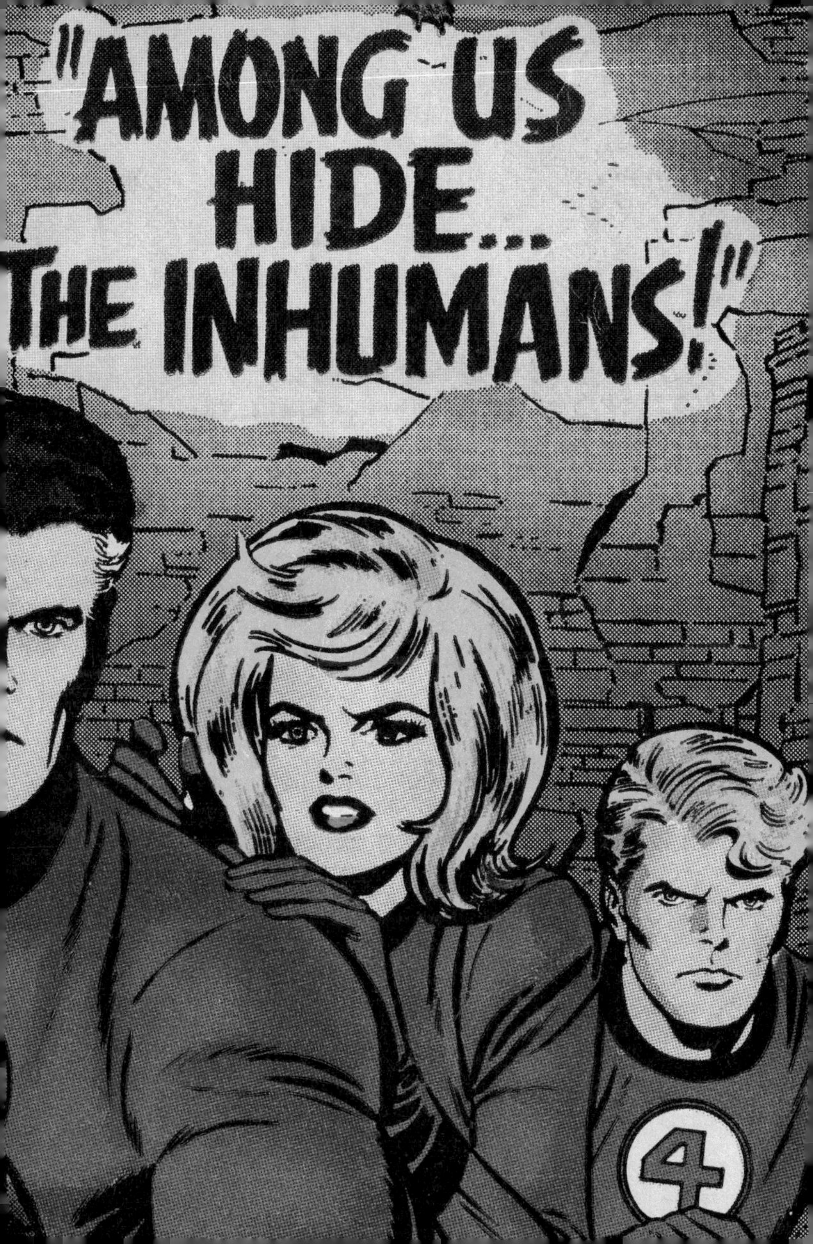
"AMONG US HIDE... THE INHUMANS!"

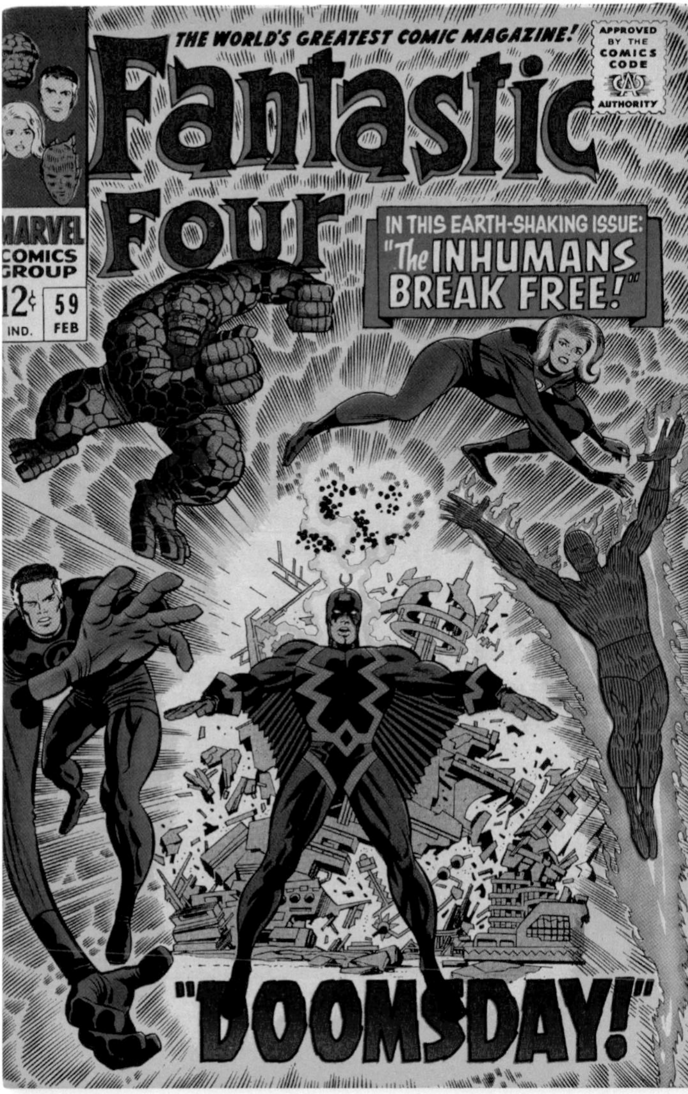
THE WORLD'S GREATEST COMIC MAGAZINE!
APPROVED BY THE COMICS CODE AUTHORITY
Fantastic Four
MARVEL COMICS GROUP
12¢ IND.
59 FEB
IN THIS EARTH-SHAKING ISSUE:
"The INHUMANS BREAK FREE!"
"DOOMSDAY!"

FANTASTIC FOUR No. 45

Pages 92–93: *Cover; pencils, Jack Kirby; inks, Joe Sinnott; December 1965.*

FANTASTIC FOUR No. 59

Opposite: *Cover; pencils, Jack Kirby; inks, Joe Sinnott; February 1967.* "Jack's point of view...became the governing philosophy of the entire publishing company and, beyond the publishing company, of the entire field," veteran artist Gil Kane told *The Comics Journal* in 1986. "[Marvel] would get artists, regardless of whether they had done romance or anything else and they taught them the ABCs, which amounted to learning Jack Kirby....Jack was like the Holy Scripture."

MASTER OF THE INKWELL

Above: *Photograph, ca. 1960s.* Joe Sinnott was a talented artist whose association with Lee dated back to the Atlas era. In the 1960s his inking brought a sophisticated gloss and techno-logical punch to Kirby's pencils on the *Fantastic Four*, which he inked consistently until 1981, along with almost every other title Marvel produced.

SLOWLY, CALMLY, IRREVOCABLY-- THE SILENT SOVEREIGN *BRACES* HIMSELF--

THEN, WITH HEAD HELD HIGH, HIS MOUTH *OPENS*--

AND THE *VOICE OF BLACK BOLT* IS HEARD THRUOUT THE LAND--!

FANTASTIC FOUR No. 59

Above and opposite: *Interiors, "Doomsday"; script, Stan Lee; pencils, Jack Kirby; inks, Joe Sinnott; February 1967.* Black Bolt, ruler of the Inhumans, is one of the most tragic characters to enter the Marvel pantheon. Possessed of sonic powers so great that his newborn cries destroyed the Inhumans' city, he lives his first eighteen years in isolation — and must vow to spend his entire life in absolute silence. Thus the Inhumans always knew he had the means to escape their captivity, but the price to pay was great. In the end, noble Black Bolt protects his evil brother, Maximus — the Inhuman Cain to his Abel — who was the cause of all of this.

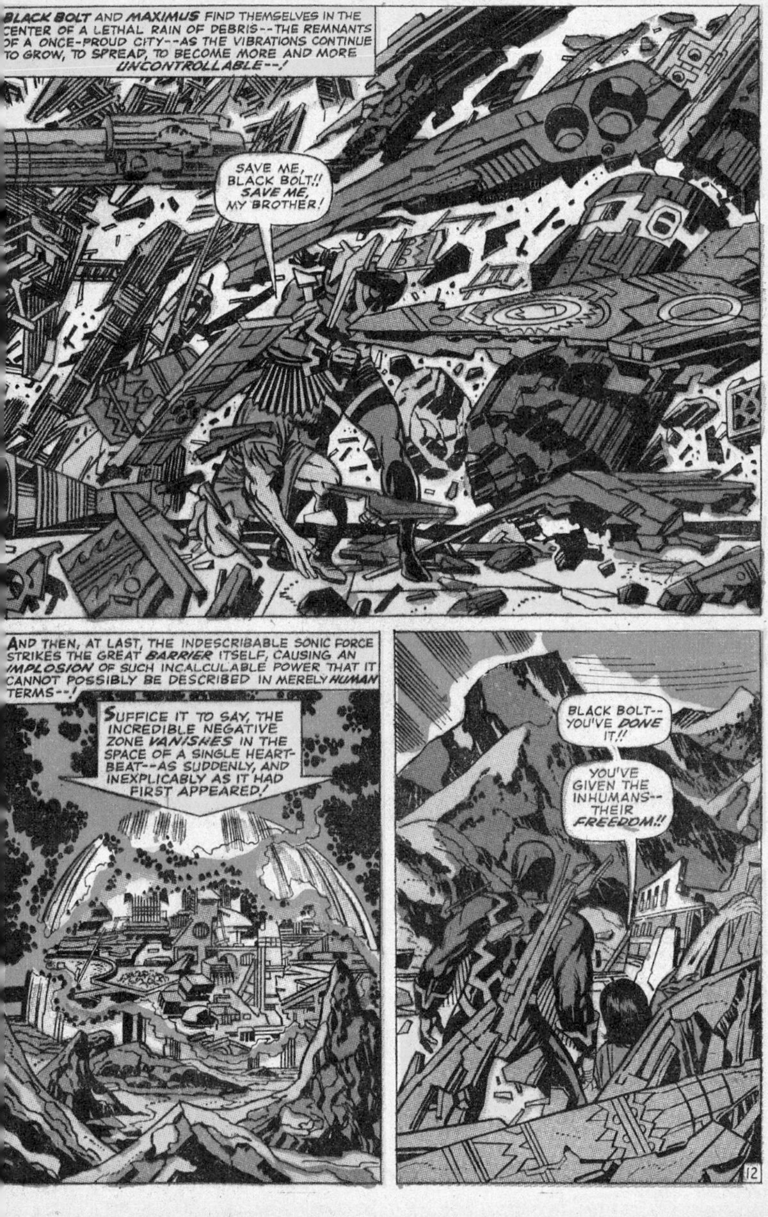

BLACK BOLT AND MAXIMUS FIND THEMSELVES IN THE CENTER OF A LETHAL RAIN OF DEBRIS--THE REMNANTS OF A ONCE-PROUD CITY--AS THE VIBRATIONS CONTINUE TO GROW, TO SPREAD, TO BECOME MORE AND MORE UNCONTROLLABLE--!
SAVE ME, BLACK BOLT!! SAVE ME, MY BROTHER!
AND THEN, AT LAST, THE INDESCRIBABLE SONIC FORCE STRIKES THE GREAT BARRIER ITSELF, CAUSING AN IMPLOSION OF SUCH INCALCULABLE POWER THAT IT CANNOT POSSIBLY BE DESCRIBED IN MERELY HUMAN TERMS--!
SUFFICE IT TO SAY, THE INCREDIBLE NEGATIVE ZONE VANISHES IN THE SPACE OF A SINGLE HEART-BEAT--AS SUDDENLY, AND INEXPLICABLY AS IT HAD FIRST APPEARED!
BLACK BOLT--YOU'VE DONE IT!!
YOU'VE GIVEN THE INHUMANS--THEIR FREEDOM!!
12

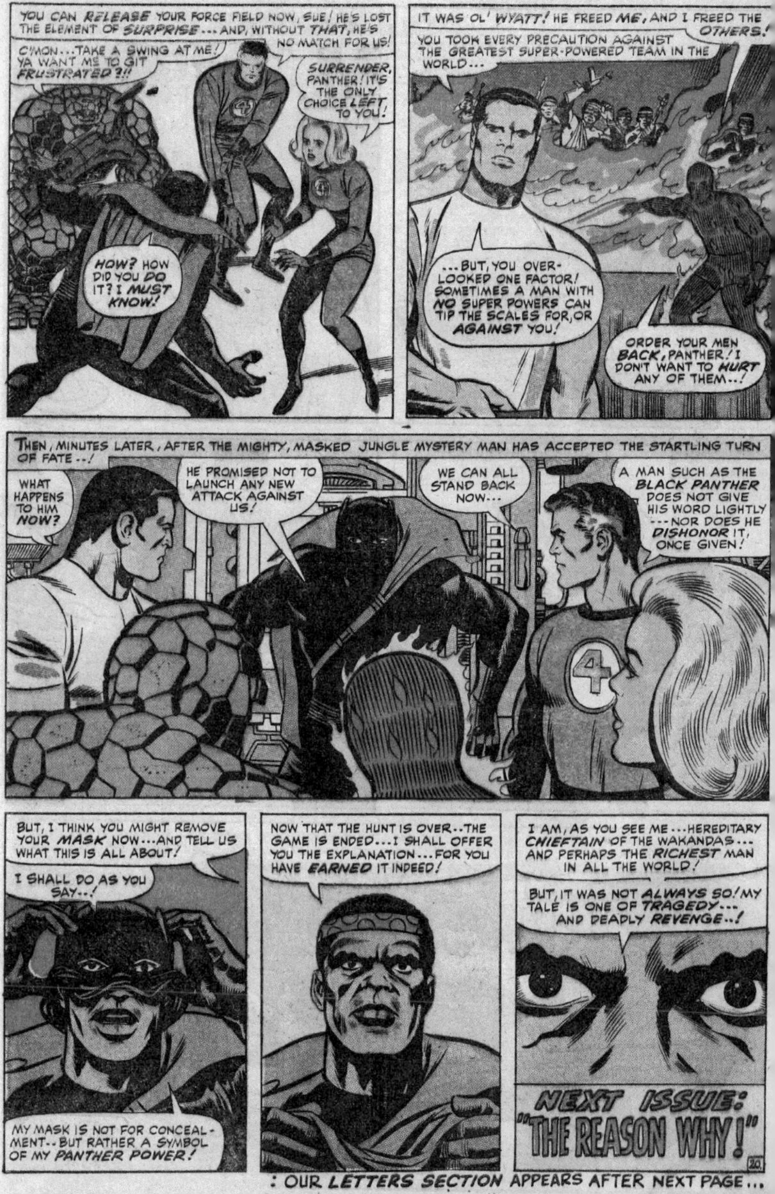
YOU CAN RELEASE YOUR FORCE FIELD NOW, SUE! HE'S LOST THE ELEMENT OF SURPRISE... AND, WITHOUT THAT, HE'S NO MATCH FOR US!
C'MON... TAKE A SWING AT ME! YA WANT ME TO GIT FRUSTRATED?!!
SURRENDER, PANTHER! IT'S THE ONLY CHOICE LEFT TO YOU!
HOW? HOW DID YOU DO IT? I MUST KNOW!
IT WAS OL' WYATT! HE FREED ME, AND I FREED THE OTHERS!
YOU TOOK EVERY PRECAUTION AGAINST THE GREATEST SUPER-POWERED TEAM IN THE WORLD...
...BUT, YOU OVER-LOOKED ONE FACTOR! SOMETIMES A MAN WITH NO SUPER POWERS CAN TIP THE SCALES FOR, OR AGAINST YOU!
ORDER YOUR MEN BACK, PANTHER! I DON'T WANT TO HURT ANY OF THEM..!
THEN, MINUTES LATER, AFTER THE MIGHTY, MASKED JUNGLE MYSTERY MAN HAS ACCEPTED THE STARTLING TURN OF FATE..!
WHAT HAPPENS TO HIM NOW?
HE PROMISED NOT TO LAUNCH ANY NEW ATTACK AGAINST US!
WE CAN ALL STAND BACK NOW...
A MAN SUCH AS THE BLACK PANTHER DOES NOT GIVE HIS WORD LIGHTLY ---NOR DOES HE DISHONOR IT, ONCE GIVEN!
BUT, I THINK YOU MIGHT REMOVE YOUR MASK NOW... AND TELL US WHAT THIS IS ALL ABOUT!
I SHALL DO AS YOU SAY..!
MY MASK IS NOT FOR CONCEAL-MENT.. BUT RATHER A SYMBOL OF MY PANTHER POWER!
NOW THAT THE HUNT IS OVER.. THE GAME IS ENDED... I SHALL OFFER YOU THE EXPLANATION... FOR YOU HAVE EARNED IT INDEED!
I AM, AS YOU SEE ME... HEREDITARY CHIEFTAIN OF THE WAKANDAS... AND PERHAPS THE RICHEST MAN IN ALL THE WORLD!
BUT, IT WAS NOT ALWAYS SO! MY TALE IS ONE OF TRAGEDY... AND DEADLY REVENGE..!
NEXT ISSUE:
"THE REASON WHY!"
20

: OUR LETTERS SECTION APPEARS AFTER NEXT PAGE...

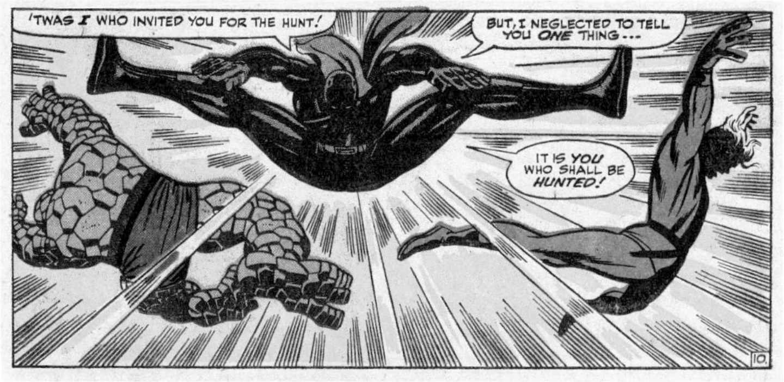
'TWAS I WHO INVITED YOU FOR THE HUNT!
BUT, I NEGLECTED TO TELL YOU ONE THING---
IT IS YOU WHO SHALL BE HUNTED!
10

FANTASTIC FOUR No. 52

Opposite and above: *Interiors, "The Black Panther!"; script, Stan Lee; pencils, Jack Kirby; inks, Joe Sinnott; July 1966.* "If ever there was a compelling black superhero that appeared directly drawn from the political moment yet presented an Afrofuturist sensibility, T'Chall[a], the Black Panther superhero of Marvel comics, is such a character. In 1966 the Lowndes County Freedom Organization first used an image of a black panther to symbolize their black political independence and self-determination in opposition to the Alabama Democratic Party's white rooster. In October of the same year the Black Panther Party for Self-Defense was created and adopted the black panther emblem as the namesake."
—Adilifu Nama

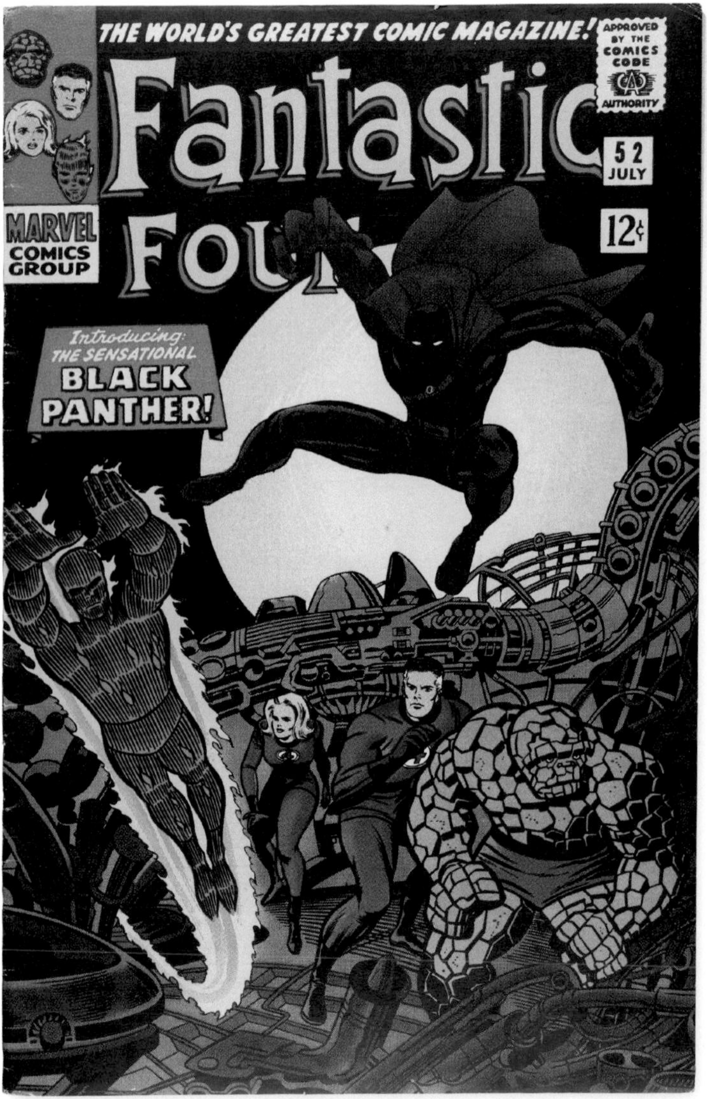
THE WORLD'S GREATEST COMIC MAGAZINE!
APPROVED BY THE COMICS CODE AUTHORITY
Fantastic Four
52 JULY
MARVEL COMICS GROUP
12¢
Introducing: THE SENSATIONAL BLACK PANTHER!

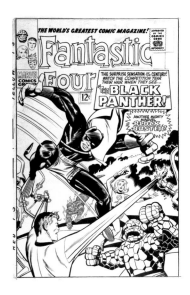

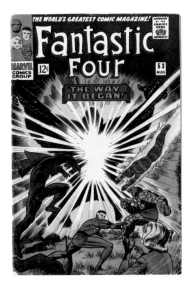

THE WORLD'S GREATEST COMIC MAGAZINE!
Fantastic Four
MARVEL COMICS GROUP
12¢
THE SURPRISE SENSATION OF THE CENTURY! WATCH THE COMPETITION TEAR THEIR HAIR WHEN THEY SEE...
"THE BLACK PANTHER!"
ANOTHER MIGHTY MARVEL BLOCK BUSTER!

THE WORLD'S GREATEST COMIC MAGAZINE!
Fantastic Four
MARVEL COMICS GROUP
12¢
53 AUG
THE WAY IT BEGAN!

FANTASTIC FOUR No. 52

Opposite: *Cover; pencils, Jack Kirby; inks, Joe Sinnott; July 1966.*

THE BLACK PANTHER

Above left: *Original cover art (unpublished),* Fantastic Four *No. 52; pencils, Jack Kirby; inks, Joe Sinnott; July 1966.* The Black Panther's debut was important enough to warrant Stan Lee tinkering with the hero's costume and cover layout. Originally designed with a half-mask, the published version had the Panther's face completely covered. But was the change made to make him look more mysterious, or was it a directive of the publisher, who may have feared the title would not be distributed by dealers in the American South of the mid-1960s? The final cover design, including the teaser copy ("Watch the competition tear their hair...") was also modified.

FANTASTIC FOUR No. 53

Above right: *Cover; pencils, Jack Kirby; inks, Joe Sinnott; August 1966.* In the origin of the Black Panther, king of Wakanda, Stan Lee and Jack Kirby treat T'Challa as an equal to the Fantastic Four, a dignified, intelligent, and resourceful man. He could be compared to actor Sidney Poitier, upon whom Kirby based his appearance.

FALL ISSUE
THE HUMAN TORCH
10¢
NO. 16
COMICS
TOKIO OIL REFINERY
PLUS SUB-MARINER
OSAKA

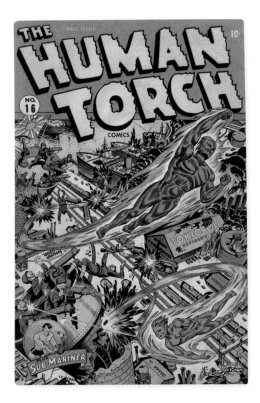

THE ORIGINAL TORCH

Above: *Cover;* The Human Torch *No. 16; pencils and inks, Alex Schomburg; Fall 1944.* The original Human Torch, created by Carl Burgos, was a flaming android. He was, in fact, the cover star of the company's very first comic book—*Marvel Comics* No. 1, in October 1939!

FANTASTIC FOUR ANNUAL No. 4

Opposite: *Interior, "The Torch That Was!"; script, Stan Lee; pencils, Jack Kirby; inks, Joe Sinnott; November 1966.* This Annual, and later *Sub-Mariner* issues 8 and 14, plus *Captain America* No. 153, contained the only stories to address the original continuity of the Timely era. Timely's android Torch faces the FF's Johnny Storm with no real explanation of where he has been all these years.

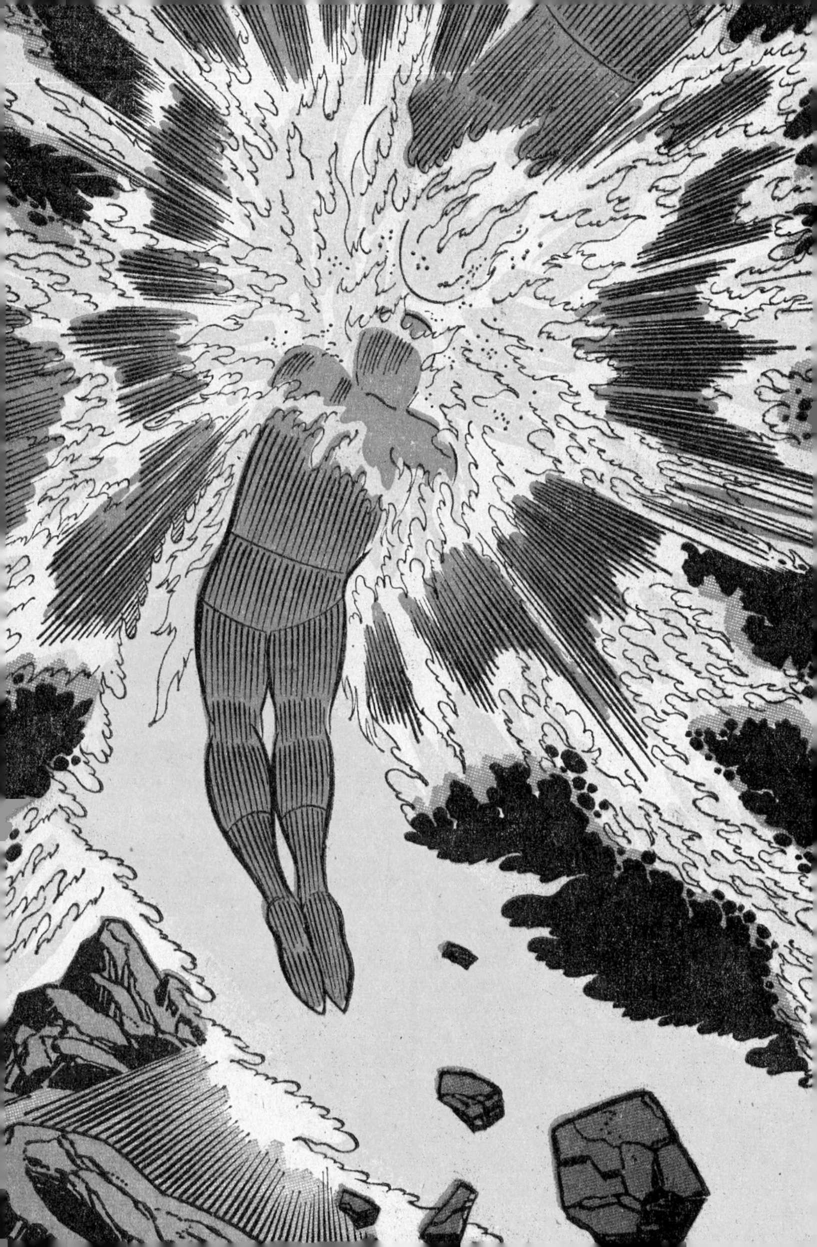

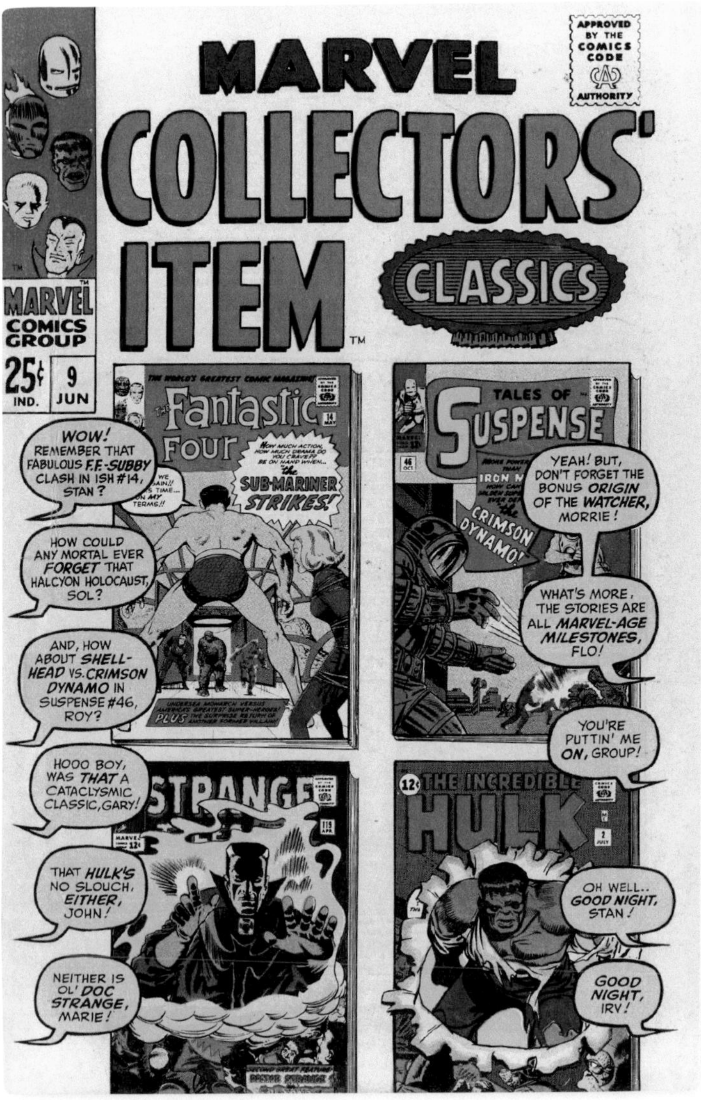

MARVEL COLLECTORS' ITEM CLASSICS
APPROVED BY THE COMICS CODE AUTHORITY
MARVEL COMICS GROUP
25¢ IND.
9 JUN
WOW! REMEMBER THAT FABULOUS F.F.-SUBBY CLASH IN ISH #14, STAN?
HOW COULD ANY MORTAL EVER FORGET THAT HALCYON HOLOCAUST, SOL?
AND, HOW ABOUT SHELL-HEAD VS. CRIMSON DYNAMO IN SUSPENSE #46, ROY?
HOOO BOY, WAS THAT A CATACLYSMIC CLASSIC, GARY!
THAT HULK'S NO SLOUCH, EITHER, JOHN!
NEITHER IS OL' DOC STRANGE, MARIE!
YEAH! BUT, DON'T FORGET THE BONUS ORIGIN OF THE WATCHER, MORRIE!
WHAT'S MORE, THE STORIES ARE ALL MARVEL-AGE MILESTONES, FLO!
YOU'RE PUTTIN' ME ON, GROUP!
OH WELL.. GOOD NIGHT, STAN!
GOOD NIGHT, IRV!
Fantastic Four
SUB-MARINER STRIKES!
TALES OF SUSPENSE
CRIMSON DYNAMO!
STRANGE
THE INCREDIBLE HULK

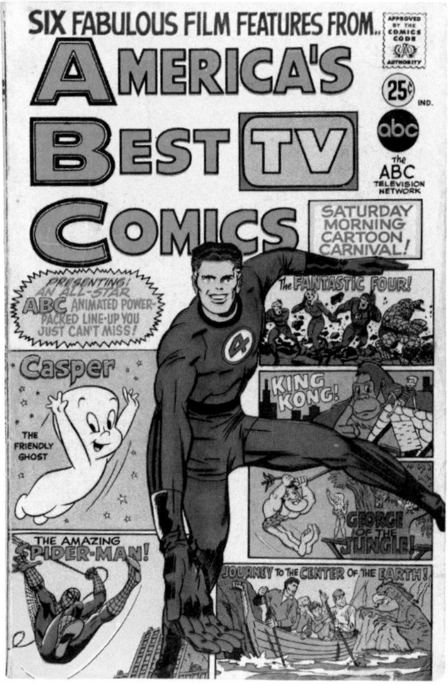
SIX FABULOUS FILM FEATURES FROM..
APPROVED BY THE COMICS CODE AUTHORITY
AMERICA'S BEST TV COMICS
25¢ IND.
abc
The ABC TELEVISION NETWORK
SATURDAY MORNING CARTOON CARNIVAL!
PRESENTING! AN ALL-STAR ABC ANIMATED POWER-PACKED LINE-UP YOU JUST CAN'T MISS!
The FANTASTIC FOUR!
Casper
THE FRIENDLY GHOST
KING KONG!
GEORGE OF THE JUNGLE!
THE AMAZING SPIDER-MAN!
JOURNEY TO THE CENTER OF THE EARTH!

ENTER THE REPRINTS!

Opposite: *Cover,* Marvel Collectors' Item Classics *No. 9; pencils, Jack Kirby and Steve Ditko; inks, Dick Ayers and Steve Ditko; June 1967.* Marvel's heroes were popular enough by 1966 to rate a line of reprints of material published only a few years earlier. Cover designs frequently included small reproductions of the original covers. The cover copy emphasizes the lighthearted, self-deprecating humor that had become a Marvel trademark, and manages to mention many staff members, including several of the production department's unsung heroes.

AMERICA'S BEST TV COMICS No. 1

Above: *Cover; pencils, Jack Kirby with various artists; inks, attributed George Roussos; Summer 1966.* Marvel produced a one-off comic to promote ABC's fall cartoon lineup, which, not surprisingly, featured the debut of both the Fantastic Four and Spidey's cartoons. ABC also used the comic to hawk their prime-time lineup, and Marvel artists such as George Tuska and John Tartaglione drew ads featuring the Flying Nun and even their competitor, Batman!

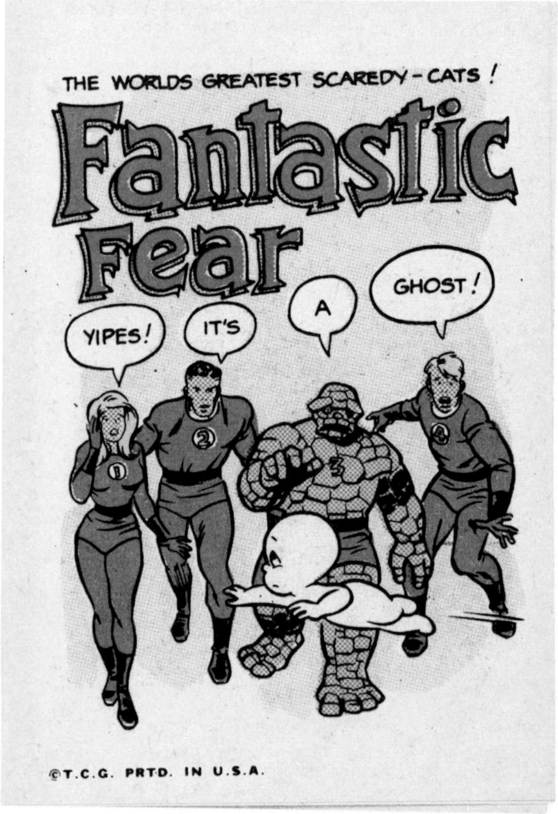
THE WORLDS GREATEST SCAREDY-CATS!
Fantastic Fear
YIPES!
IT'S
A
GHOST!
©T.C.G. PRT'D. IN U.S.A.

KRAZY LITTLE COMICS

Above: *Covers,* Topps Krazy Little Comics; *dialogue, Len Brown; pencils and inks, Wally Wood; 1967.* Len Brown and Roy Thomas teamed up with Wally Wood and Gil Kane for a line of mini-comics for Topps, which included parodies of Marvel characters and back cover ads by Art Spiegelman. They were test marketed but did not receive national distribution.

BRAND ECHH No. 1

Opposite: *Cover; pencils, Jack Kirby; inks, Mike Esposito; August 1967.*

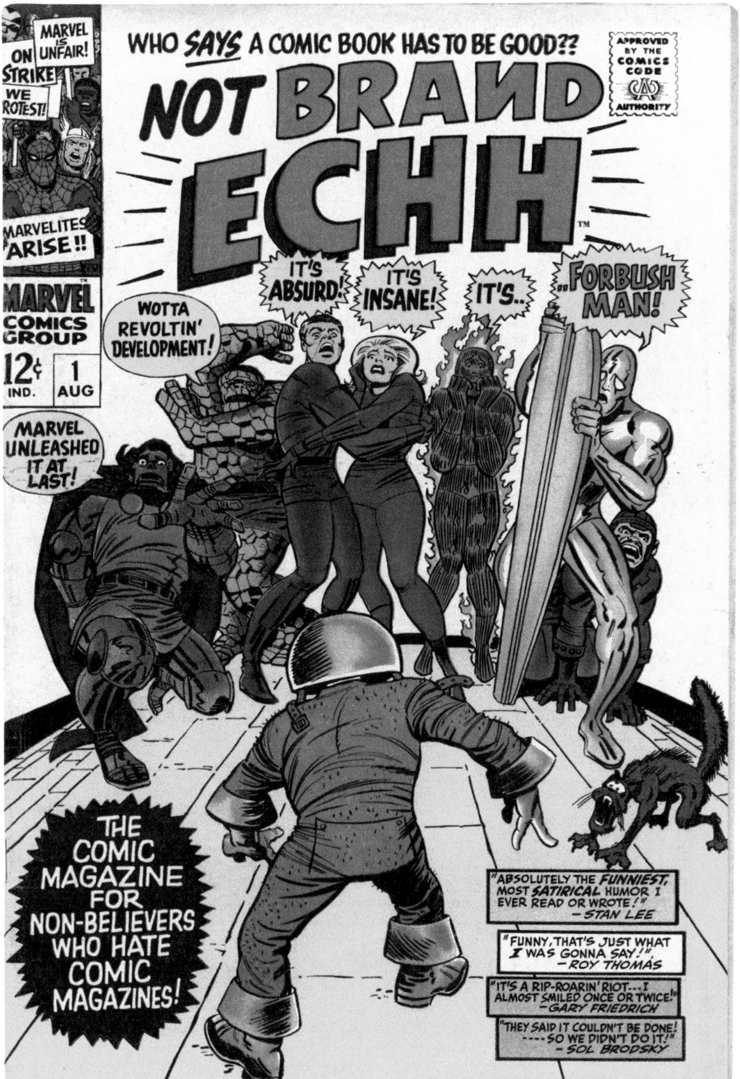

WHO SAYS A COMIC BOOK HAS TO BE GOOD??
NOT BRAND ECHH
APPROVED BY THE COMICS CODE AUTHORITY
MARVEL IS UNFAIR!
ON STRIKE
WE PROTEST!
MARVELITES ARISE!!
MARVEL COMICS GROUP
12¢ IND.
1 AUG
IT'S ABSURD!
IT'S INSANE!
IT'S..
..FORBUSH MAN!
WOTTA REVOLTIN' DEVELOPMENT!
MARVEL UNLEASHED IT AT LAST!
THE COMIC MAGAZINE FOR NON-BELIEVERS WHO HATE COMIC MAGAZINES!
"ABSOLUTELY THE FUNNIEST, MOST SATIRICAL HUMOR I EVER READ OR WROTE!" —STAN LEE
"FUNNY, THAT'S JUST WHAT I WAS GONNA SAY!" —ROY THOMAS
"IT'S A RIP-ROARIN' RIOT... I ALMOST SMILED ONCE OR TWICE!" —GARY FRIEDRICH
"THEY SAID IT COULDN'T BE DONE! ---- SO WE DIDN'T DO IT!" —SOL BRODSKY

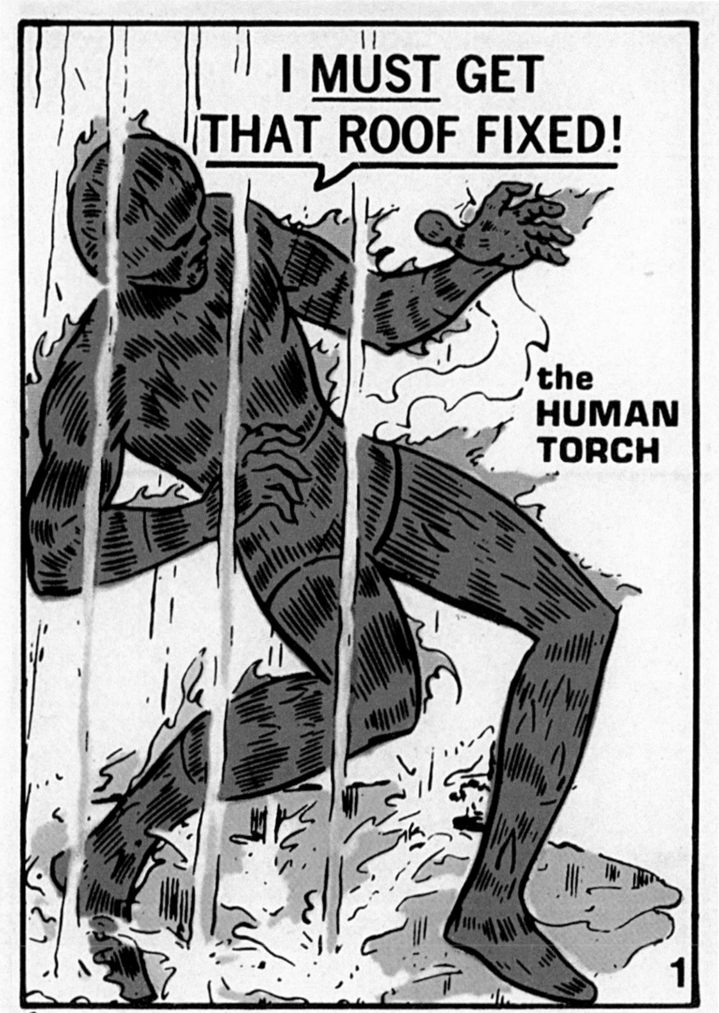
I MUST GET THAT ROOF FIXED!
the HUMAN TORCH
1
©1967 MARVEL COMICS GROUP ©P.C.G.C. PRINTED IN U.S.A.

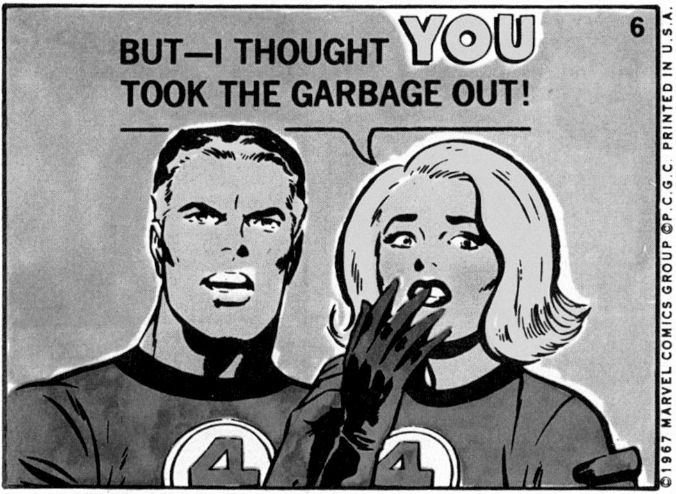
6
BUT—I THOUGHT YOU TOOK THE GARBAGE OUT!
©1967 MARVEL COMICS GROUP ©P.C.G.C. PRINTED IN U.S.A.

ALL THIS AND A STICK OF GUM!

Opposite, above, and pages 110–11: *Super Hero stickers, 1967.* Donruss may have released the first Marvel trading card set a year earlier, but the Philadelphia Chewing Gum Company was the first to produce a set of Marvel Comics trading cards that were all stickers (55 of them in total). They featured Marvel's most popular super heroes, using art from the comic books and adding funny captions. For just a nickel kids could go to the corner drugstore and buy a pack, which consisted of five stickers and a stick of gum.

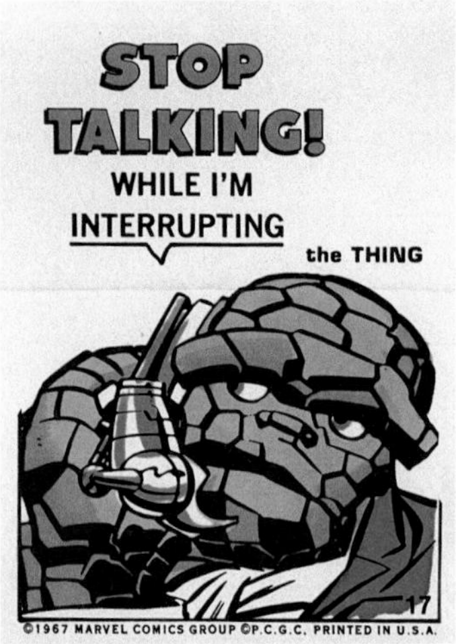
STOP TALKING!
WHILE I'M INTERRUPTING
the THING
17
©1967 MARVEL COMICS GROUP ©P.C.G.C. PRINTED IN U.S.A.

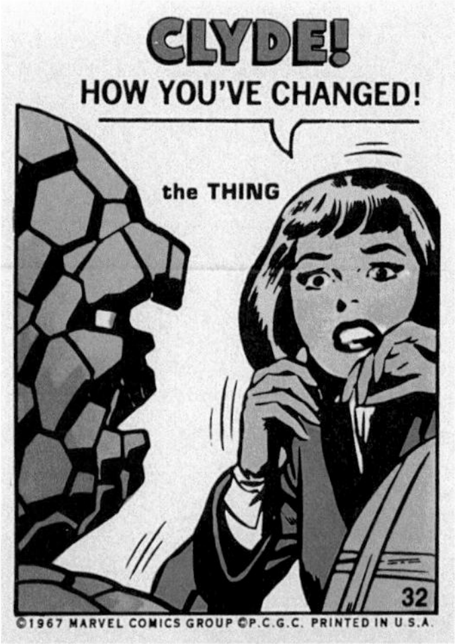
CLYDE!
HOW YOU'VE CHANGED!
the THING
32
©1967 MARVEL COMICS GROUP ©P.C.G.C. PRINTED IN U.S.A.

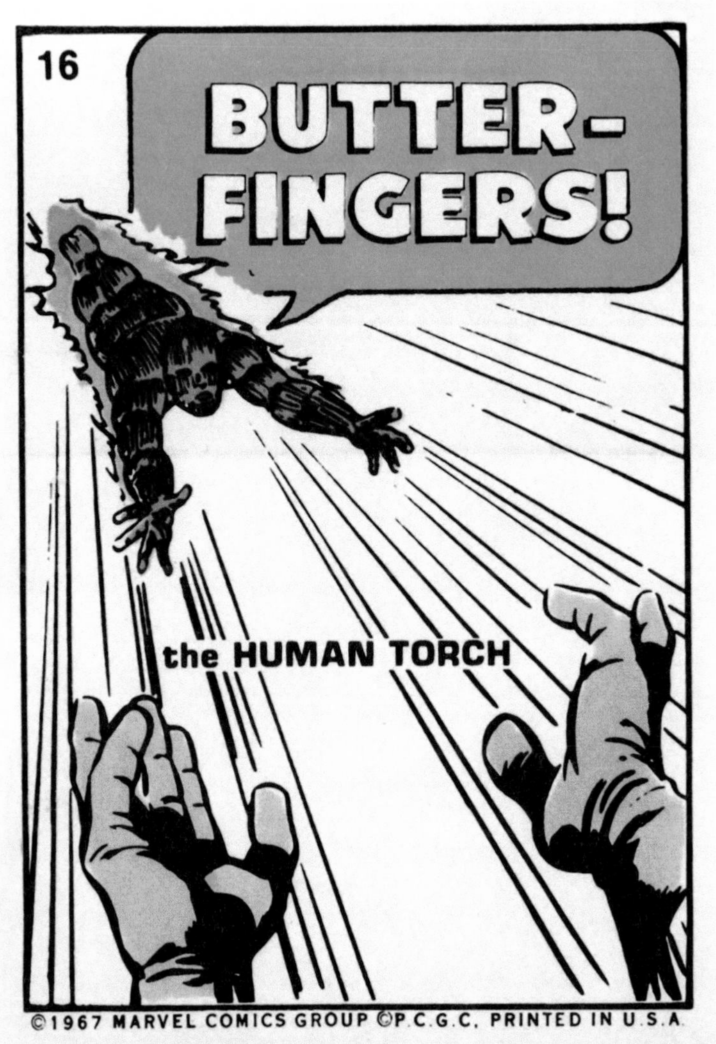
16
BUTTER-FINGERS!
the HUMAN TORCH
©1967 MARVEL COMICS GROUP ©P.C.G.C. PRINTED IN U.S.A.

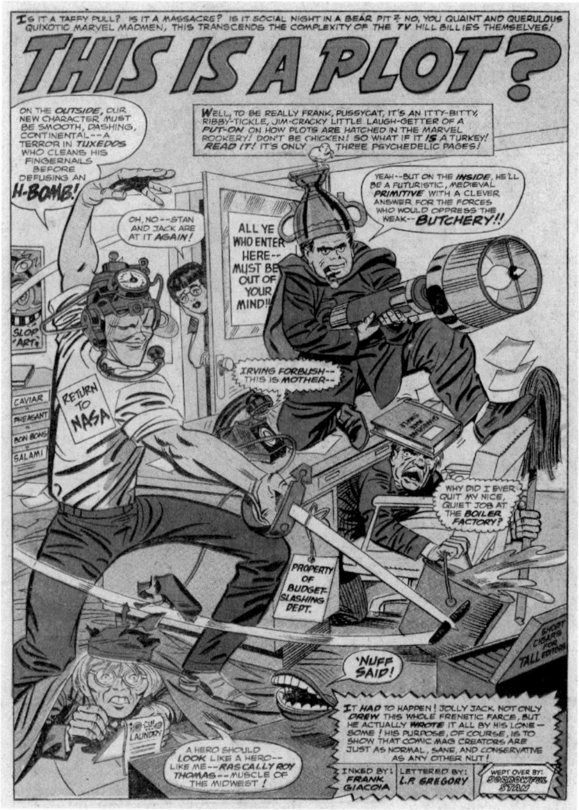
IS IT A TAFFY PULL? IS IT A MASSACRE? IS IT SOCIAL NIGHT IN A BEAR PIT? NO, YOU QUAINT AND QUERULOUS QUIXOTIC MARVEL MADMEN, THIS TRANSCENDS THE COMPLEXITY OF THE TV HILL BILLIES THEMSELVES!
THIS IS A PLOT?
ON THE OUTSIDE, OUR NEW CHARACTER MUST BE SMOOTH, DASHING, CONTINENTAL--A TERROR IN TUXEDOS WHO CLEANS HIS FINGERNAILS BEFORE DEFUSING AN H-BOMB!
WELL, TO BE REALLY FRANK, PUSSYCAT, IT'S AN ITTY-BITTY, RIBBY-TICKLE, JIM-CRACKY LITTLE LAUGH-GETTER OF A PUT-ON ON HOW PLOTS ARE HATCHED IN THE MARVEL ROOKERY! DON'T BE CHICKEN! SO WHAT IF IT IS A TURKEY! READ IT! IT'S ONLY THREE PSYCHEDELIC PAGES!
YEAH--BUT ON THE INSIDE, HE'LL BE A FUTURISTIC, MEDIEVAL PRIMITIVE WITH A CLEVER ANSWER FOR THE FORCES WHO WOULD OPPRESS THE WEAK--BUTCHERY!!
OH, NO--STAN AND JACK ARE AT IT AGAIN!
ALL YE WHO ENTER HERE--MUST BE OUT OF YOUR MIND!!
SLOP ART
RETURN TO NASA
CAVIAR
PHEASANT
BON BONS
SALAMI
IRVING FORBUSH--THIS IS MOTHER--
WHY DID I EVER QUIT MY NICE, QUIET JOB AT THE BOILER FACTORY?
PROPERTY OF BUDGET-SLASHING DEPT.
SHORT CIGARS FOR TALL EDITORS
'NUFF SAID!
IT HAD TO HAPPEN! JOLLY JACK NOT ONLY DREW THIS WHOLE FRENETIC FARCE, BUT HE ACTUALLY WROTE IT ALL BY HIS LONE-SOME! HIS PURPOSE, OF COURSE, IS TO SHOW THAT COMIC MAG CREATORS ARE JUST AS NORMAL, SANE, AND CONSERVATIVE AS ANY OTHER NUT!
LAUNDRY
A HERO SHOULD LOOK LIKE A HERO--LIKE ME--RASCALLY ROY THOMAS--MUSCLE OF THE MIDWEST!
INKED BY: FRANK GIACOIA
LETTERED BY: L.P. GREGORY
WEPT OVER BY: SORROWFUL STAN

FANTASTIC FOUR ANNUAL No. 5

Above: *Interior, "This Is a Plot?"; script and pencils, Jack Kirby; inks, Frank Giacoia; Summer 1968.*

NOT BRAND ECHH No. 11

Opposite: *Interior, "Auntie Goose Rhymes Dept."; script, Roy Thomas; pencils and inks, John Verpoorten; December 1968.* Roy Thomas and Verpoorten transform the nursery rhyme "Little Miss Muffett" into a satirical tribute to Jack Kirby that shows a parade of Marvel characters who come to life at his drawing board.

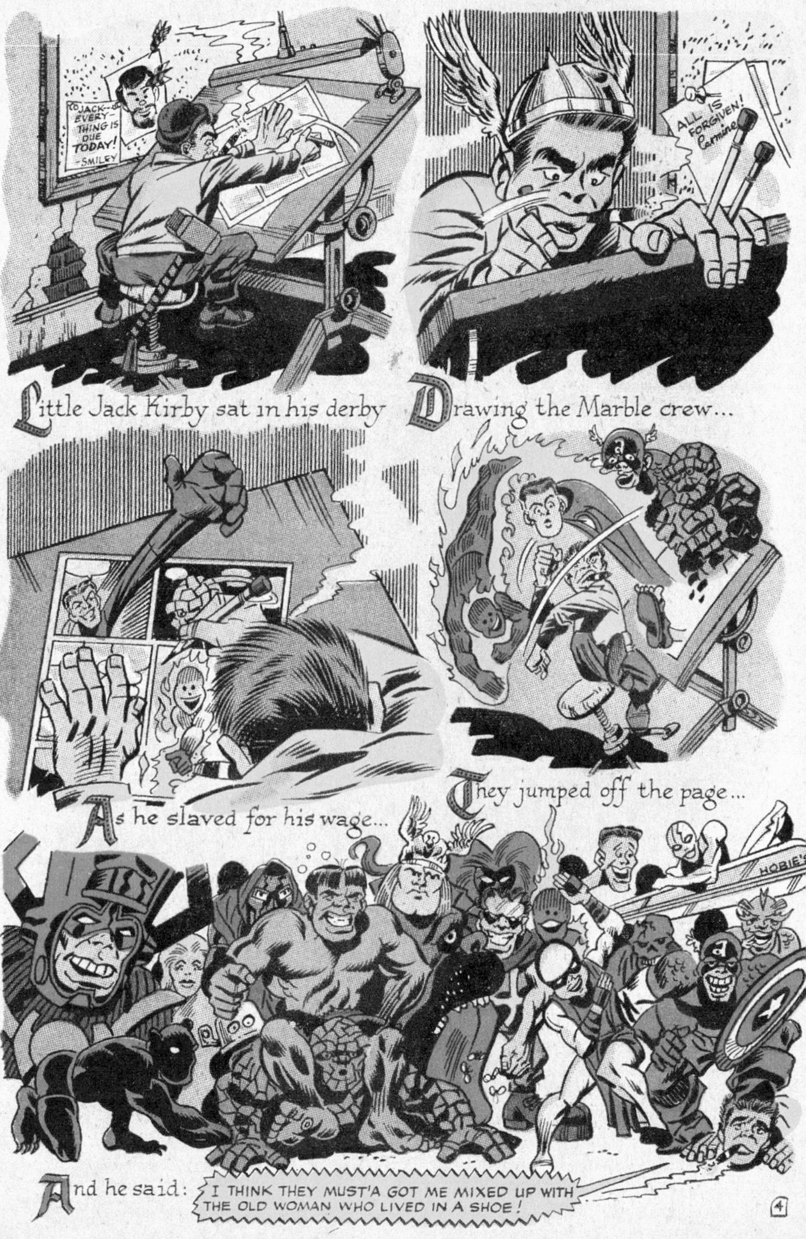
TO JACK-- EVERY-THING IS DUE TODAY! -SMILEY
Little Jack Kirby sat in his derby
ALL IS FORGIVEN! Carmine
Drawing the Marble crew...
As he slaved for his wage...
They jumped off the page...
HOBIE'S
And he said:
I THINK THEY MUST'A GOT ME MIXED UP WITH THE OLD WOMAN WHO LIVED IN A SHOE!
4

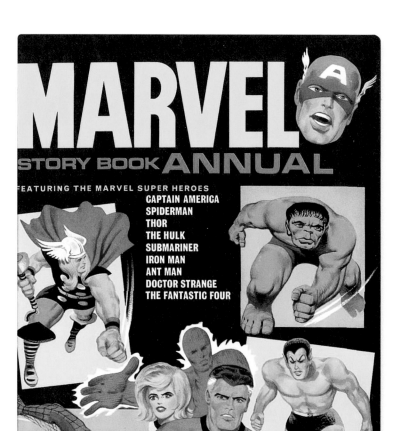

MARVEL

STORY BOOK ANNUAL

FEATURING THE MARVEL SUPER HEROES

CAPTAIN AMERICA
SPIDERMAN
THOR
THE HULK
SUBMARINER
IRON MAN
ANT MAN
DOCTOR STRANGE
THE FANTASTIC FOUR

MARVEL STORY BOOK ANNUAL 1967

Opposite: *Cover; artist unkown; World Distributors, Manchester, ca. 1967.*

THE FANTASTIC FOUR IN THE HOUSE OF HORRORS

Below: *Cover; pencils, Herb Trimpe; inks, John Verpoorten; Whitman, 1968.*

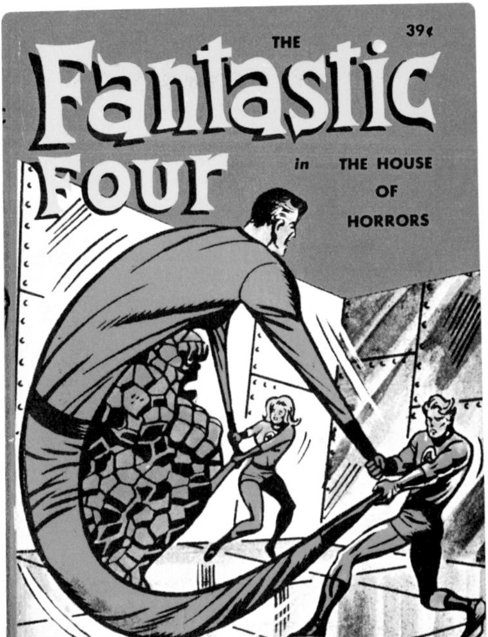
39¢
THE
Fantastic
Four
in
THE HOUSE
OF
HORRORS

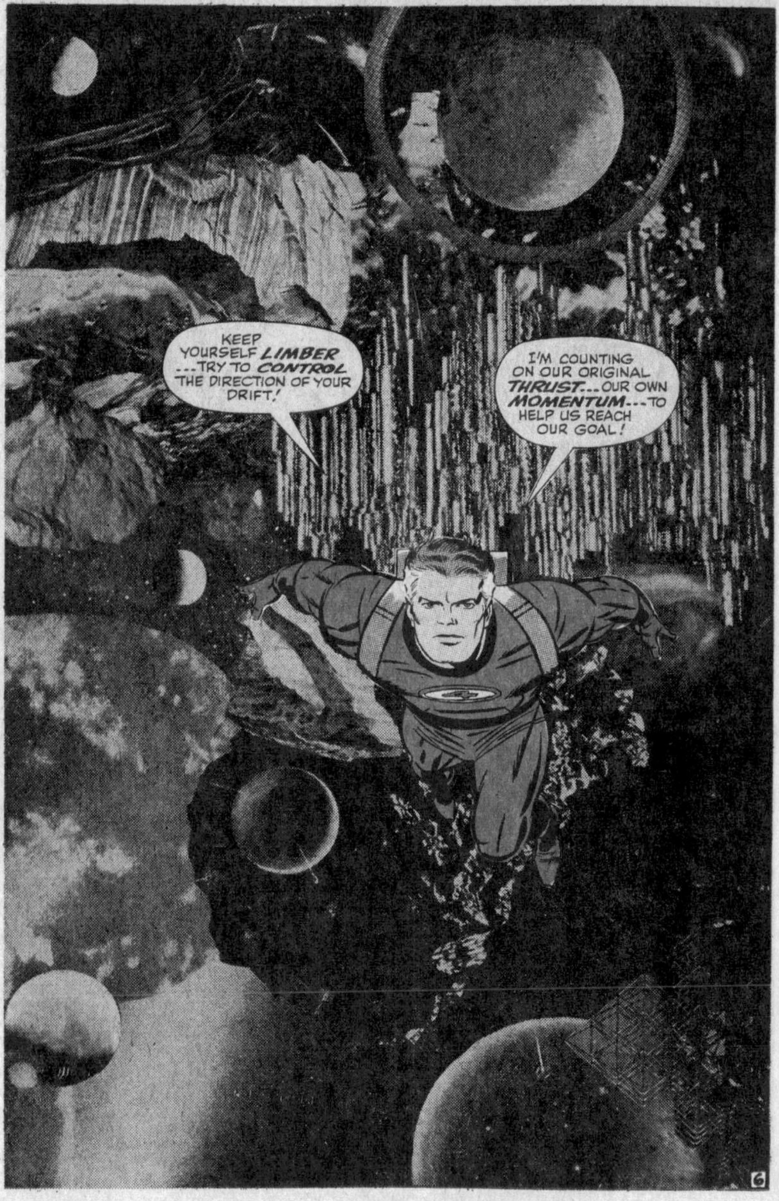
KEEP YOURSELF LIMBER ...TRY TO CONTROL THE DIRECTION OF YOUR DRIFT!
I'M COUNTING ON OUR ORIGINAL THRUST... OUR OWN MOMENTUM...TO HELP US REACH OUR GOAL!
6

GOAL? WHAT ABOUT THAT SPINNIN' VORTEX THAT ALMOST BLEW US UP LIKE FIRE-CRACKERS LAST TIME WE WUZ HERE?
IT'S SMACK-DAB IN THE CENTER OF THIS COCKEYED WORLD!
NO MATTER WHAT DIRECTION WE PICK... WE CAN'T MISS BEIN' PULLED RIGHT INTO IT!
THAT'S WHAT I LIKE ABOUT YOU, BLUE-EYES...
EVEN WHEN THINGS GET HOPE-LESS, YOU ALWAYS LOOK AT THE CHEER-FUL SIDE!
WELL, HARDY HAR HAR!

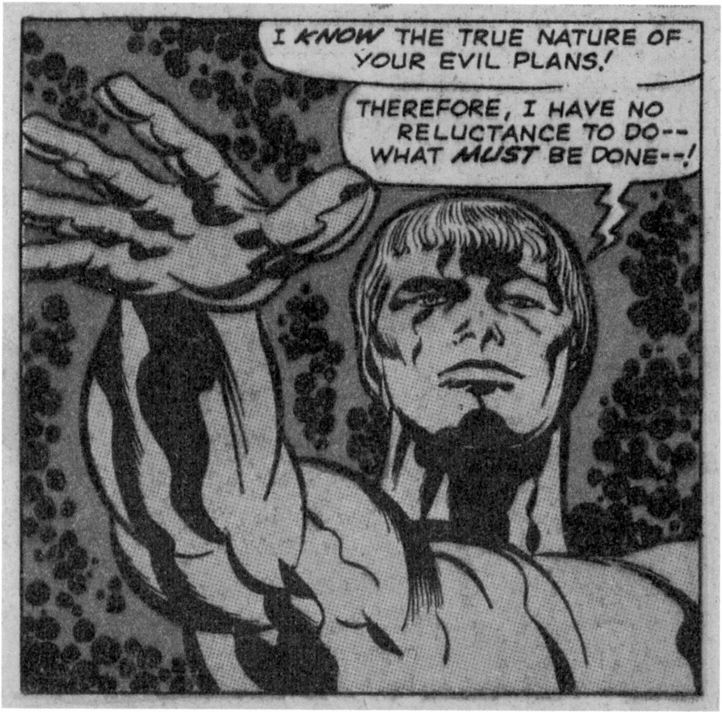
I KNOW THE TRUE NATURE OF YOUR EVIL PLANS!
THEREFORE, I HAVE NO RELUCTANCE TO DO-- WHAT MUST BE DONE--!

THE KIRBY LAB

Pages 116–17: *Interior,* Fantastic Four Annual *No. 6; script, Stan Lee; pencils and collage, Jack Kirby; inks, Joe Sinnott; November 1968.* Kirby's techniques were ahead of their time, and the current technology was typically unable to reproduce his photo collages anywhere near how he intended them. For one thing, they were printed in black-and-white!

FANTASTIC FOUR No. 67

Above: *Interior, "When Opens the Cocoon!"; script, Stan Lee; pencils, Jack Kirby; inks, Joe Sinnott; October 1967.* Him is introduced, a new life-form. He turns on his creators, for creating him with evil intent.

FANTASTIC FOUR No. 72

Opposite: *Cover; pencils, Jack Kirby; inks, Joe Sinnott, March 1968.*

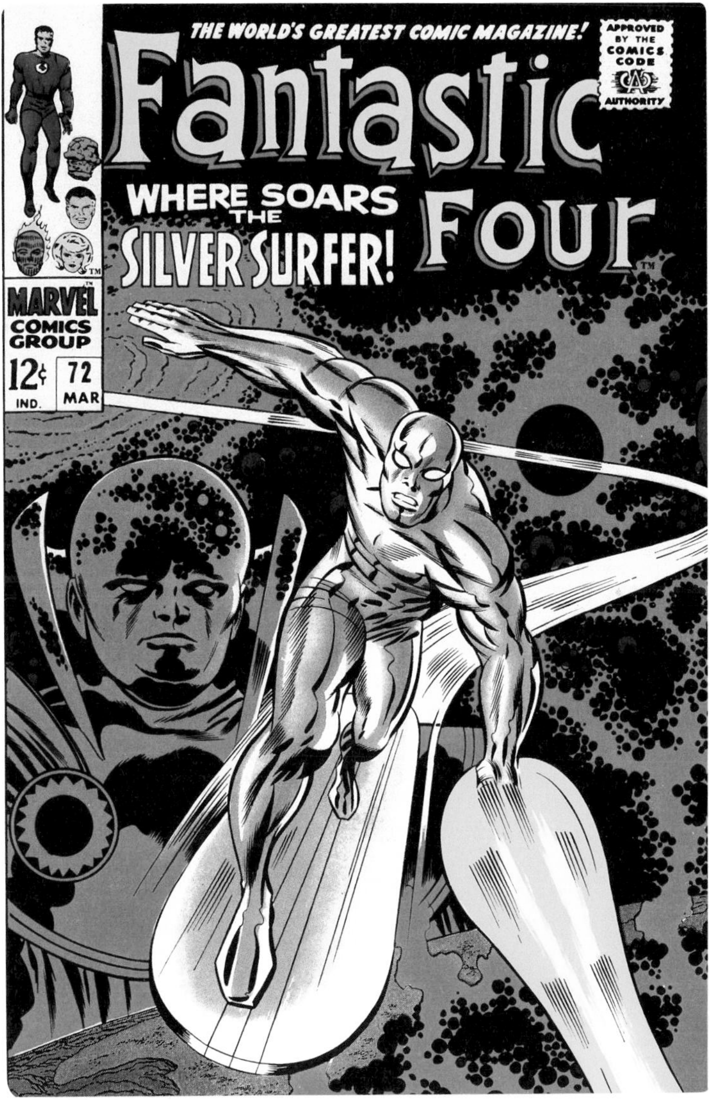
THE WORLD'S GREATEST COMIC MAGAZINE!
Fantastic Four
WHERE SOARS THE SILVER SURFER!
APPROVED BY THE COMICS CODE AUTHORITY
MARVEL COMICS GROUP
12¢ IND.
72 MAR

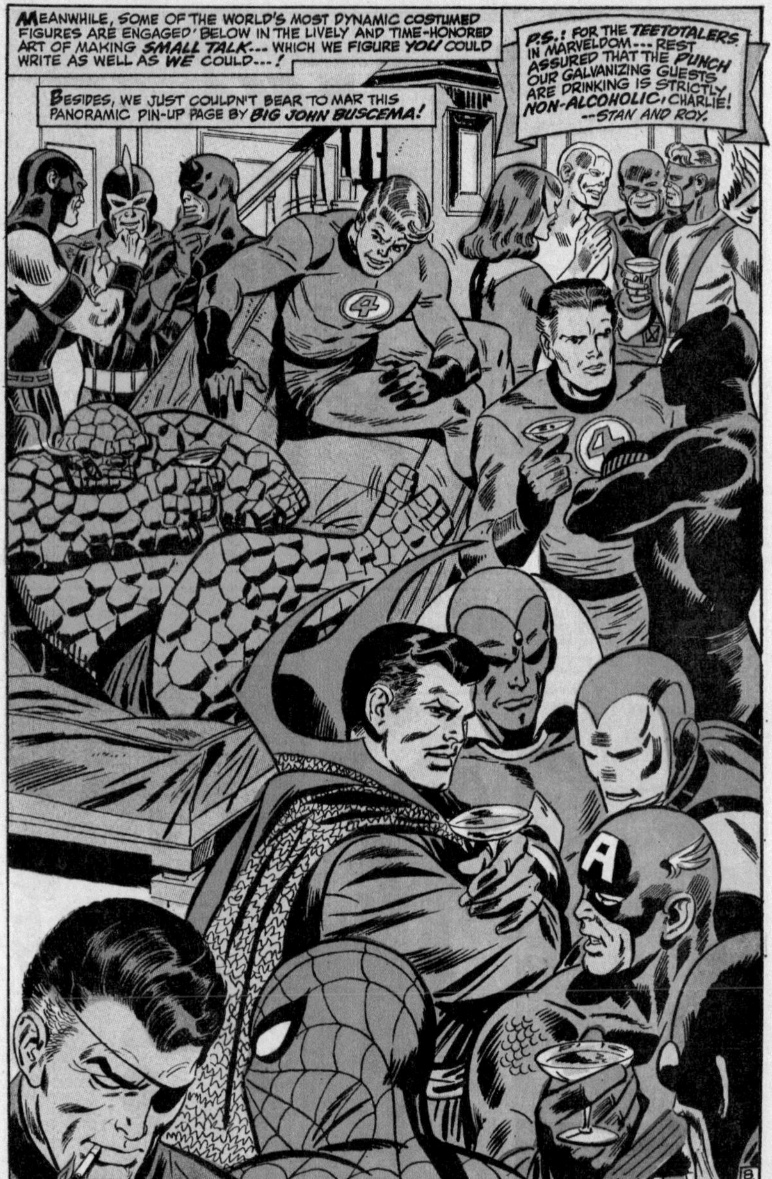

MEANWHILE, SOME OF THE WORLD'S MOST DYNAMIC COSTUMED FIGURES ARE ENGAGED BELOW IN THE LIVELY AND TIME-HONORED ART OF MAKING SMALL TALK... WHICH WE FIGURE YOU COULD WRITE AS WELL AS WE COULD...!
BESIDES, WE JUST COULDN'T BEAR TO MAR THIS PANORAMIC PIN-UP PAGE BY BIG JOHN BUSCEMA!
P.S.: FOR THE TEETOTALERS IN MARVELDOM... REST ASSURED THAT THE PUNCH OUR GALVANIZING GUESTS ARE DRINKING IS STRICTLY NON-ALCOHOLIC, CHARLIE! --STAN AND ROY.
8.

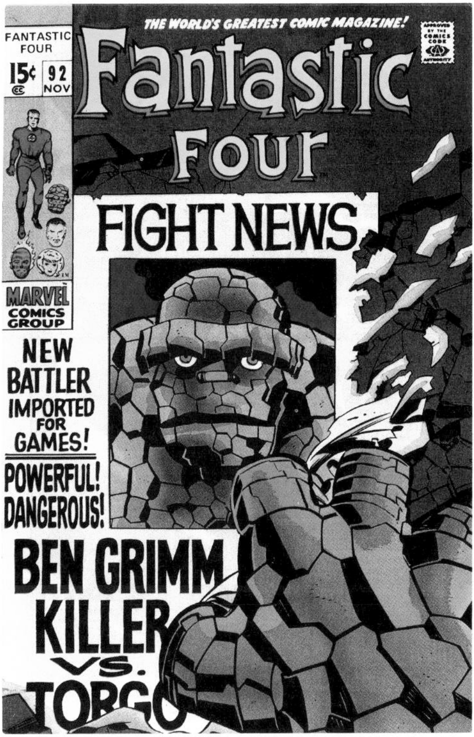
THE WORLD'S GREATEST COMIC MAGAZINE!
FANTASTIC FOUR
15¢ 92 NOV
APPROVED BY THE COMICS CODE AUTHORITY
Fantastic Four
FIGHT NEWS
MARVEL COMICS GROUP
NEW BATTLER IMPORTED FOR GAMES!
POWERFUL! DANGEROUS!
BEN GRIMM KILLER VS. TORGO

THE AVENGERS No. 60

Opposite: *Interior, "Till Death Do Us Part!"; script, Roy Thomas; pencils, John Buscema; inks, Mike Esposito; January 1969.* The wedding of Hank Pym and Janet Van Dyne was an excuse for Marvel's heroes to socialize together. Coincidentally, Roy Thomas was on a honeymoon cruise to the Caribbean when writing the dialogue for this issue. This particular panel demonstrates John Buscema's ability to show emotions and personality through pantomime, letting the image tell the story.

FANTASTIC FOUR No. 92

Above: *Cover; pencils, Jack Kirby; inks, Joe Sinnott; November 1969.*

FANTASTIC FOUR No. 79

Below: *Cover; pencils, Jack Kirby; inks, Joe Sinnott; October 1968.* The Thing's tragic nature was such that, even when he was cured of his monstrous appearance, he could never live a normal life as Ben Grimm. His sense of responsibility — to his teammates, and to the world at large — always forced him to return to his monstrous form.

ALL IN A DAY'S WORK

Opposite: *Interior original Photostat;* Fantastic Four *No. 77; pencils, Jack Kirby; August 1968.* This Photostat of Kirby's original pencils shows his marginal notes, offering a brief explanation for each corresponding panel, for Stan Lee to reference as he wrote the final dialogue. Stan often used Kirby's notes as a rough guide, expanding on, revising — and sometimes completely ignoring them — in order to achieve the necessary continuity of storyline and consistent characterization. What's truly fantastic is that, by all accounts, Kirby likely drew several other pages the same day he did this one!

THE WORLD'S GREATEST COMIC MAGAZINE!
Fantastic Four
THIS MONSTER FOREVER!
MARVEL COMICS GROUP
12¢ IND.
79 OCT

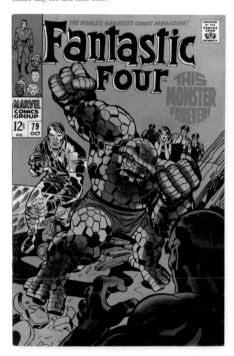

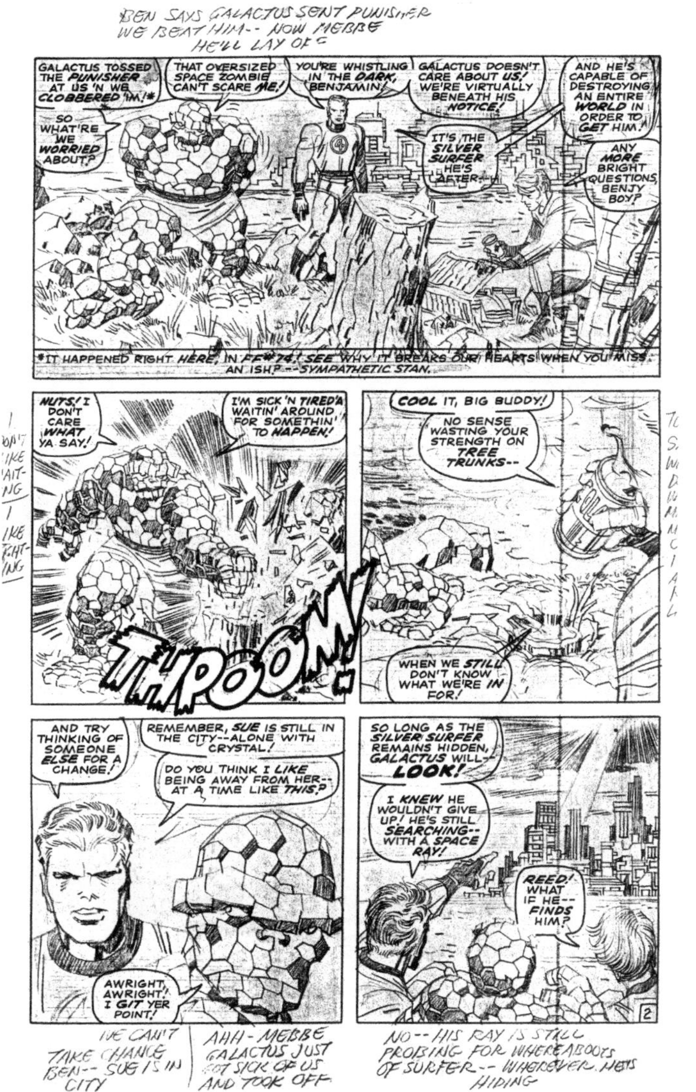
BEN SAYS GALACTUS SENT PUNISHER WE BEAT HIM-- NOW MEBBE HE'LL LAY OFF
GALACTUS TOSSED THE PUNISHER AT US 'N WE CLOBBERED 'IM!*
SO WHAT'RE WE WORRIED ABOUT?
THAT OVERSIZED SPACE ZOMBIE CAN'T SCARE ME!
YOU'RE WHISTLING IN THE DARK, BENJAMIN!
GALACTUS DOESN'T CARE ABOUT US! WE'RE VIRTUALLY BENEATH HIS NOTICE!
IT'S THE SILVER SURFER HE'S AFTER--
AND HE'S CAPABLE OF DESTROYING AN ENTIRE WORLD IN ORDER TO GET HIM!
ANY MORE BRIGHT QUESTIONS, BENJY BOY?
*IT HAPPENED RIGHT HERE, IN FF#74! SEE WHY IT BREAKS OUR HEARTS WHEN YOU MISS AN ISH? --SYMPATHETIC STAN.
NUTS! I DON'T CARE WHAT YA SAY!
I'M SICK 'N TIRED 'A WAITIN' AROUND FOR SOMETHIN' TO HAPPEN!
THOOOM!
COOL IT, BIG BUDDY!
NO SENSE WASTING YOUR STRENGTH ON TREE TRUNKS--
WHEN WE STILL DON'T KNOW WHAT WE'RE IN FOR!
AND TRY THINKING OF SOMEONE ELSE FOR A CHANGE!
REMEMBER, SUE IS STILL IN THE CITY--ALONE WITH CRYSTAL!
DO YOU THINK I LIKE BEING AWAY FROM HER-- AT A TIME LIKE THIS?
AWRIGHT, AWRIGHT! I GIT YER POINT!
SO LONG AS THE SILVER SURFER REMAINS HIDDEN, GALACTUS WILL-- LOOK!
I KNEW HE WOULDN'T GIVE UP! HE'S STILL SEARCHING-- WITH A SPACE RAY!
REED! WHAT IF HE-- FINDS HIM?
2
WE CAN'T TAKE CHANCE BEN-- SUE IS IN CITY
AHH-MEBBE GALACTUS JUST GOT SICK OF US AND TOOK OFF
NO-- HIS RAY IS STILL PROBING FOR WHEREABOUTS OF SURFER-- WHEREVER HE'S HIDING

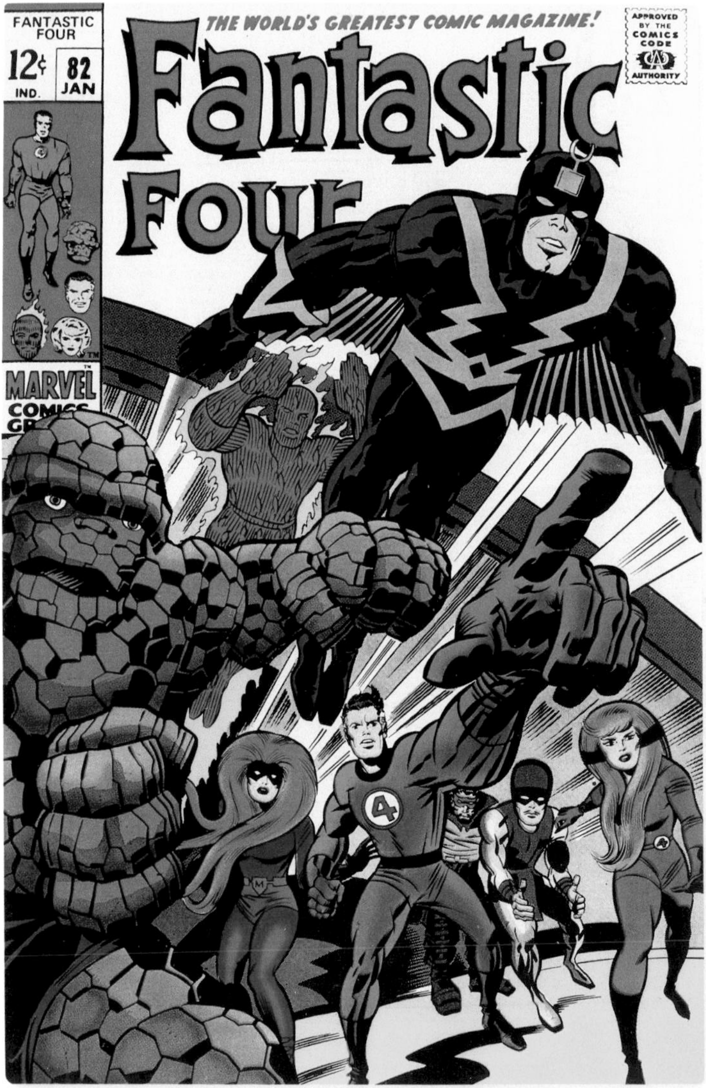
FANTASTIC FOUR
12¢
IND.
82
JAN
MARVEL COMICS GR
THE WORLD'S GREATEST COMIC MAGAZINE!
Fantastic Four
APPROVED BY THE COMICS CODE AUTHORITY

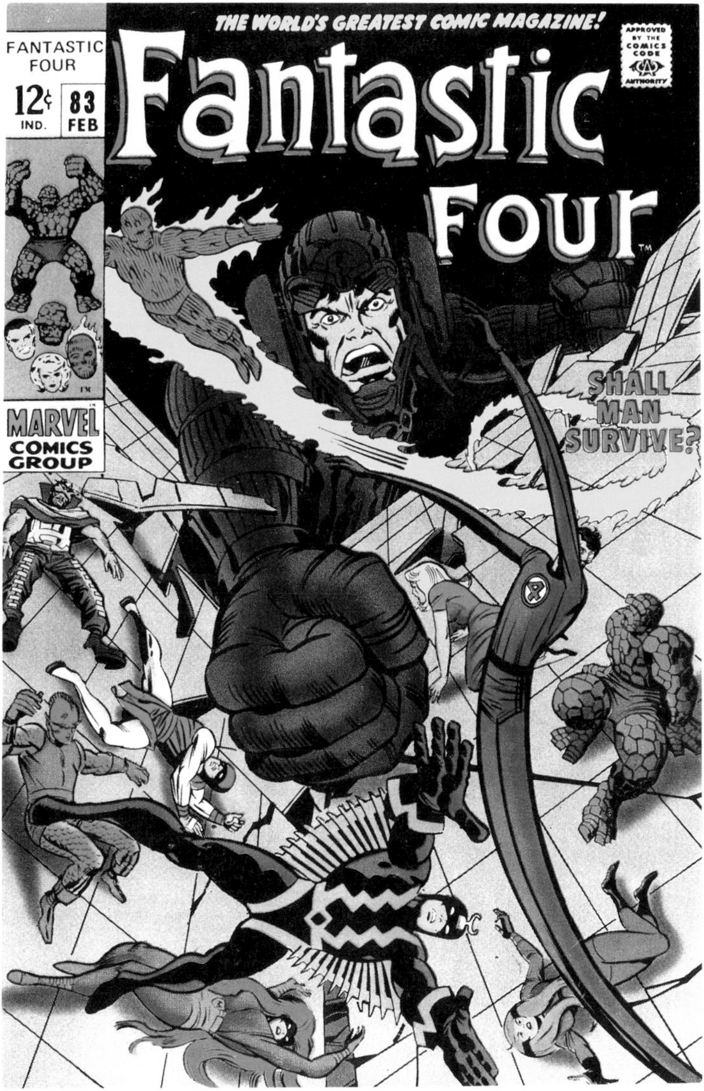
THE WORLD'S GREATEST COMIC MAGAZINE!
FANTASTIC FOUR
12¢ IND.
83 FEB
APPROVED BY THE COMICS CODE AUTHORITY
Fantastic Four™
MARVEL COMICS GROUP
SHALL MAN SURVIVE?

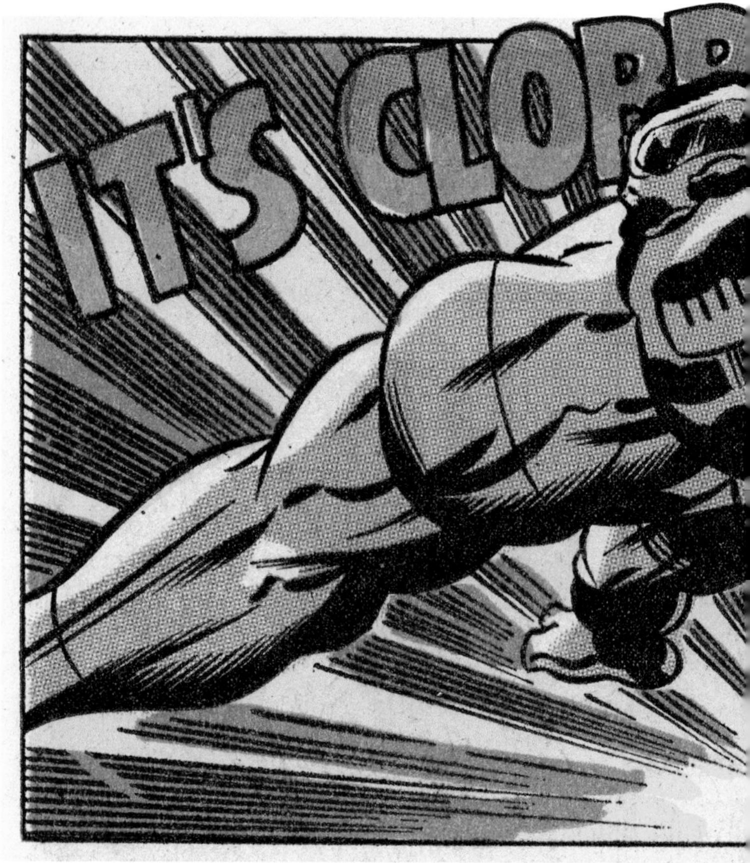

FANTASTIC FOUR No. 82

Page 124: *Cover; pencils, Jack Kirby; inks, Joe Sinnott; January 1969.*

FANTASTIC FOUR No. 83

Page 125: *Cover; pencils, Jack Kirby; inks, Joe Sinnott; February 1969.* Fantastic Four cohorts the Inhumans received a TV series on ABC in 2017.

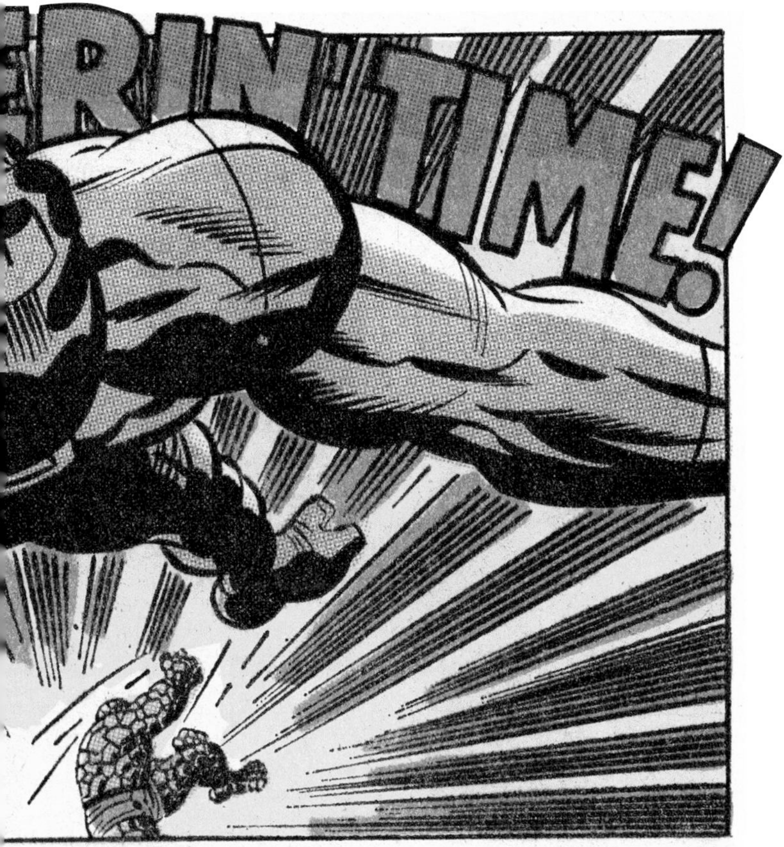
ERIN' TIME!

FANTASTIC FOUR No. 83

Above: *Interior, "Shall Man Survive?"; script, Stan Lee; pencils, Jack Kirby; inks, Joe Sinnott; February 1969.* "It's Clobberin' Time!" became the Thing's catchphrase whenever he went into action — he certainly packed a punch! He also seemed to leap off the page, thanks to Kirby's incredible mastery of perspective.

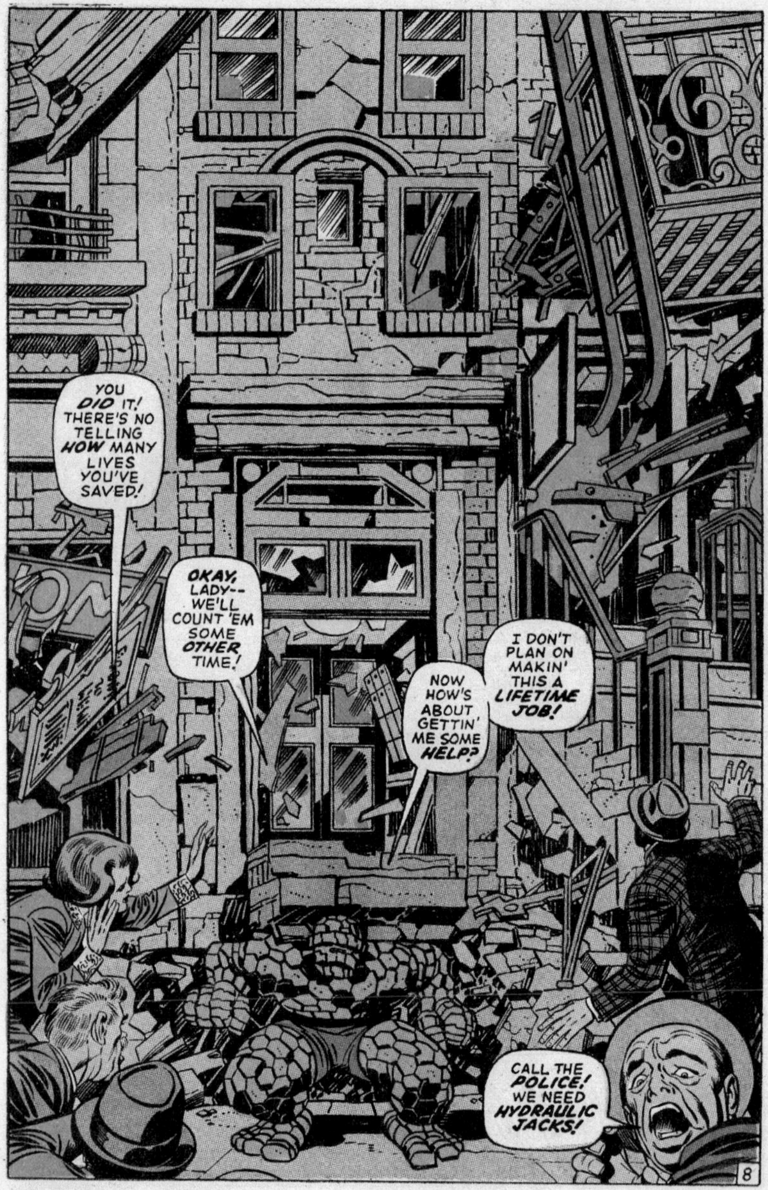
YOU DID IT! THERE'S NO TELLING HOW MANY LIVES YOU'VE SAVED!
OKAY, LADY-- WE'LL COUNT 'EM SOME OTHER TIME!
I DON'T PLAN ON MAKIN' THIS A LIFETIME JOB!
NOW HOW'S ABOUT GETTIN' ME SOME HELP?
CALL THE POLICE! WE NEED HYDRAULIC JACKS!
8

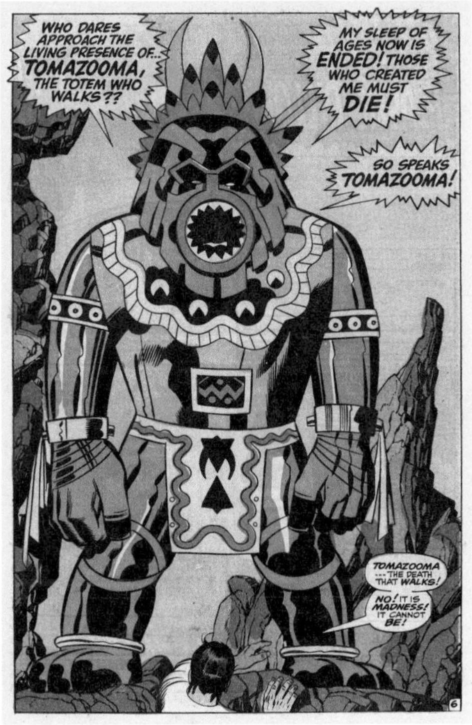
WHO DARES APPROACH THE LIVING PRESENCE OF... TOMAZOOMA, THE TOTEM WHO WALKS??
MY SLEEP OF AGES NOW IS ENDED! THOSE WHO CREATED ME MUST DIE!
SO SPEAKS TOMAZOOMA!
TOMAZOOMA ---THE DEATH THAT WALKS!
NO! IT IS MADNESS! IT CANNOT BE!
6

FANTASTIC FOUR No. 95

Opposite: *Interior, "Tomorrow... World War Three!"; script, Stan Lee; pencils, Jack Kirby; inks, Joe Sinnott; February 1970.* "Of course, Jack had a lot of detail, but I probably even added more to his buildings. Jack was so great with those bricks he used to put in, and I'd put little cracks in the bricks and things like that." — Joe Sinnott

FANTASTIC FOUR No. 80

Above: *Interior, "Where Treads the Living Totem!"; script, Stan Lee; pencils, Jack Kirby; inks, Joe Sinnott; November 1968.* Lee and Kirby harken back to an earlier time—only seven short years!—with the "living totem" Tomazooma, who was very much in the mold of their Atlas-era monsters.

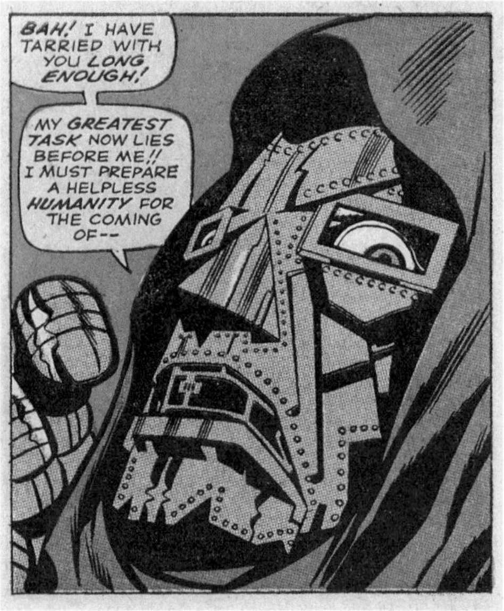
BAH! I HAVE TARRIED WITH YOU LONG ENOUGH!
MY GREATEST TASK NOW LIES BEFORE ME!! I MUST PREPARE A HELPLESS HUMANITY FOR THE COMING OF--

FANTASTIC FOUR No. 59

Above: *Interior, "Doomsday!"; script, Stan Lee; pencils, Jack Kirby; inks, Joe Sinnott; February 1967.*

FANTASTIC FOUR No. 74

Opposite: *Interior, "When Calls Galactus!"; script, Stan Lee; pencils, Jack Kirby; inks, Joe Sinnott; May 1968.* A starving Galactus searches for his former herald. Kirby's latest signature, the full-page illustrated portrait, still manages to convey Galactus's power—even in his weakened state—but perhaps the close-up also betrays a hint of his sadness...and humanity?

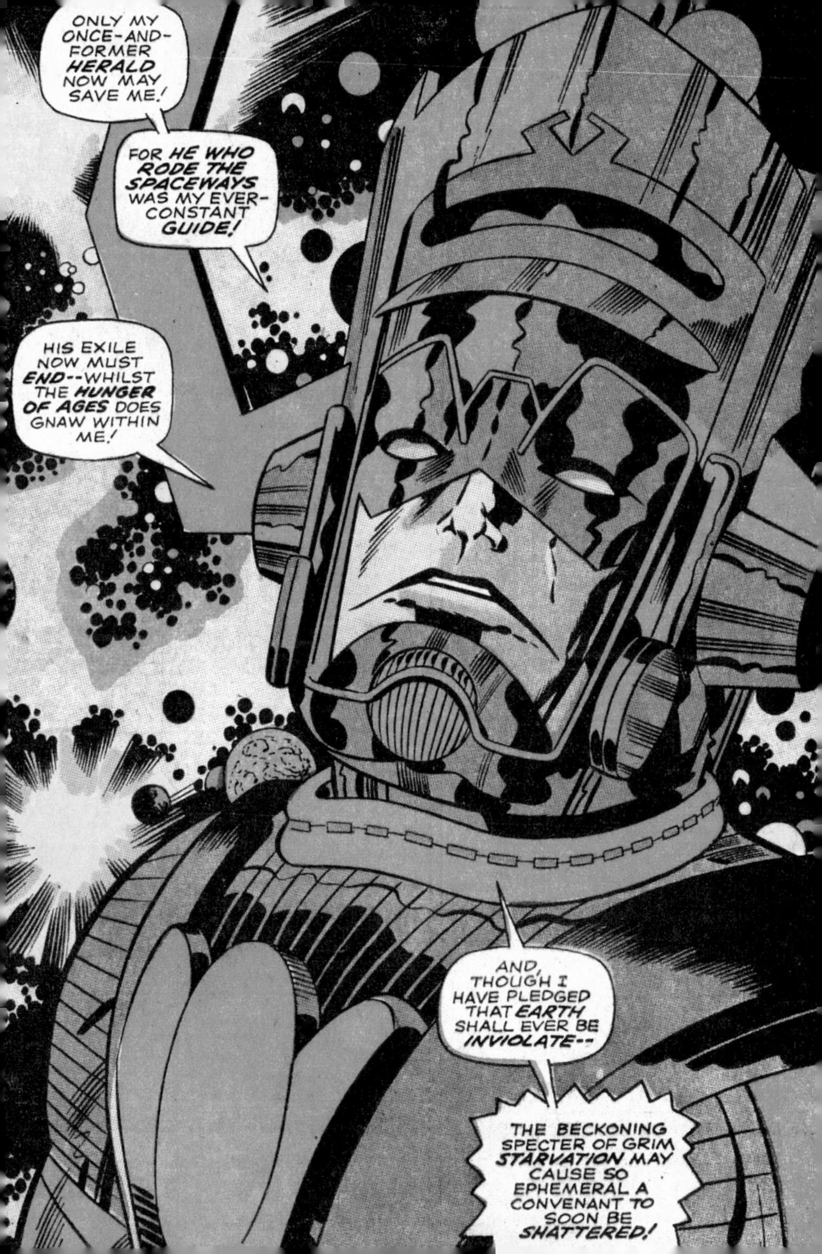
ONLY MY ONCE-AND-FORMER HERALD NOW MAY SAVE ME!
FOR HE WHO RODE THE SPACEWAYS WAS MY EVER-CONSTANT GUIDE!
HIS EXILE NOW MUST END--WHILST THE HUNGER OF AGES DOES GNAW WITHIN ME!
AND, THOUGH I HAVE PLEDGED THAT EARTH SHALL EVER BE INVIOLATE--
THE BECKONING SPECTER OF GRIM STARVATION MAY CAUSE SO EPHEMERAL A CONVENANT TO SOON BE SHATTERED!

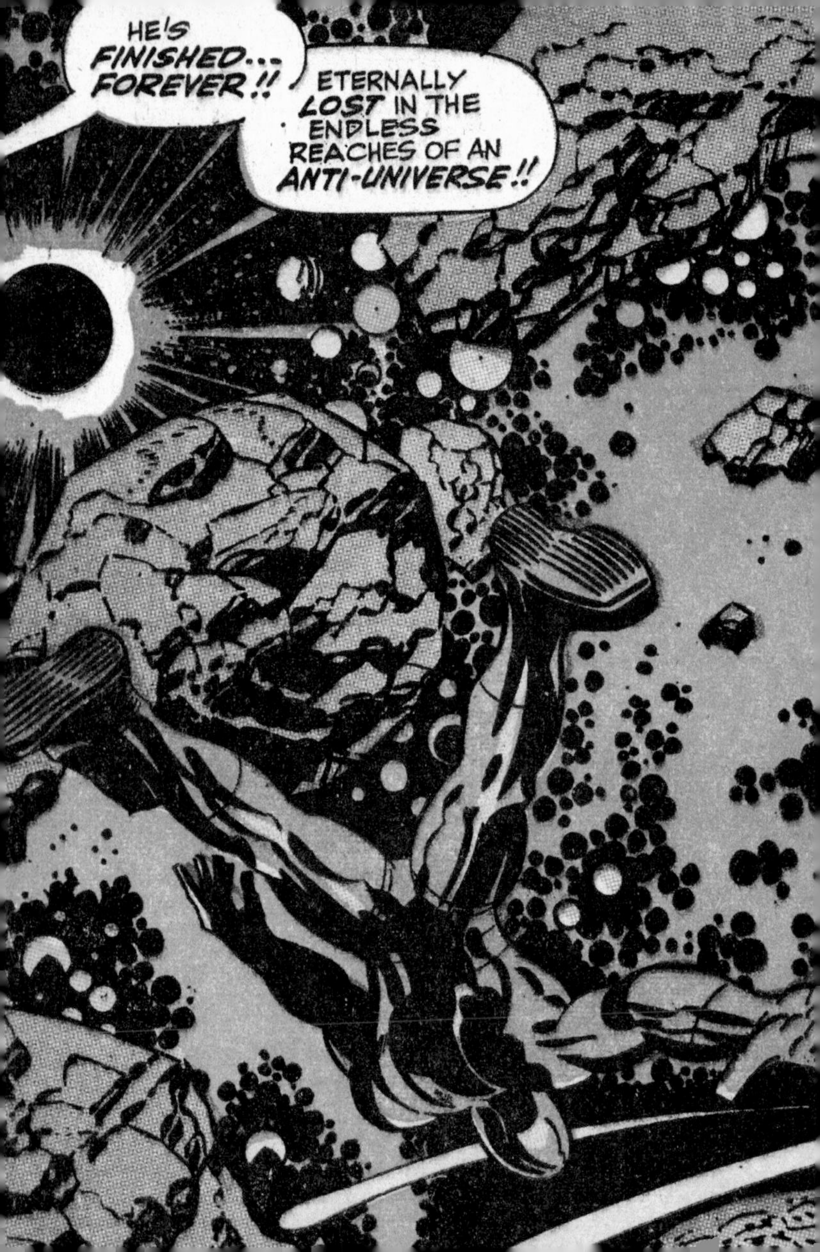
HE'S FINISHED... FOREVER!!
ETERNALLY LOST IN THE ENDLESS REACHES OF AN ANTI-UNIVERSE!!

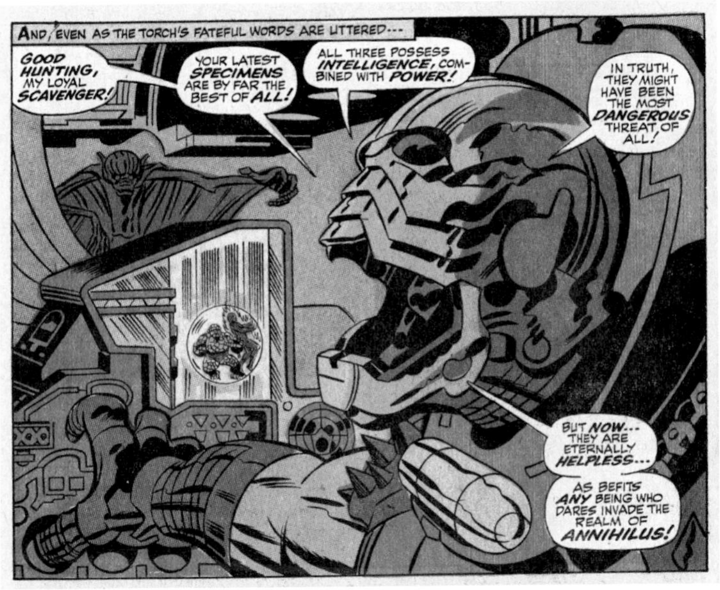
AND, EVEN AS THE TORCH'S FATEFUL WORDS ARE UTTERED---
GOOD HUNTING, MY LOYAL SCAVENGER!
YOUR LATEST SPECIMENS ARE BY FAR THE BEST OF ALL!
ALL THREE POSSESS INTELLIGENCE, COMBINED WITH POWER!
IN TRUTH, THEY MIGHT HAVE BEEN THE MOST DANGEROUS THREAT OF ALL!
BUT NOW... THEY ARE ETERNALLY HELPLESS...
AS BEFITS ANY BEING WHO DARES INVADE THE REALM OF ANNIHILUS!

FANTASTIC FOUR No. 71

Opposite: *Interior, "And So It Ends…"; script, Stan Lee; pencils, Jack Kirby; inks, Joe Sinnott; February 1967.* The Mad Thinker's android is sent into the Negative Zone, an area outside the normal sphere of our galaxy, studied extensively by Reed Richards. The antimatter universe—sparsely populated, though with a preponderance of villains, most famously Annihilus and Blastaar—became an effective threat for the FF, and offered a demise of sorts for villains that technically couldn't be killed based on the strictures of the Comics Code Authority.

FANTASTIC FOUR ANNUAL No. 6

Above: *Interior, "Let There Be Life!"; script, Stan Lee; pencils, Jack Kirby; inks, Joe Sinnott; Summer 1968.* Annihilus was an alien creature whose visual look appeared to be an amalgamation of an insect and Nosferatu, Max Schreck's iconic vampire, from director F. W. Murnau's eerie 1922 silent film.

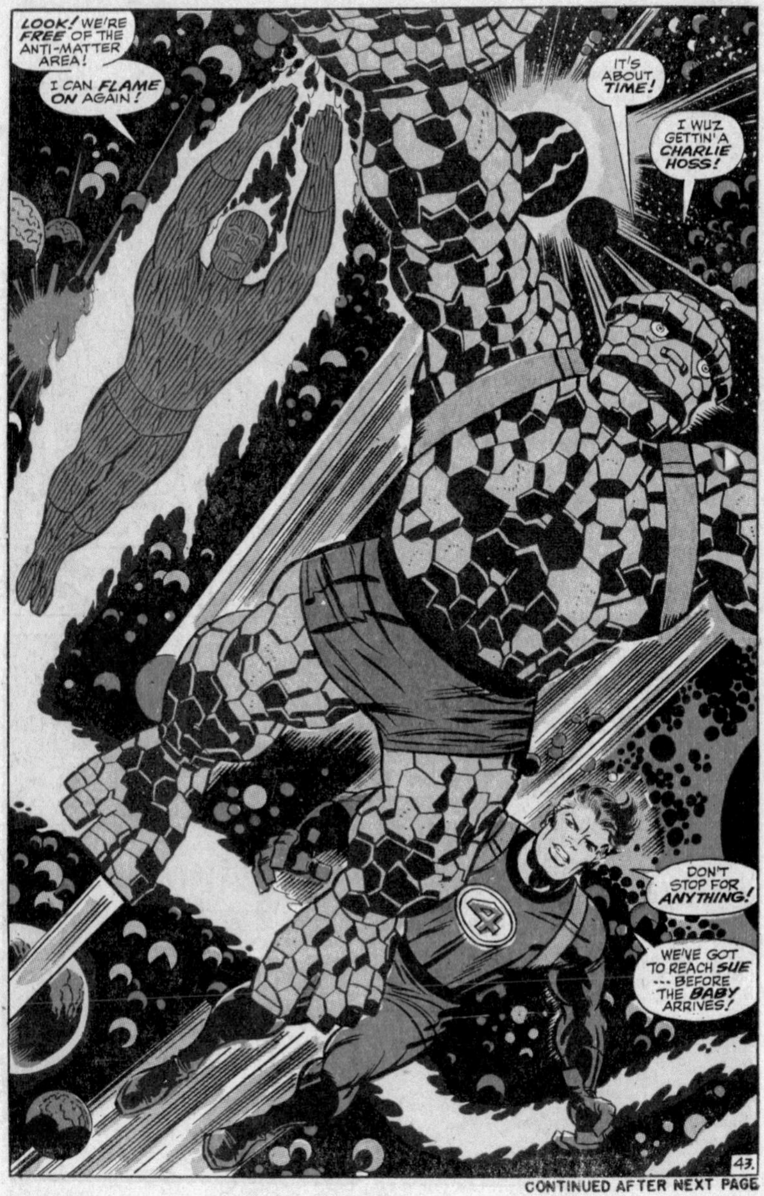
LOOK! WE'RE FREE OF THE ANTI-MATTER AREA!
I CAN FLAME ON AGAIN!
IT'S ABOUT TIME!
I WUZ GETTIN' A CHARLIE HOSS!
DON'T STOP FOR ANYTHING!
WE'VE GOT TO REACH SUE --- BEFORE THE BABY ARRIVES!
43.

CONTINUED AFTER NEXT PAGE

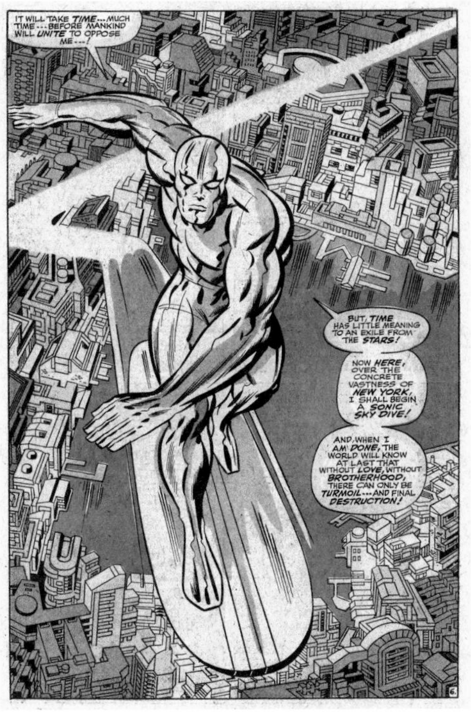
IT WILL TAKE TIME...MUCH TIME---BEFORE MANKIND WILL UNITE TO OPPOSE ME---!
BUT, TIME HAS LITTLE MEANING TO AN EXILE FROM THE STARS!
NOW HERE, OVER THE CONCRETE VASTNESS OF NEW YORK, I SHALL BEGIN A SONIC SKY DIVE!
AND, WHEN I AM DONE, THE WORLD WILL KNOW AT LAST THAT WITHOUT LOVE, WITHOUT BROTHERHOOD, THERE CAN ONLY BE TURMOIL---AND FINAL DESTRUCTION!
6

FANTASTIC FOUR ANNUAL No. 6

Opposite: *Interior, "Let There Be Life!"; script, Stan Lee; pencils, Jack Kirby; inks, Joe Sinnott; Summer 1968.*

FANTASTIC FOUR No. 72

Above: *Interior, "Where Soars the Silver Surfer!"; script, Stan Lee; pencils, Jack Kirby; inks, Joe Sinnott; March 1968.*

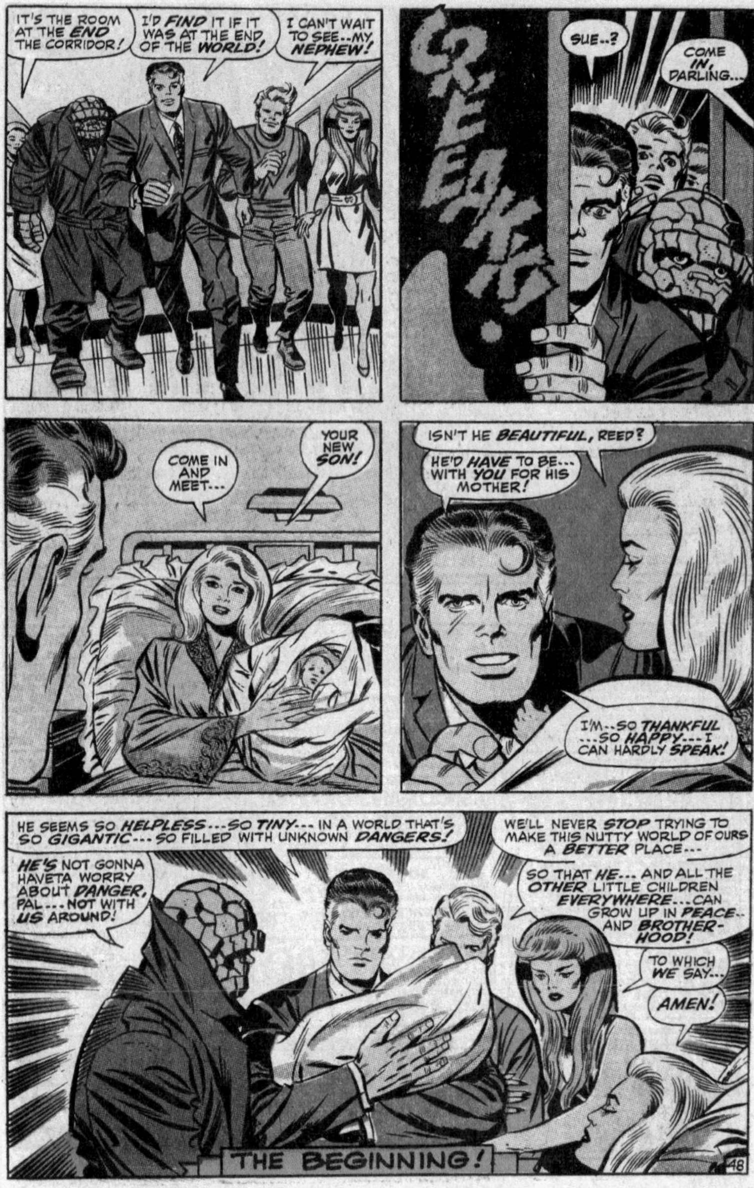

IT'S THE ROOM AT THE END THE CORRIDOR!
I'D FIND IT IF IT WAS AT THE END OF THE WORLD!
I CAN'T WAIT TO SEE...MY NEPHEW!
CREEAK!
SUE..?
COME IN, DARLING...
COME IN AND MEET...
YOUR NEW SON!
ISN'T HE BEAUTIFUL, REED?
HE'D HAVE TO BE... WITH YOU FOR HIS MOTHER!
I'M...SO THANKFUL ...SO HAPPY...I CAN HARDLY SPEAK!
HE SEEMS SO HELPLESS...SO TINY...IN A WORLD THAT'S SO GIGANTIC...SO FILLED WITH UNKNOWN DANGERS!
HE'S NOT GONNA HAVETA WORRY ABOUT DANGER, PAL...NOT WITH US AROUND!
WE'LL NEVER STOP TRYING TO MAKE THIS NUTTY WORLD OF OURS A BETTER PLACE...
SO THAT HE...AND ALL THE OTHER LITTLE CHILDREN EVERYWHERE...CAN GROW UP IN PEACE.. AND BROTHER-HOOD!
TO WHICH WE SAY...
AMEN!
THE BEGINNING!
48

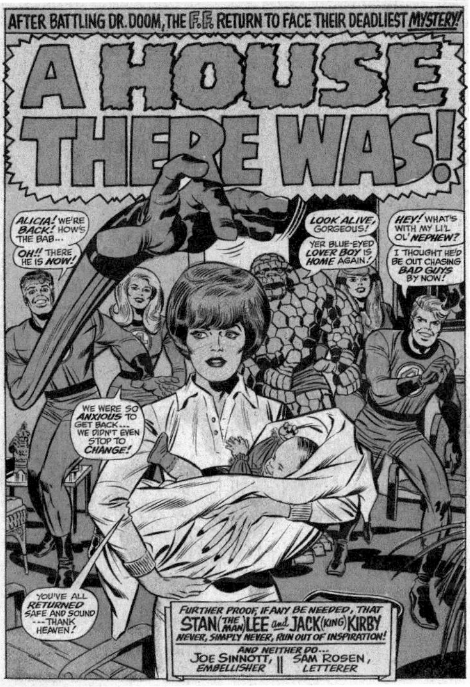
AFTER BATTLING DR. DOOM, THE F.F. RETURN TO FACE THEIR DEADLIEST MYSTERY!
A HOUSE THERE WAS!
ALICIA! WE'RE BACK! HOW'S THE BAB...
OH!! THERE HE IS NOW!
LOOK ALIVE, GORGEOUS!
YER BLUE-EYED LOVER BOY IS HOME AGAIN!
HEY! WHAT'S WITH MY LI'L OL' NEPHEW?
I THOUGHT HE'D BE OUT CHASING BAD GUYS BY NOW!
WE WERE SO ANXIOUS TO GET BACK... WE DIDN'T EVEN STOP TO CHANGE!
YOU'VE ALL RETURNED SAFE AND SOUND ---THANK HEAVEN!
FURTHER PROOF, IF ANY BE NEEDED, THAT STAN (THE MAN) LEE and JACK (KING) KIRBY NEVER, SIMPLY NEVER, RUN OUT OF INSPIRATION!
AND NEITHER DO... JOE SINNOTT, EMBELLISHER || SAM ROSEN, LETTERER

FANTASTIC FOUR ANNUAL No. 6

Opposite: *Interior, "Let There Be Life!"; script, Stan Lee; pencils, Jack Kirby; inks, Joe Sinnott; Summer 1968.* Sue Storm and Reed Richards welcome their first child, Franklin, who will go on to be one of the most powerful mutants in the Marvel Universe.

FANTASTIC FOUR No. 88

Above: *Interior, "A House There Was!"; script, Stan Lee; pencils, Jack Kirby; inks, Joe Sinnott; July 1969.* Although Kirby is known for his larger-than-life characters and depictions of science fiction spectacle, he was also a master of quiet, everyday moments, such as this splash page showing the FF arriving to greet comics' first baby, Franklin Richards. It was quotidian scenes like these that allowed readers to connect with Marvel's characters—and especially with the Fantastic Four and Spider-Man—on a very human level.

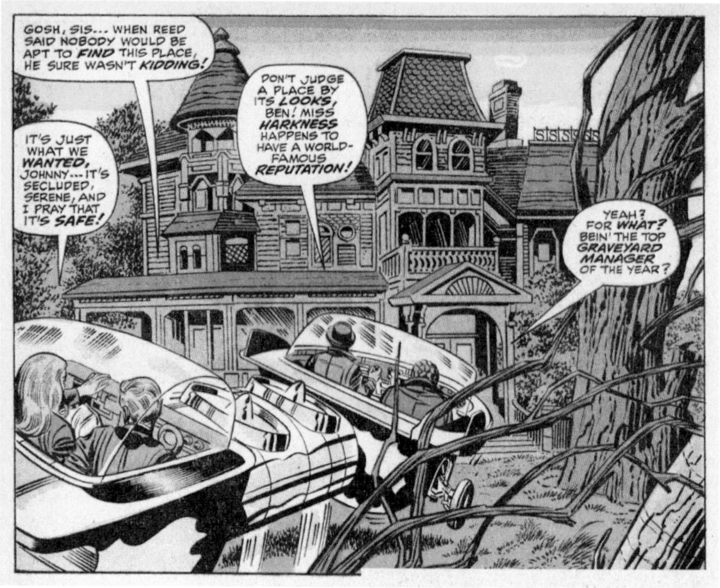
GOSH, SIS... WHEN REED SAID NOBODY WOULD BE APT TO *FIND* THIS PLACE, HE SURE WASN'T *KIDDING!*
IT'S JUST WHAT WE *WANTED,* JOHNNY... IT'S SECLUDED, SERENE, AND I PRAY THAT IT'S *SAFE!*
DON'T JUDGE A PLACE BY ITS *LOOKS,* BEN! MISS *HARKNESS* HAPPENS TO HAVE A WORLD-FAMOUS *REPUTATION!*
YEAH? FOR *WHAT?* BEIN' THE TOP *GRAVEYARD MANAGER* OF THE YEAR?

FANTASTIC FOUR No. 94

Above and opposite: *Interiors, "The Return of the Frightful Four!"; script, Stan Lee; pencils, Jack Kirby; inks, Joe Sinnott; January 1970.* Having drawn his share of stories in the mystery/supernatural genre, including *Black Magic* and *House of Mystery*, Jack Kirby was more than capable of creating fearsome images when called upon. The popularity of the supernatural TV soap opera *Dark Shadows* probably provided inspiration, and Lee kept the mood light with references to pop culture figures from Vincent Price to TV's favorite vampire, Barnabas Collins. Agatha Harkness (opposite) was introduced as a nanny for Reed and Sue's baby—but she was no ordinary babysitter! Harkness was a witch who used her powers for good, adding a new, offbeat addition to the book's cast of characters.

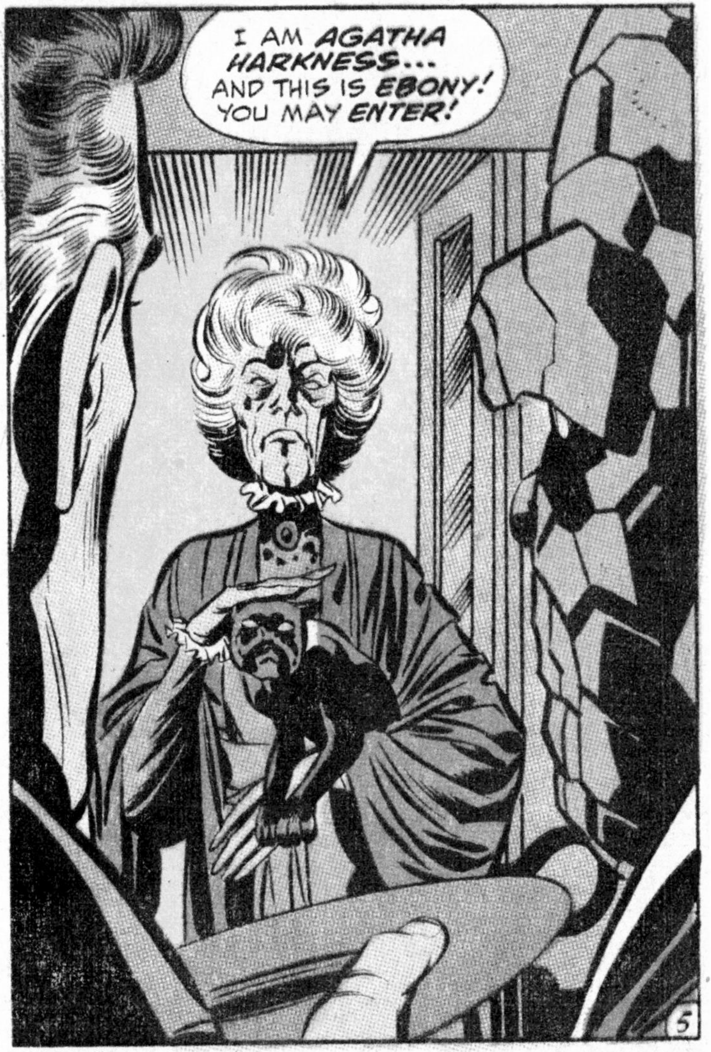
I AM AGATHA HARKNESS... AND THIS IS EBONY! YOU MAY ENTER!
5

AH, BUT EBONY IS...
FAR, FAR MORE...
THAN JUST AN ALLEY CAT!
BEFORE MY EYES... IT KEEPS GROWING... I'VE GOT TO FLY... GOT TO GET AWAY..!!
KRASH!
THERE'S NO ESCAPING IT... NO MATTER WHERE I GO!!
14

FANTASTIC FOUR No. 94

Above: *Interior, "The Return of the Frightful Four!"; script, Stan Lee; pencils, Jack Kirby; inks, Joe Sinnott; January 1970.*

FANTASTIC FOUR ANNUAL No. 14

Opposite: *Interior, "Cat's-Paw!"; plot and script, Marv Wolfman; plot and pencils, George Pérez; inks, Pablo Marcos; 1979.* Being a super hero's kid required a powerful governess. Franklin Richards' nanny was one of the original witches from the Salem witch trials!

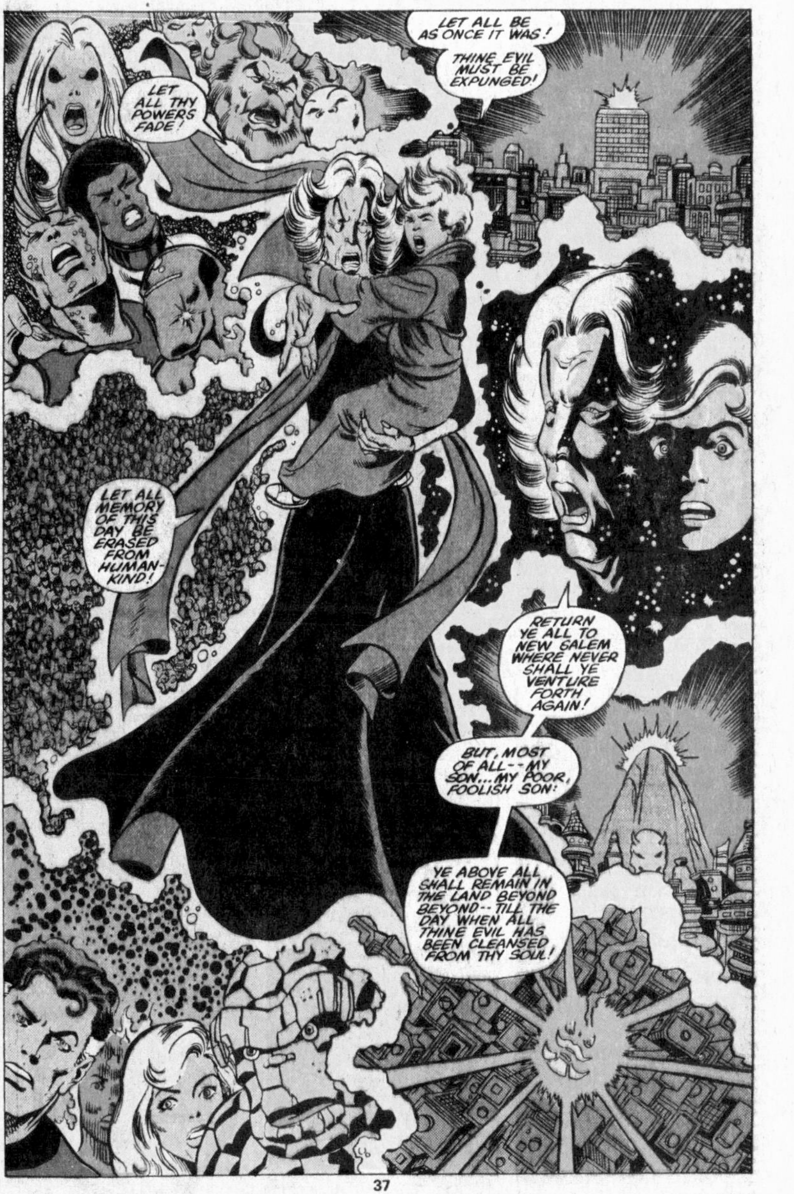
LET ALL THY POWERS FADE!
LET ALL BE AS ONCE IT WAS!
THINE EVIL MUST BE EXPUNGED!
LET ALL MEMORY OF THIS DAY BE ERASED FROM HUMAN-KIND!
RETURN YE ALL TO NEW SALEM WHERE NEVER SHALL YE VENTURE FORTH AGAIN!
BUT, MOST OF ALL-- MY SON... MY POOR, FOOLISH SON!
YE ABOVE ALL SHALL REMAIN IN THE LAND BEYOND BEYOND-- TILL THE DAY WHEN ALL THINE EVIL HAS BEEN CLEANSED FROM THY SOUL!

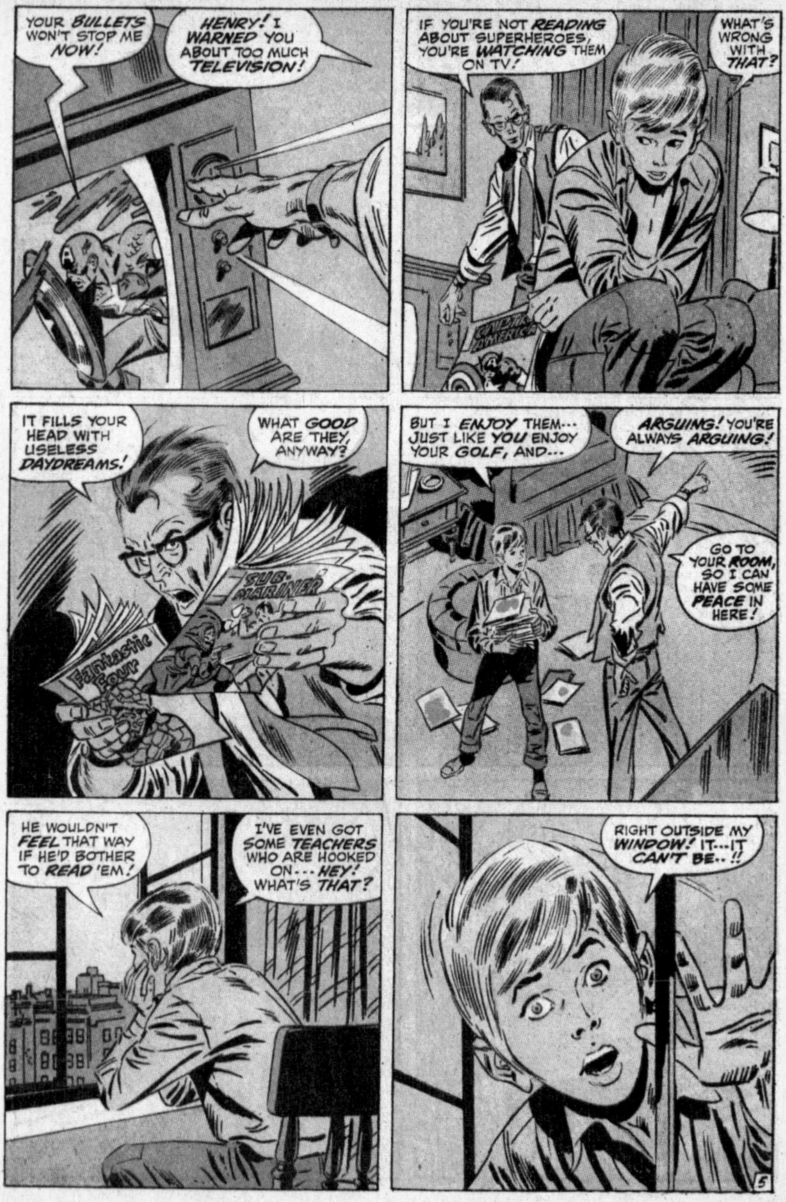
YOUR BULLETS WON'T STOP ME NOW!
HENRY! I WARNED YOU ABOUT TOO MUCH TELEVISION!
IF YOU'RE NOT READING ABOUT SUPERHEROES, YOU'RE WATCHING THEM ON TV!
WHAT'S WRONG WITH THAT?
CAPTAIN AMERICA
IT FILLS YOUR HEAD WITH USELESS DAYDREAMS!
WHAT GOOD ARE THEY, ANYWAY?
SUB-MARINER
Fantastic Four
BUT I ENJOY THEM... JUST LIKE YOU ENJOY YOUR GOLF, AND...
ARGUING! YOU'RE ALWAYS ARGUING!
GO TO YOUR ROOM, SO I CAN HAVE SOME PEACE IN HERE!
HE WOULDN'T FEEL THAT WAY IF HE'D BOTHER TO READ 'EM!
I'VE EVEN GOT SOME TEACHERS WHO ARE HOOKED ON... HEY! WHAT'S THAT?
RIGHT OUTSIDE MY WINDOW! IT... IT CAN'T BE..!!
5

SILVER SURFER No. 14

Opposite: *Interior, "The Surfer and the Spider!"; script, Stan Lee; pencils, John Buscema; inks, Dan Adkins; March 1970.* Like the Surfer's conflicted character—born to soar through the universe, yet trapped on Earth—this short sequence seems to speak to many kids' deep connection to comics. The stigma associated with "these childish things" still figured strongly in the minds of most adults, even as Marvel's comics were striving—and succeeding—to reinvent the medium as a more sophisticated entertainment.

SUB-MARINER No. 8

Below: *Interior, "In the Rage of Battle!"; script, Roy Thomas; pencils, John Buscema; inks, Dan Adkins; December 1968.*

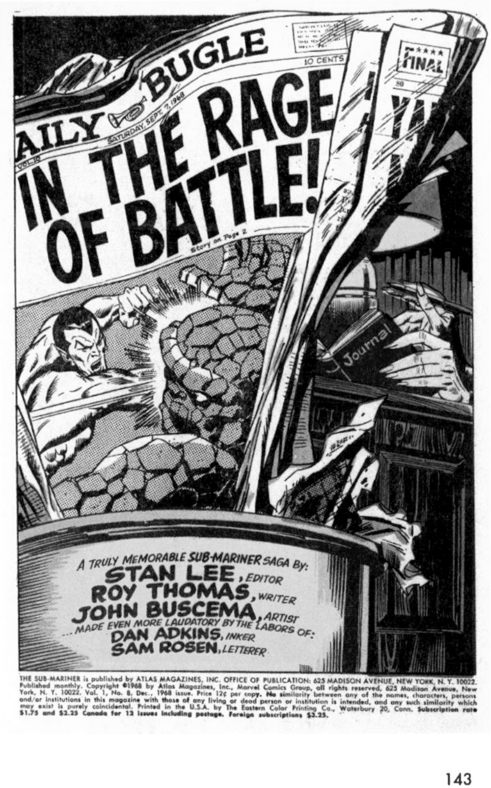

AILY BUGLE
10 CENTS
SATURDAY, SEPT. 7, 1968
FINAL
IN THE RAGE OF BATTLE!
Story on Page 2
Journal
A TRULY MEMORABLE SUB-MARINER SAGA By:
STAN LEE, EDITOR
ROY THOMAS, WRITER
JOHN BUSCEMA, ARTIST
... MADE EVEN MORE LAUDATORY BY THE LABORS OF:
DAN ADKINS, INKER
SAM ROSEN, LETTERER
THE SUB-MARINER is published by ATLAS MAGAZINES, INC. OFFICE OF PUBLICATION: 625 MADISON AVENUE, NEW YORK, N. Y. 10022. Published monthly. Copyright ©1968 by Atlas Magazines, Inc., Marvel Comics Group, all rights reserved, 625 Madison Avenue, New York, N. Y. 10022. Vol. 1, No. 8, Dec., 1968 issue. Price 12¢ per copy. No similarity between any of the names, characters, persons and/or institutions in this magazine with those of any living or dead person or institution is intended, and any such similarity which may exist is purely coincidental. Printed in the U.S.A. by The Eastern Color Printing Co., Waterbury 20, Conn. Subscription rate $1.75 and $2.25 Canada for 12 issues including postage. Foreign subscriptions $3.25.

MARVEL No. 1

Below: *Cover; pencils, Jack Kirby; inks, Paul Reinman; Editions Lug, April 1970.*

LOS 4 FANTASTICOS No. 3

Opposite: *Cover; pencils and inks, attributed Rafael López Espí; Ediciones Vértice, Barcelona, November 1969.*

FANTASTIC FOUR No. 98

Pages 146–47: *Interior, "Mystery on the Moon!"; script, Stan Lee; pencils, Jack Kirby; inks, Joe Sinnott; May 1970.* The extraordinary achievement of landing two men on the moon and returning them home safely was the pride of many Americans, including Kirby and Lee, who leapt at the chance to have their characters contribute in their own small way. A few issues later, they received the following reply from the Apollo 11 team: "Quite contrary to your popular beliefs, the United States is perfectly able to make a round trip to the moon without any help from the Fantastic Four. Man makes it to another world only to find out that the whole thing wouldn't have been possible if not for a group of superheroes. Next time, butt out of our business!" Marvel printed the letter, "because it just might be genuine and we don't want to get into a running feud with three of the great guys of our time." Better safe than sorry, even if "the address on the envelope read 'Akron, Ohio,' and not Houston at all!"

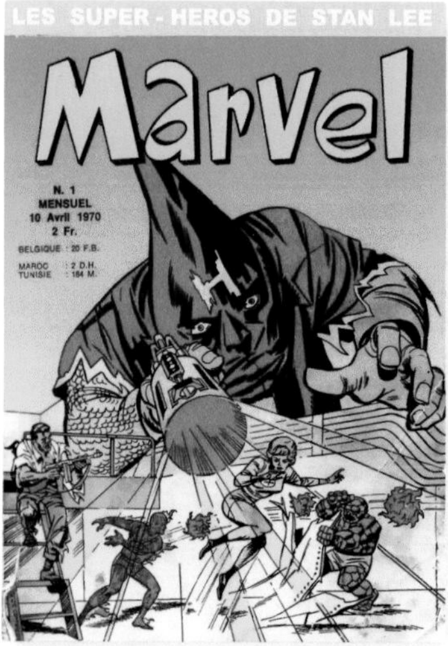
LES SUPER-HEROS DE STAN LEE
Marvel
N. 1
MENSUEL
10 Avril 1970
2 Fr.
BELGIQUE : 20 F.B.
MAROC : 2 D.H.
TUNISIE : 184 M.

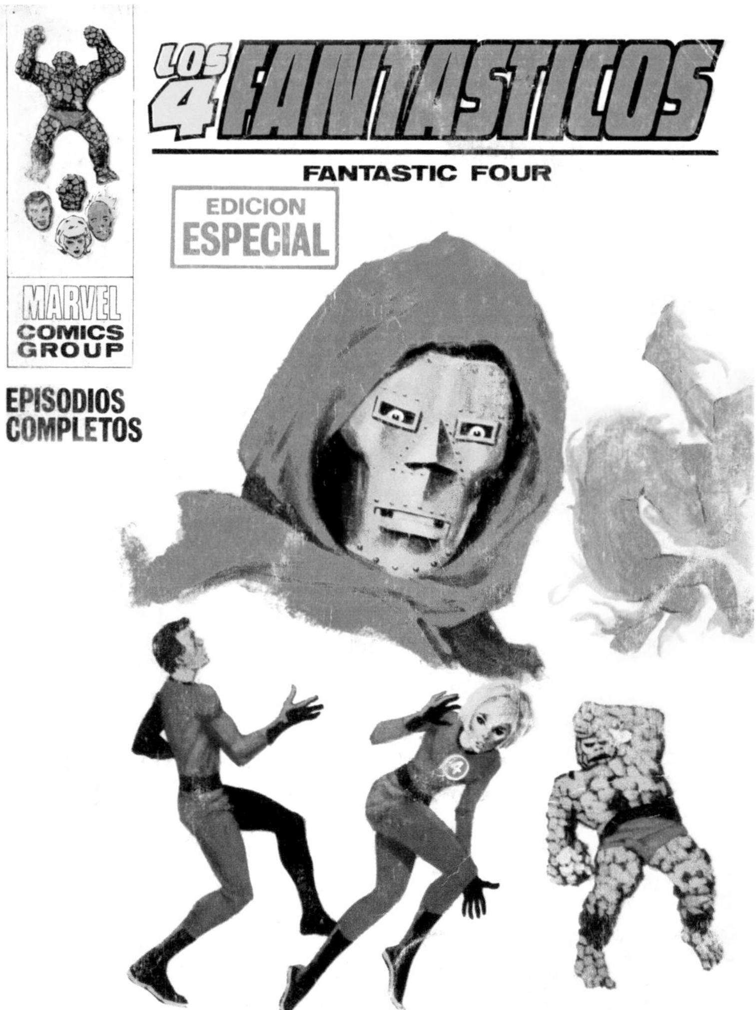
LOS 4 FANTASTICOS
FANTASTIC FOUR
EDICION ESPECIAL
MARVEL COMICS GROUP
EPISODIOS COMPLETOS
HISTORIAS GRAFICAS PARA ADULTOS
CONTRA EL DR. MUERTE

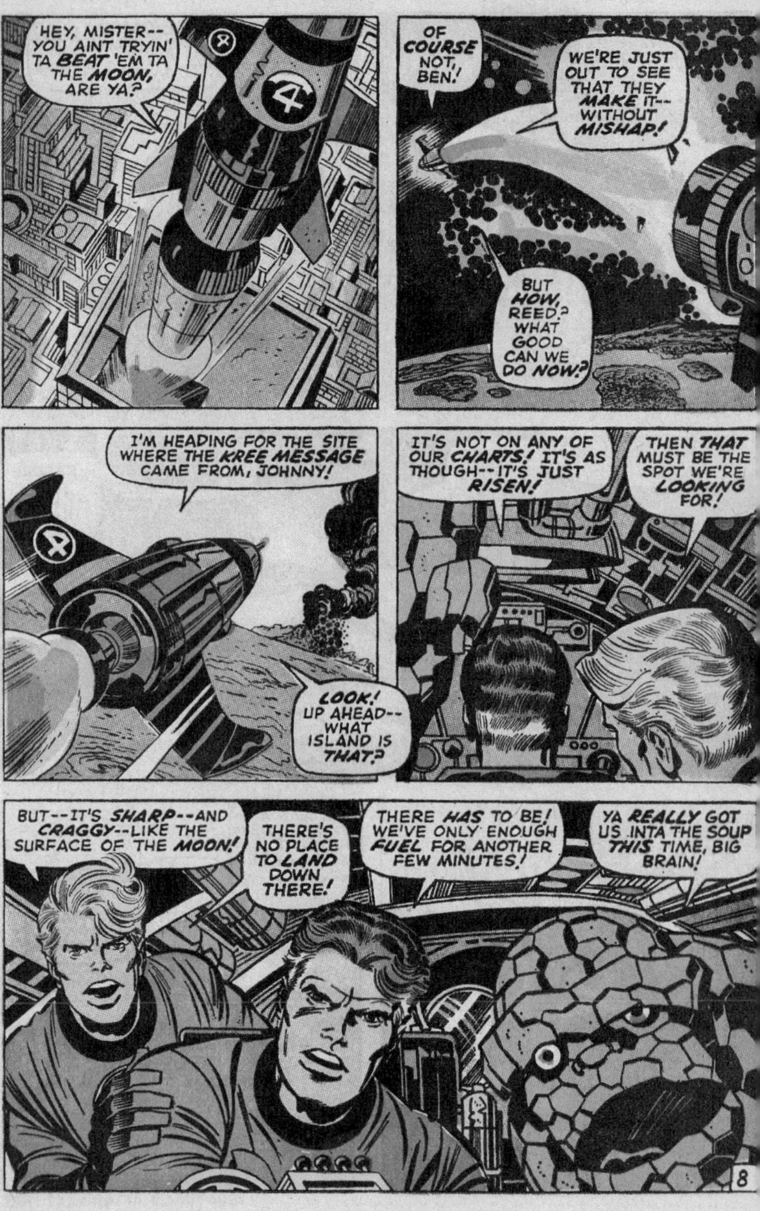

HEY, MISTER-- YOU AINT TRYIN' TA BEAT 'EM TA THE MOON, ARE YA?
OF COURSE NOT, BEN.!
WE'RE JUST OUT TO SEE THAT THEY MAKE IT-- WITHOUT MISHAP!
BUT HOW, REED? WHAT GOOD CAN WE DO NOW?
I'M HEADING FOR THE SITE WHERE THE KREE MESSAGE CAME FROM, JOHNNY!
LOOK! UP AHEAD-- WHAT ISLAND IS THAT?
IT'S NOT ON ANY OF OUR CHARTS! IT'S AS THOUGH--IT'S JUST RISEN!
THEN THAT MUST BE THE SPOT WE'RE LOOKING FOR!
BUT--IT'S SHARP--AND CRAGGY--LIKE THE SURFACE OF THE MOON!
THERE'S NO PLACE TO LAND DOWN THERE!
THERE HAS TO BE! WE'VE ONLY ENOUGH FUEL FOR ANOTHER FEW MINUTES!
YA REALLY GOT US INTA THE SOUP THIS TIME, BIG BRAIN!
8

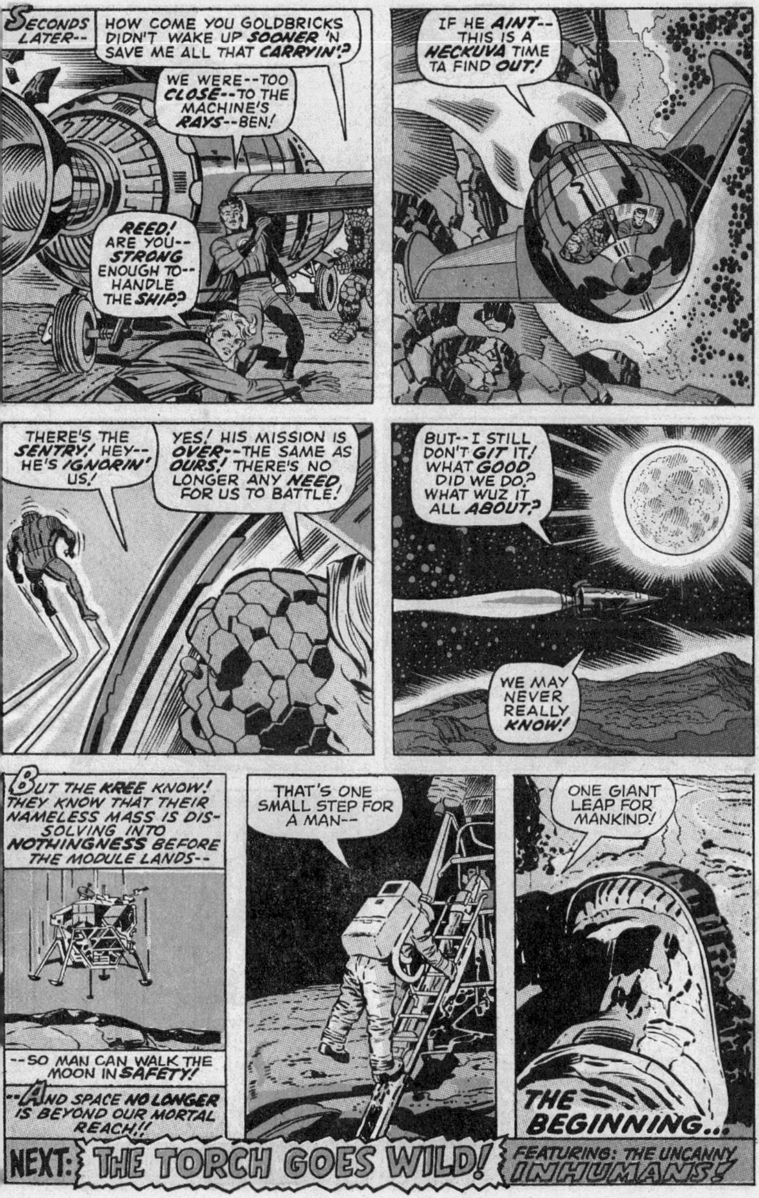
SECONDS LATER--
HOW COME YOU GOLDBRICKS DIDN'T WAKE UP SOONER 'N SAVE ME ALL THAT CARRYIN'?
WE WERE--TOO CLOSE--TO THE MACHINE'S RAYS--BEN!
REED! ARE YOU--STRONG ENOUGH TO--HANDLE THE SHIP?
IF HE AINT--THIS IS A HECKUVA TIME TA FIND OUT!
THERE'S THE SENTRY! HEY--HE'S IGNORIN' US!
YES! HIS MISSION IS OVER--THE SAME AS OURS! THERE'S NO LONGER ANY NEED FOR US TO BATTLE!
BUT--I STILL DON'T GIT IT! WHAT GOOD DID WE DO? WHAT WUZ IT ALL ABOUT?
WE MAY NEVER REALLY KNOW!
BUT THE KREE KNOW! THEY KNOW THAT THEIR NAMELESS MASS IS DISSOLVING INTO NOTHINGNESS BEFORE THE MODULE LANDS--
--SO MAN CAN WALK THE MOON IN SAFETY!
--AND SPACE NO LONGER IS BEYOND OUR MORTAL REACH!!
THAT'S ONE SMALL STEP FOR A MAN--
ONE GIANT LEAP FOR MANKIND!
THE BEGINNING...
NEXT: THE TORCH GOES WILD! FEATURING: THE UNCANNY INHUMANS!

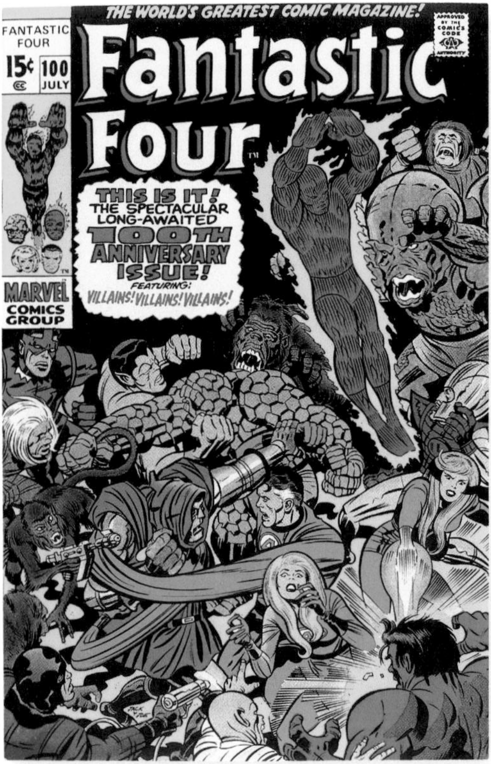
THE WORLD'S GREATEST COMIC MAGAZINE!
FANTASTIC FOUR
15¢ 100 JULY
Fantastic Four
MARVEL COMICS GROUP
THIS IS IT! THE SPECTACULAR LONG-AWAITED 100TH ANNIVERSARY ISSUE! FEATURING: VILLAINS! VILLAINS! VILLAINS!

FANTASTIC FOUR No. 100

Above: *Cover; pencils, Jack Kirby; inks, Joe Sinnott; July 1970.* The series reaches No. 100 with Lee and Kirby as its sole creative team.

GIANT- SIZE FANTASTIC FOUR No. 2

Opposite: *Interior, "Time Enough for Death!"; script, Gerry Conway; pencils, John Buscema; inks, Chic Stone; August 1974.* Hello, Dalí! In what was by now a long-standing tradition, the surreal landscapes of Salvador Dalí's iconic painting *The Persistence of Memory* are parodied in the FF's romp through the looking glass, chasing no less august a personage than Stan Lee's beloved postman, Willie Lumpkin.

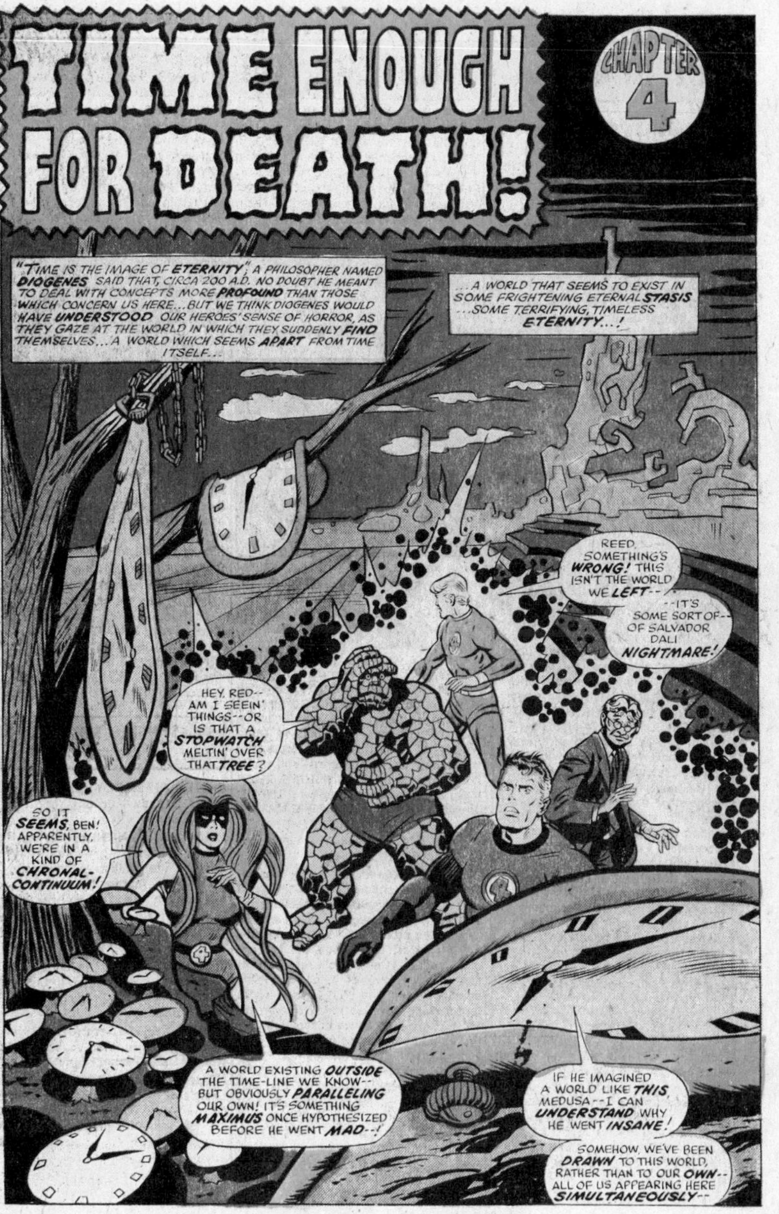

TIME ENOUGH FOR DEATH!
CHAPTER 4
"TIME IS THE IMAGE OF ETERNITY," A PHILOSOPHER NAMED DIOGENES SAID THAT, CIRCA 200 A.D. NO DOUBT HE MEANT TO DEAL WITH CONCEPTS MORE PROFOUND THAN THOSE WHICH CONCERN US HERE... BUT WE THINK DIOGENES WOULD HAVE UNDERSTOOD OUR HEROES' SENSE OF HORROR, AS THEY GAZE AT THE WORLD IN WHICH THEY SUDDENLY FIND THEMSELVES... A WORLD WHICH SEEMS APART FROM TIME ITSELF...
...A WORLD THAT SEEMS TO EXIST IN SOME FRIGHTENING ETERNAL STASIS ...SOME TERRIFYING, TIMELESS ETERNITY...!
REED, SOMETHING'S WRONG! THIS ISN'T THE WORLD WE LEFT--
--IT'S SOME SORT OF--OF SALVADOR DALI NIGHTMARE!
HEY, RED--AM I SEEIN' THINGS--OR IS THAT A STOPWATCH MELTIN' OVER THAT TREE?
SO IT SEEMS, BEN! APPARENTLY, WE'RE IN A KIND OF CHRONAL-CONTINUUM!
A WORLD EXISTING OUTSIDE THE TIME-LINE WE KNOW--BUT OBVIOUSLY PARALLELING OUR OWN! IT'S SOMETHING MAXIMUS ONCE HYPOTHESIZED BEFORE HE WENT MAD--!
IF HE IMAGINED A WORLD LIKE THIS, MEDUSA--I CAN UNDERSTAND WHY HE WENT INSANE!
SOMEHOW, WE'VE BEEN DRAWN TO THIS WORLD, RATHER THAN TO OUR OWN--ALL OF US APPEARING HERE SIMULTANEOUSLY--

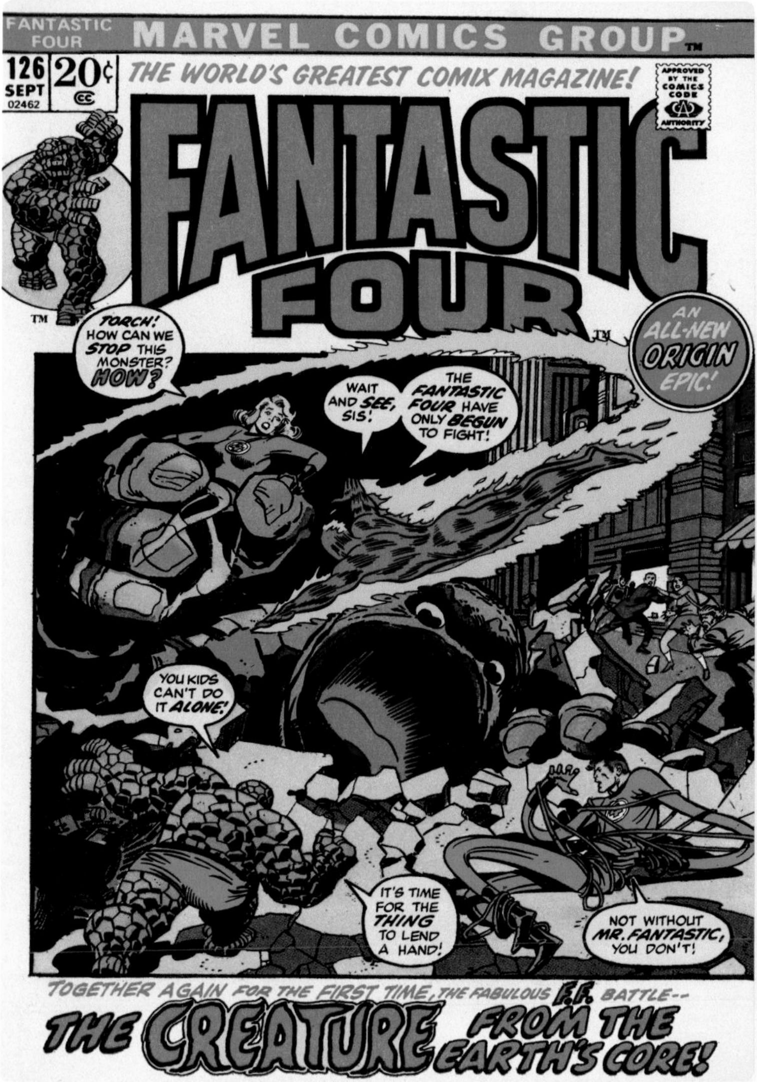

FANTASTIC FOUR
MARVEL COMICS GROUP
126 SEPT 02462
20¢
THE WORLD'S GREATEST COMIX MAGAZINE!
APPROVED BY THE COMICS CODE AUTHORITY
FANTASTIC FOUR
AN ALL-NEW ORIGIN EPIC!
TORCH! HOW CAN WE STOP THIS MONSTER? HOW?
WAIT AND SEE, SIS!
THE FANTASTIC FOUR HAVE ONLY BEGUN TO FIGHT!
YOU KIDS CAN'T DO IT ALONE!
IT'S TIME FOR THE THING TO LEND A HAND!
NOT WITHOUT MR. FANTASTIC, YOU DON'T!
TOGETHER AGAIN FOR THE FIRST TIME, THE FABULOUS F.F. BATTLE--
THE CREATURE FROM THE EARTH'S CORE!

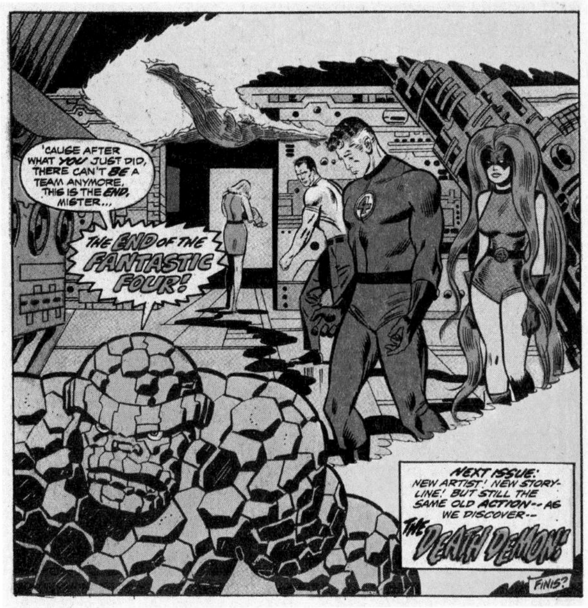
'CAUSE AFTER WHAT YOU JUST DID, THERE CAN'T BE A TEAM ANYMORE. THIS IS THE END, MISTER...
THE END OF THE FANTASTIC FOUR!
NEXT ISSUE: NEW ARTIST! NEW STORY-LINE! BUT STILL THE SAME OLD ACTION-- AS WE DISCOVER--
THE DEATH DEMON!
FINIS?

FANTASTIC FOUR No. 126

Opposite: *Cover; pencils, John Buscema; inks, Joe Sinnott; September 1972.* This cover's layout is a direct homage to the very first issue of *Fantastic Four*. "*Fantastic Four* No. 1 changed my life," said Gerry Conway, who would later write for the title. "After reading that comic (and running back to the candy store around the corner to see if they had any more, and amazingly enough, finding out they had one leftover copy of *Fantastic Four* No. 3...) I suddenly knew what I wanted to do with my life."

FANTASTIC FOUR No. 141

Above: *Interior, "The End of the Fantastic Four!"; script, Gerry Conway; pencils, John Buscema; inks, Joe Sinnott; December 1973.* Fantastic Four no more? As the ever-increasing complexities of life in a modernizing society began seeping into comics, even Marvel's first family was not immune to the specter of divorce, infidelity (Namor wasn't hanging around for his health!), and child abuse (Reed having literally shot his young son Franklin with a giant ray gun...).

ON THE RADIO

Below: *Vinyl record, "The Adventures of the Fantastic Four," 1975.* With scripts taken directly from the comic books, the adventures were chopped up into five-minute segments memorable mostly for the presence of Bill Murray, who gave voice to the Human Torch in the short-lived Marvel venture. He likely shed no sizzling tears, since he followed it up with the second season of *Saturday Night Live*.

AVENGERS (FANS) ASSEMBLE!

Opposite: *Poster, Mighty Marvel Comicon; pencils, John Buscema; inks, Joe Sinnott; 1975.*

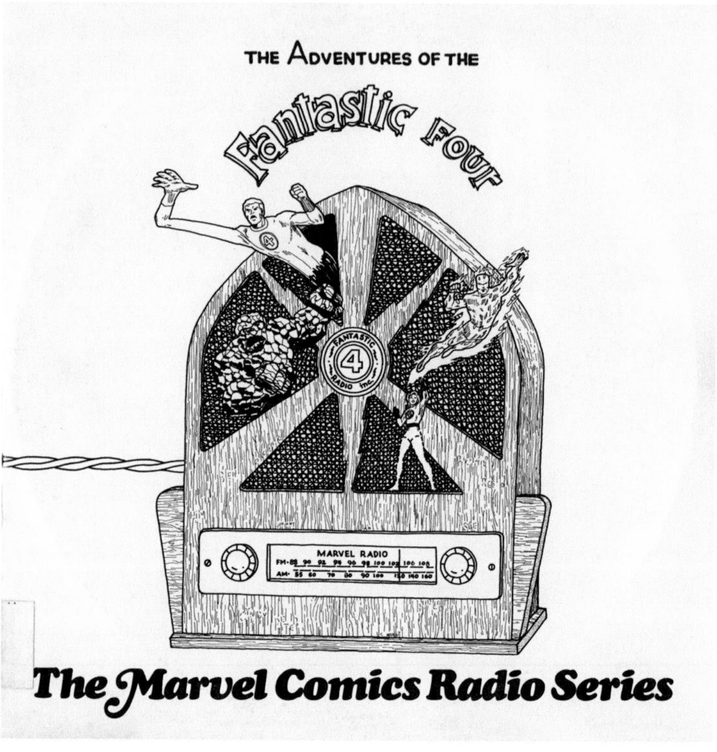
THE ADVENTURES OF THE
Fantastic Four
FANTASTIC
4
RADIO Inc.
MARVEL RADIO
The Marvel Comics Radio Series

GET YOURS IN THE MARVEL ROOM

MIGHTY MARVEL COMICON 1975!

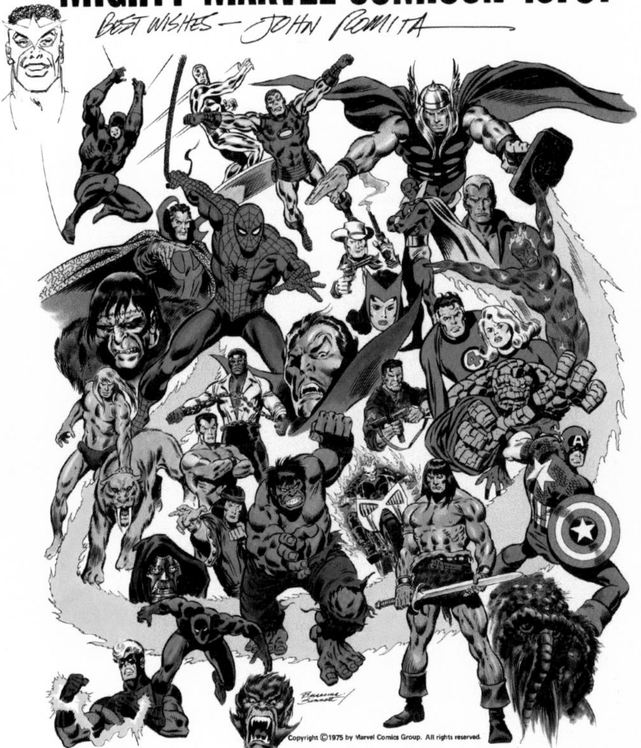
BEST WISHES — JOHN ROMITA
Copyright ©1975 by Marvel Comics Group. All rights reserved.

JOHN ROMITA

SATURDAY, MARCH 22 – MONDAY, MARCH 24

HOTEL COMMODORE, PARK AVENUE & 42 STREET

MARVEL MARCHES ON!

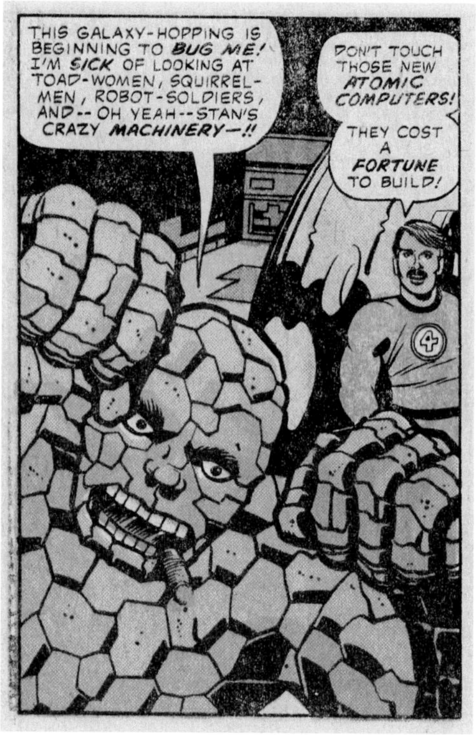
THIS GALAXY-HOPPING IS BEGINNING TO BUG ME! I'M SICK OF LOOKING AT TOAD-WOMEN, SQUIRREL-MEN, ROBOT-SOLDIERS, AND-- OH YEAH--STAN'S CRAZY MACHINERY—!!
DON'T TOUCH THOSE NEW ATOMIC COMPUTERS!
THEY COST A FORTUNE TO BUILD!

WHAT IF? No. 11

Above, opposite, and pages 156–57: *Cover; pencils, Jack Kirby; inks, Joe Sinnott. Interiors, "What If the Original Marvel Bullpen Had Become the Fantastic Four?"; script and pencils, Jack Kirby; inks, Mike Royer and Bill Wray; October 1978.* In this odd and nostalgic "What If...?" story, Kirby characteristically positioned himself as the Thing. Asked by *The Comics Journal* in 1990 whether he had put some of himself into the rock-steady FF clobberer, Kirby said it was an association others made before he did and then added, "I suppose I must be a lot like Ben Grimm. I never duck out of a fight; I don't care what the hell the odds are, and I'm rough at times, but I try to be a decent guy all the time." Lee and Sol Brodsky, both then still with the company, were Mr. Fantastic and the Human Torch. And Kirby had not forgotten Flo Steinberg, who had left Marvel in 1968—she landed the Invisible Girl role.

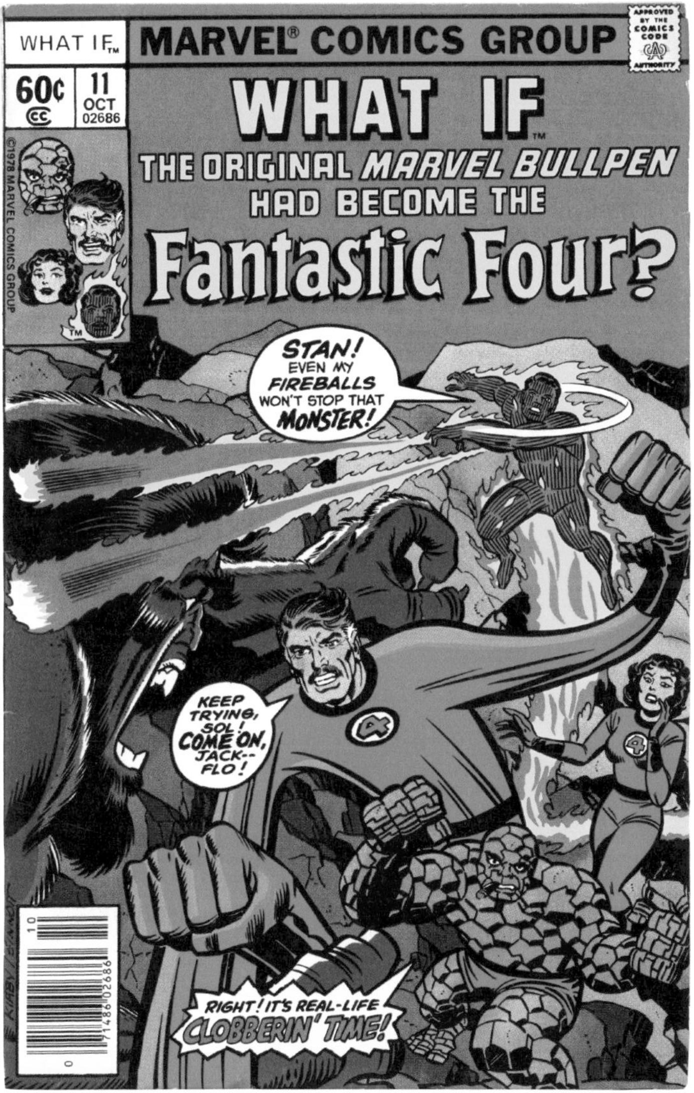
WHAT IF
MARVEL® COMICS GROUP
APPROVED BY THE COMICS CODE AUTHORITY
60¢
11 OCT 02686
WHAT IF
THE ORIGINAL MARVEL BULLPEN HAD BECOME THE
Fantastic Four?
©1978 MARVEL COMICS GROUP
STAN! EVEN MY FIREBALLS WON'T STOP THAT MONSTER!
KEEP TRYING, SOL! COME ON, JACK-- FLO!
RIGHT! IT'S REAL-LIFE CLOBBERIN' TIME!

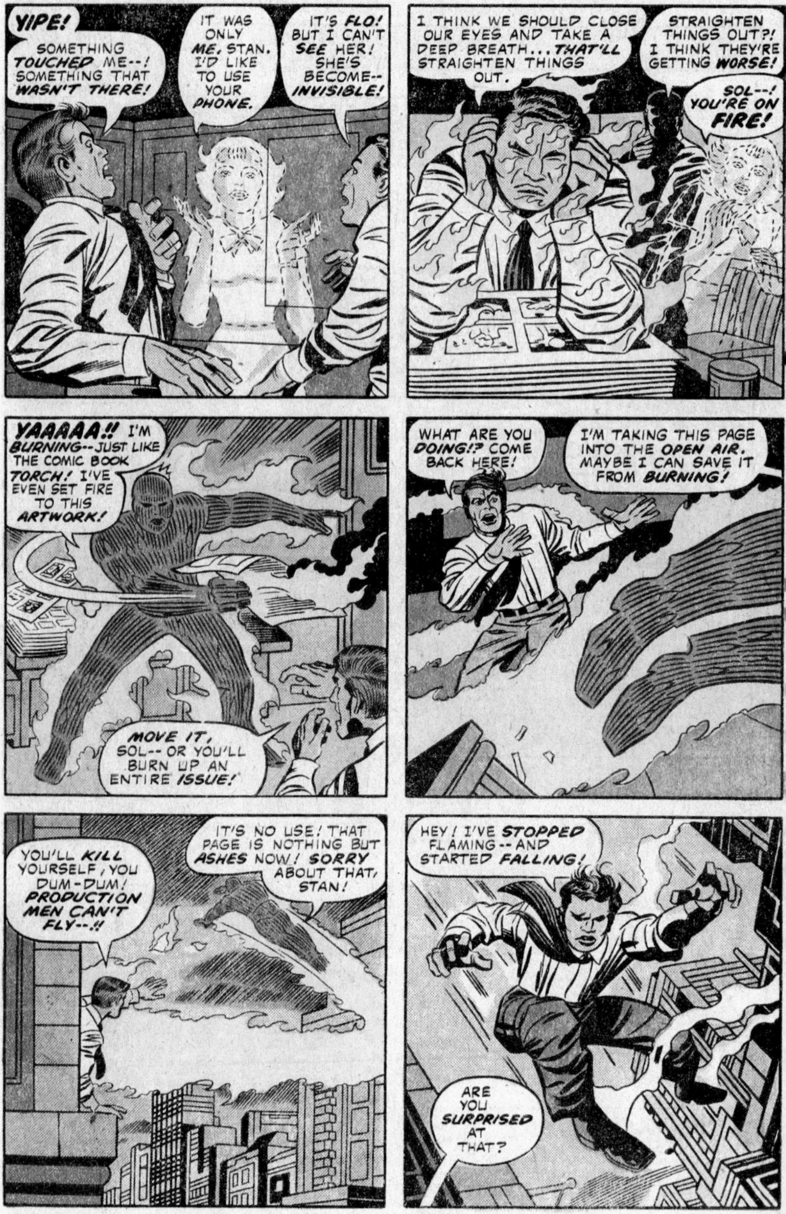
YIPE!
SOMETHING TOUCHED ME--! SOMETHING THAT WASN'T THERE!
IT WAS ONLY ME, STAN. I'D LIKE TO USE YOUR PHONE.
IT'S FLO! BUT I CAN'T SEE HER! SHE'S BECOME-- INVISIBLE!
I THINK WE SHOULD CLOSE OUR EYES AND TAKE A DEEP BREATH....THAT'LL STRAIGHTEN THINGS OUT.
STRAIGHTEN THINGS OUT?! I THINK THEY'RE GETTING WORSE!
SOL--! YOU'RE ON FIRE!
YAAAAA!! I'M BURNING--JUST LIKE THE COMIC BOOK TORCH! I'VE EVEN SET FIRE TO THIS ARTWORK!
MOVE IT, SOL-- OR YOU'LL BURN UP AN ENTIRE ISSUE!
WHAT ARE YOU DOING!? COME BACK HERE!
I'M TAKING THIS PAGE INTO THE OPEN AIR. MAYBE I CAN SAVE IT FROM BURNING!
YOU'LL KILL YOURSELF, YOU DUM-DUM! PRODUCTION MEN CAN'T FLY--!!
IT'S NO USE! THAT PAGE IS NOTHING BUT ASHES NOW! SORRY ABOUT THAT, STAN!
HEY! I'VE STOPPED FLAMING--AND STARTED FALLING!
ARE YOU SURPRISED AT THAT?

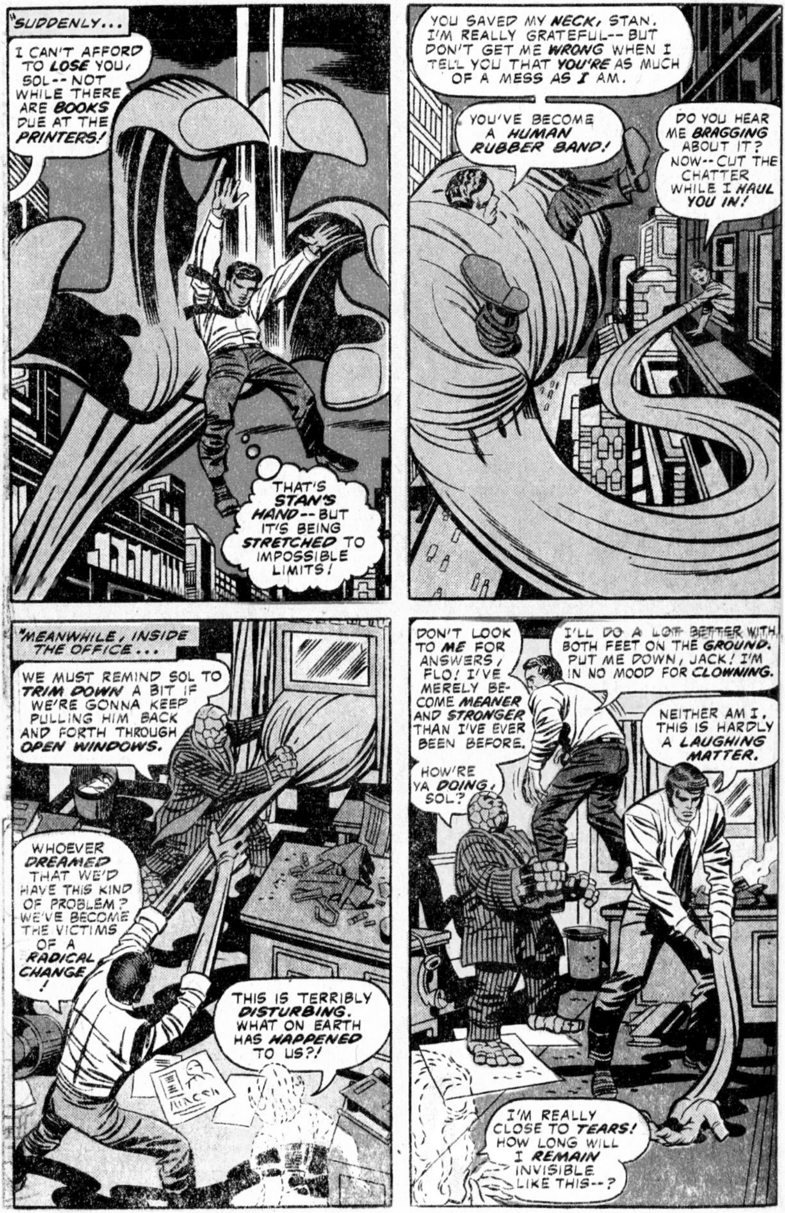
SUDDENLY...
I CAN'T AFFORD TO LOSE YOU, SOL-- NOT WHILE THERE ARE BOOKS DUE AT THE PRINTERS!
THAT'S STAN'S HAND-- BUT IT'S BEING STRETCHED TO IMPOSSIBLE LIMITS!
YOU SAVED MY NECK, STAN. I'M REALLY GRATEFUL-- BUT DON'T GET ME WRONG WHEN I TELL YOU THAT YOU'RE AS MUCH OF A MESS AS I AM.
YOU'VE BECOME A HUMAN RUBBER BAND!
DO YOU HEAR ME BRAGGING ABOUT IT? NOW-- CUT THE CHATTER WHILE I HAUL YOU IN!
MEANWHILE, INSIDE THE OFFICE...
WE MUST REMIND SOL TO TRIM DOWN A BIT IF WE'RE GONNA KEEP PULLING HIM BACK AND FORTH THROUGH OPEN WINDOWS.
WHOEVER DREAMED THAT WE'D HAVE THIS KIND OF PROBLEM? WE'VE BECOME THE VICTIMS OF A RADICAL CHANGE!
THIS IS TERRIBLY DISTURBING. WHAT ON EARTH HAS HAPPENED TO US?!
DON'T LOOK TO ME FOR ANSWERS, FLO! I'VE MERELY BECOME MEANER AND STRONGER THAN I'VE EVER BEEN BEFORE.
I'LL DO A LOT BETTER WITH BOTH FEET ON THE GROUND. PUT ME DOWN, JACK! I'M IN NO MOOD FOR CLOWNING.
HOW'RE YA DOING, SOL?
NEITHER AM I. THIS IS HARDLY A LAUGHING MATTER.
I'M REALLY CLOSE TO TEARS! HOW LONG WILL I REMAIN INVISIBLE LIKE THIS--?

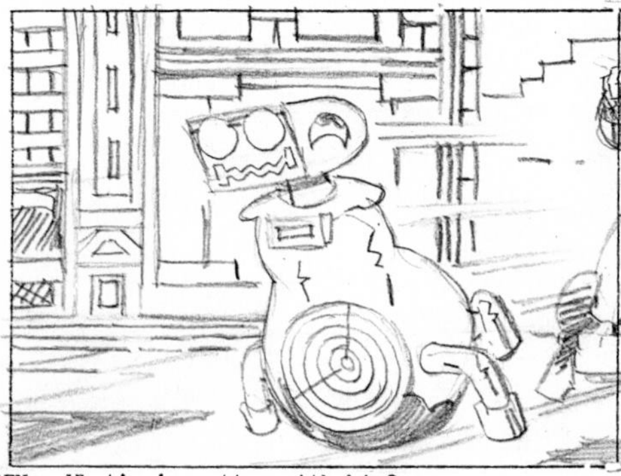

BEN: What's 'a matter with him?

REED: He seems to be trapped in some sort of force field.

HERBIE: Cannot compute . . . . cannot compute . .

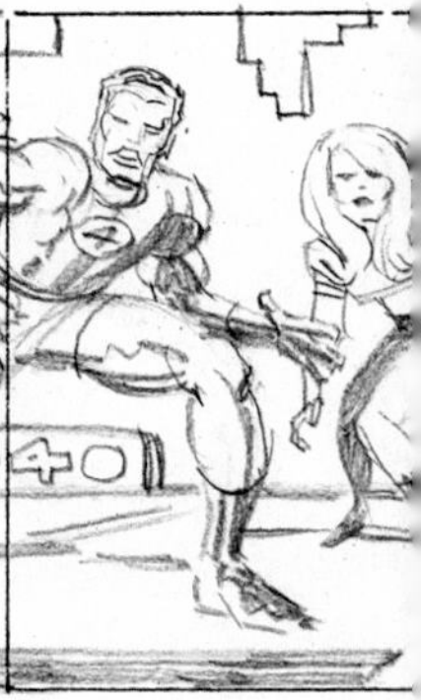

BEN: What are we goi

REED: There must be

nearby

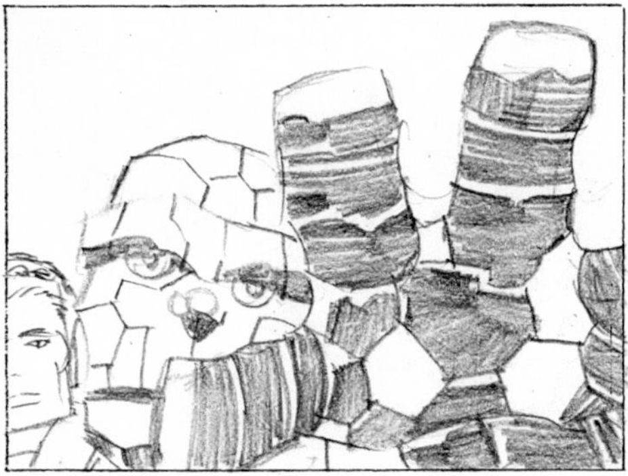

This oughta' cure him!

HERBIE: Cannot compute . . . cannot compute.

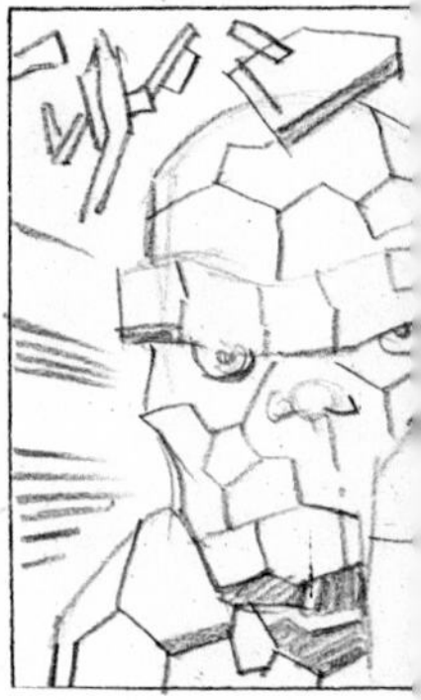

(o.s.) Cosin

equals

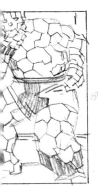

about it?

of power source

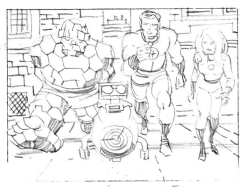

BEN: I get the idea, pal.

30 degree angle

Ahhhhhhhhhhhh.   Thank-you, Benjamine

BEN: Any time, little pal.

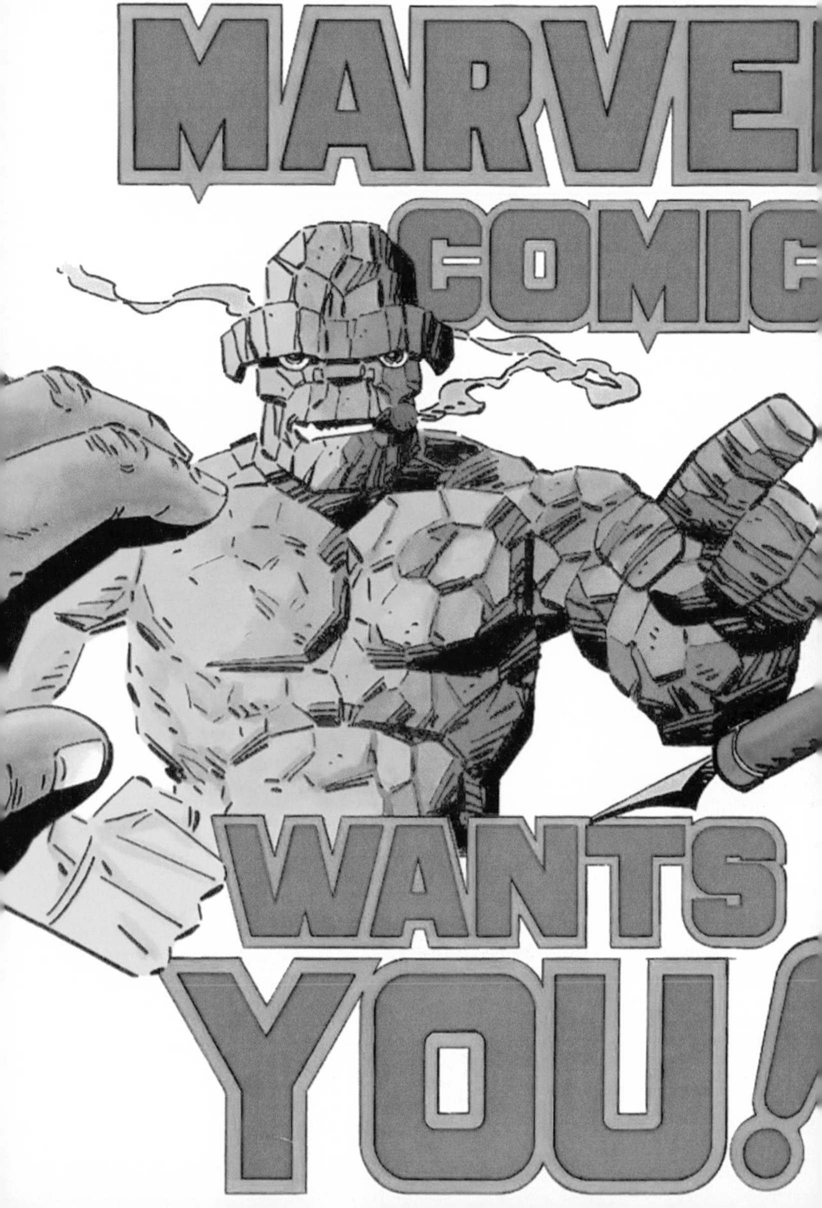
MARVE
COMIC
WANTS
YOU

THE FANTASTIC…WAIT, WHAT'S THAT?!

Pages 158–59: *Storyboard,* Fantastic Four *cartoon, NBC; art, Jack Kirby; 1978.* The Human Torch wasn't available when the Fantastic Four flew to the small screen, so Mr. Fantastic, the Invisible Woman, and the Thing were joined by H.E.R.B.I.E. the robot. And, yes, H.E.R.B.I.E. did find his way into comics —in five 1979 *FF* issues and sporadically thereafter.

MARVEL COMICS TRY-OUT BOOK No.1

Left: *House ad; art, attributed Terry Austin; 1983.*

PASSING THE TORCH

Above: *Animation cel,* Fantastic Four, *NBC; art, Jack Kirby; 1978.* NBC's *Fantastic Four* Saturday morning cartoon runs thirteen episodes. H.E.R.B.I.E. replaces the Torch, whose planned live-action show was never realized.

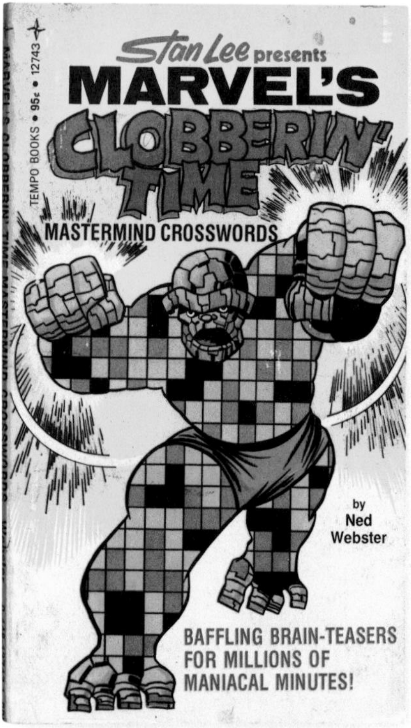

TEMPO BOOKS • 95¢ • 12743
Stan Lee presents
MARVEL'S
CLOBBERIN' TIME
MASTERMIND CROSSWORDS
by
Ned
Webster
BAFFLING BRAIN-TEASERS
FOR MILLIONS OF
MANIACAL MINUTES!

IF CROSSWORDS ARE YOUR THING

Above: *Book cover,* Marvel's Clobberin' Time Mastermind Crosswords; *art, unknown; Tempo Books; 1977.* A less-celebrated component of ex-publisher Goodman's Magazine Management, puzzle and game magazines had been a reliable staple since the 1940s. Stan Lee, wearing his publisher hat, likely saw no need to change this, and in fact seemed to have more and more fun commissioning such classic titles as *The Mighty Marvel Superheroes' Cookbook* and *The Mighty Marvel Comics Strength and Fitness Book.* When new parent Cadence industries instituted Jim Galton as president in 1978, one of his first acts was to bring licensing in-house, leading to still more Merry Marvel Madness on toy shelves and in back-to-school aisles around the world.

MARVEL TWO-IN-ONE No. 94

Opposite: *Cover; pencils, Ron Wilson; inks, Chic Stone; December 1982.*

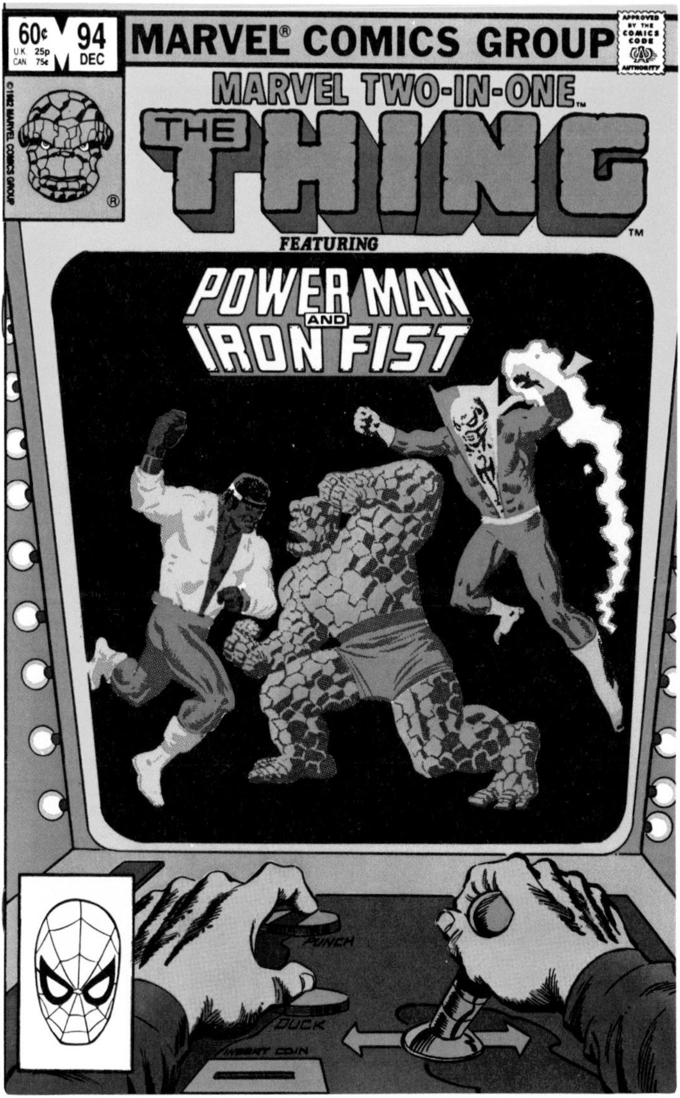
60¢
94
U.K. 25p
CAN. 75¢
DEC
MARVEL® COMICS GROUP
APPROVED BY THE COMICS CODE AUTHORITY
© 1982 MARVEL COMICS GROUP
MARVEL TWO-IN-ONE™
THE THING™
FEATURING
POWER MAN AND IRON FIST
PUNCH
DUCK
INSERT COIN

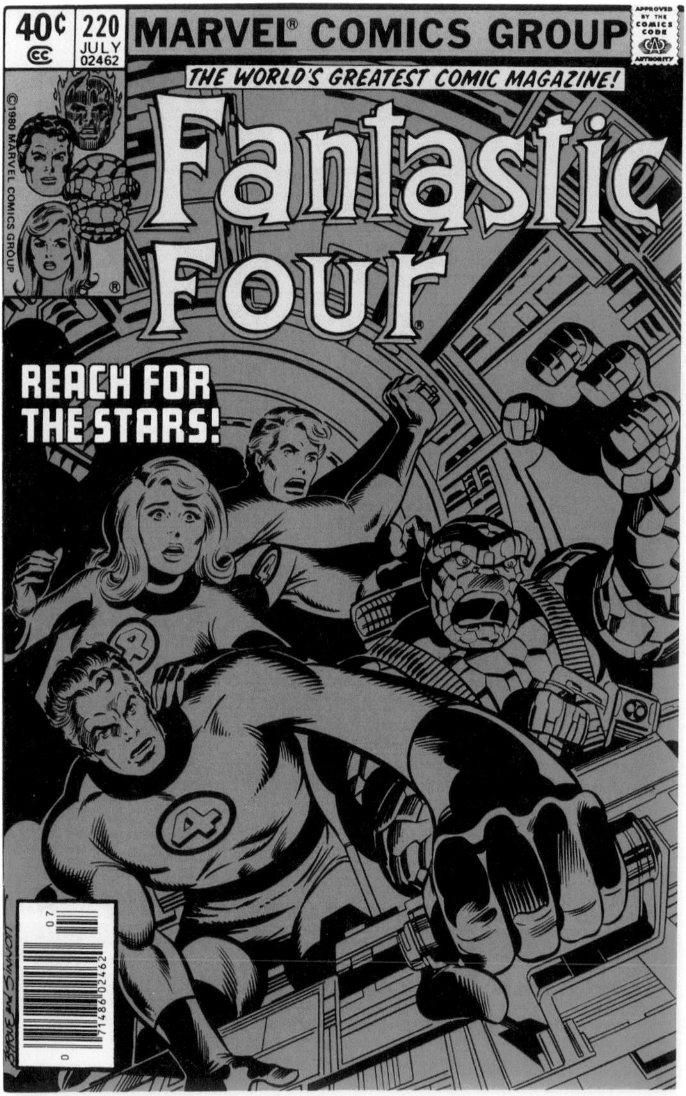
40¢
220
JULY
02462
MARVEL® COMICS GROUP
APPROVED BY THE COMICS CODE AUTHORITY
THE WORLD'S GREATEST COMIC MAGAZINE!
Fantastic Four®
©1980 MARVEL COMICS GROUP
REACH FOR THE STARS!

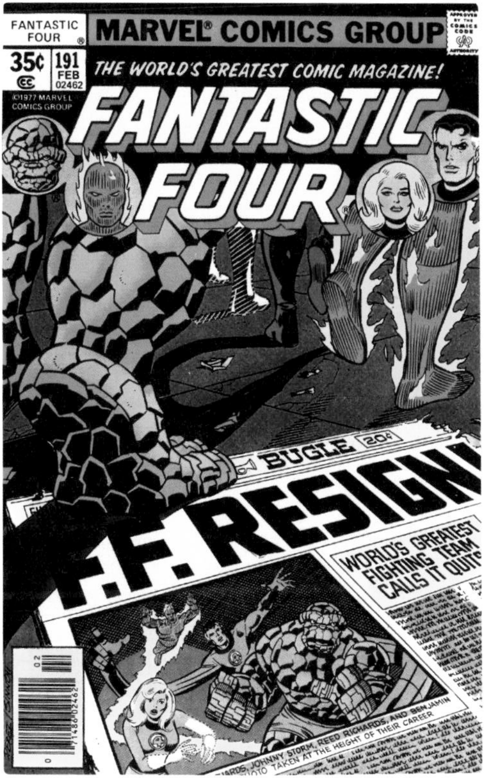
FANTASTIC FOUR
MARVEL COMICS GROUP
35¢
191
FEB
02462
©1977 MARVEL COMICS GROUP
THE WORLD'S GREATEST COMIC MAGAZINE!
FANTASTIC FOUR
BUGLE 20¢
F.F. RESIGN
WORLD'S GREATEST FIGHTING TEAM CALLS IT QUIT
JOHNNY STORM, REED RICHARDS, AND BENJAMIN
TAKEN AT THE HEIGHT OF THEIR CAREER

FANTASTIC FOUR No. 220

Opposite: *Cover; pencils, John Byrne; inks, Joe Sinnott; July 1980.* This story was originally commissioned as a never-realized promotion with Coke. By using only one color, this cover screams DANGER!

FANTASTIC FOUR No. 191

Above: *Cover; pencils, George Pérez; inks, Joe Sinnott; February 1978.* The cover says it all—the Fantastic Four disband in this issue. The next four issues would feature members' solo stories, before the team came back together in No. 196 to take on Doctor Doom.

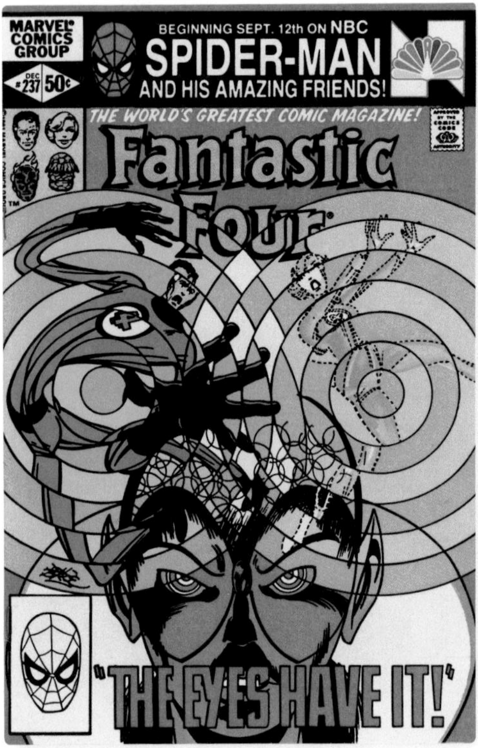
MARVEL COMICS GROUP
DEC #237 50¢
BEGINNING SEPT. 12th ON NBC
SPIDER-MAN
AND HIS AMAZING FRIENDS!
THE WORLD'S GREATEST COMIC MAGAZINE!
Fantastic Four
"THE EYES HAVE IT!"

FANTASTIC FOUR No. 237

Above: *Cover; pencils and inks, John Byrne; December 1981.*

FANTASTIC FOUR No. 262

Opposite: *Interior, "The Trial of Reed Richards"; script, pencils, and inks, John Byrne; January 1984.* "When the FF first gain their powers they looked like a bunch of folks who suddenly gain superpowers. Now they looked like rugged, muscular heroes. Even the Thing had taken on a rounded, teddy bear look. Their uniforms, which originally look like functional jumpsuits, now looked like skintight super hero clothes. In other words, they were starting to look like life imitating a comic book, instead of the other way around. So I set about restoring what I felt was missing.... With Marvel's, Shooter's and Stan's blessings, I began doing everything I could to recapture what I remembered." —John Byrne

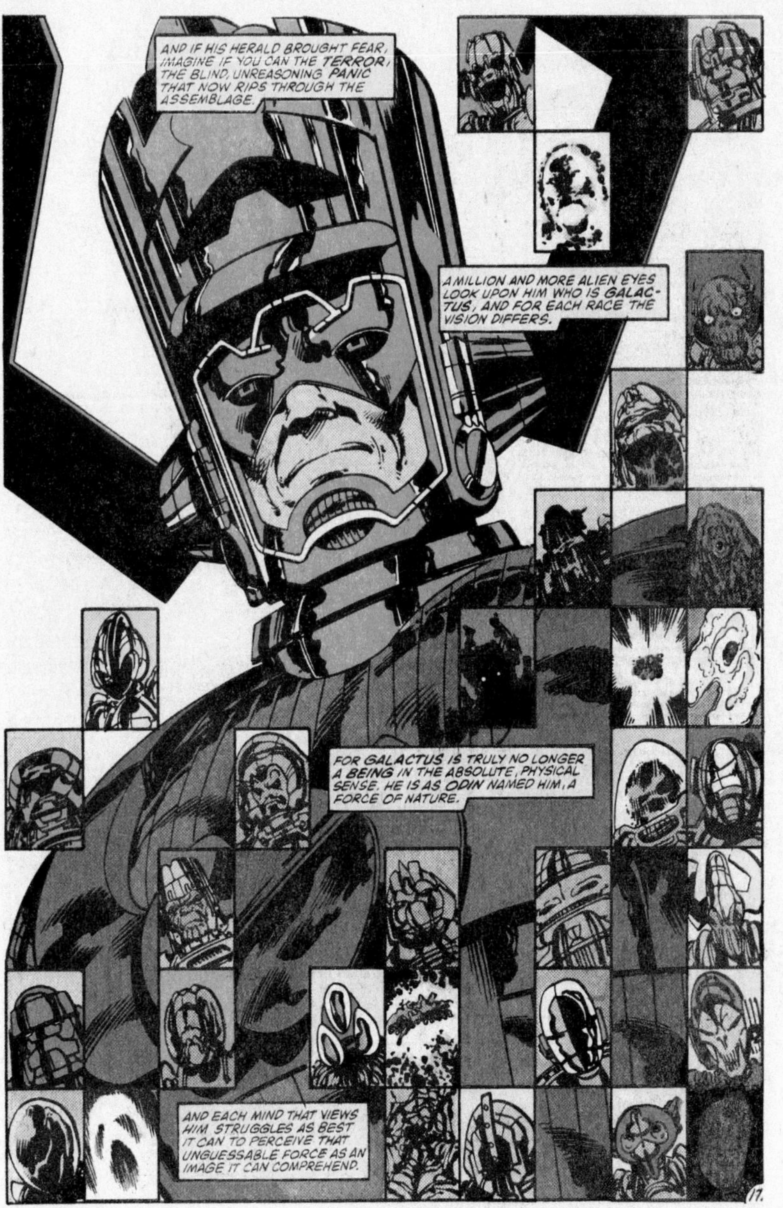
AND IF HIS HERALD BROUGHT FEAR, IMAGINE IF YOU CAN THE TERROR, THE BLIND, UNREASONING PANIC THAT NOW RIPS THROUGH THE ASSEMBLAGE.
A MILLION AND MORE ALIEN EYES LOOK UPON HIM WHO IS GALACTUS, AND FOR EACH RACE THE VISION DIFFERS.
FOR GALACTUS IS TRULY NO LONGER A BEING IN THE ABSOLUTE, PHYSICAL SENSE. HE IS AS ODIN NAMED HIM, A FORCE OF NATURE.
AND EACH MIND THAT VIEWS HIM STRUGGLES AS BEST IT CAN TO PERCEIVE THAT UNGUESSABLE FORCE AS AN IMAGE IT CAN COMPREHEND.

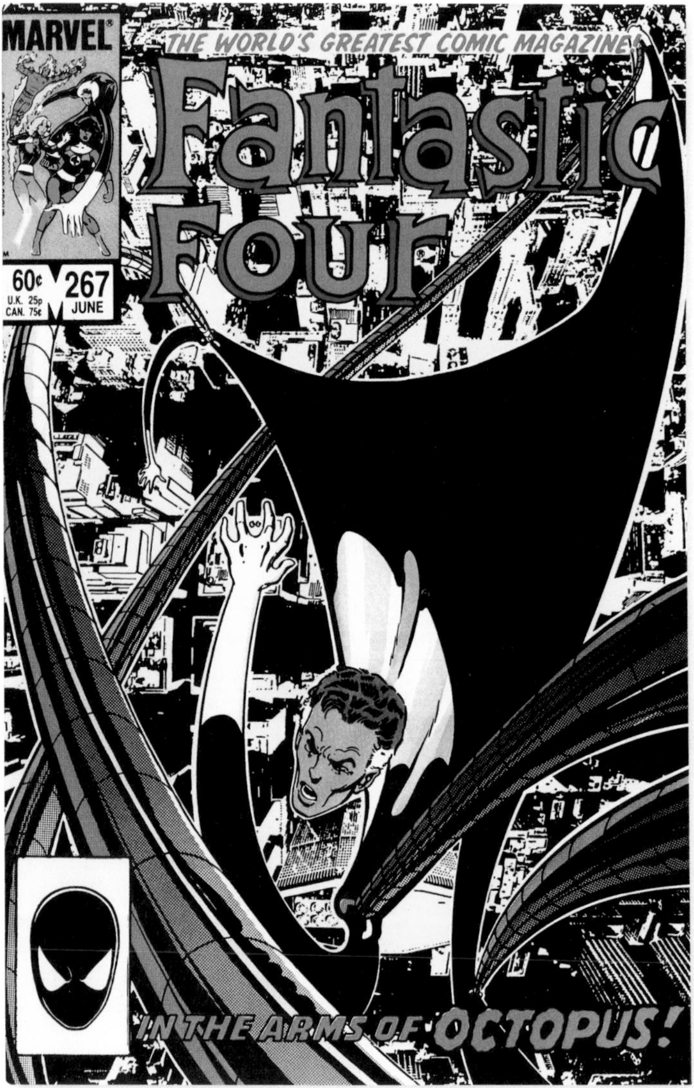
MARVEL
THE WORLD'S GREATEST COMIC MAGAZINE!
Fantastic Four
60¢
267
U.K. 25p
CAN. 75¢
JUNE
IN THE ARMS OF OCTOPUS!

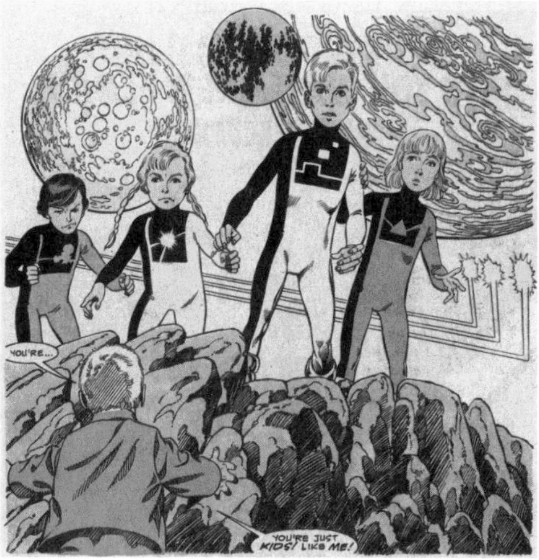
YOU'RE...
YOU'RE JUST KIDS! LIKE ME!

FANTASTIC FOUR No. 267

Opposite: *Cover; pencils and inks, John Byrne; June 1984.* Marvel worked to keep Reed's powers heroic, to set him apart from Jack Cole's forties creation, Plastic Man. He rarely stretched only his neck, and never took the form of airplanes or cars, the way Cole's comedic crimefighter would.

FANTASTIC FOUR No. 282

Above: *Interior, "Inwards to Infinity!"; script and pencils, John Byrne; inks, Jerry Ordway; September 1985.* Franklin Richards dreams of the Power Pack, four pre-teen siblings given superpowers—and their own spaceship! Written and drawn by Louise Simonson and June Brigman, it proved a surprise hit. "I thought it would be a kids' book and it turned out to be a book for everybody," recalled Simonson. "Even Alan Moore liked it. So did Chris Claremont. I was flabbergasted by that."

FANTASTIC FOUR No. 280

Below: *Cover; pencils, John Byrne; inks, Jerry Ordway; July 1985.* An homage to comic art legend Will Eisner's *Spirit* splash pages, in which the hero's name could often be found as part of the architecture of the image.

FANTASTIC FOUR No. 258

Opposite: *Cover; pencils and inks, John Byrne; September 1983.*

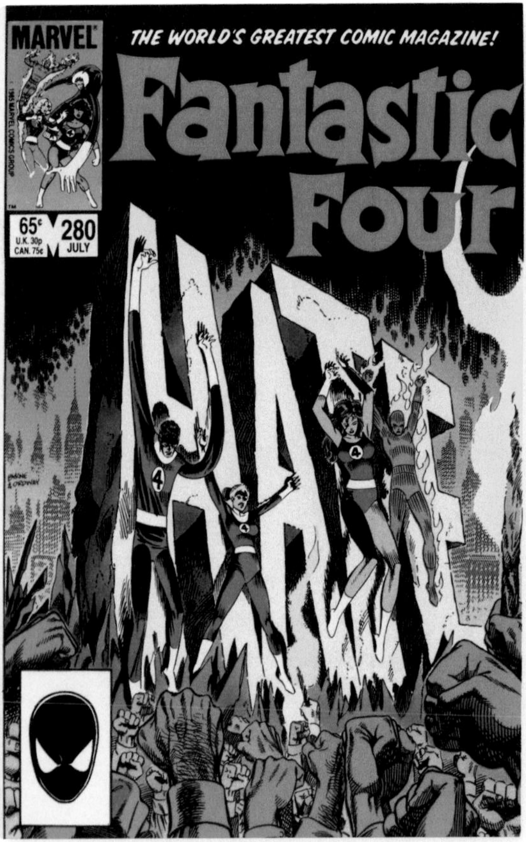
MARVEL
THE WORLD'S GREATEST COMIC MAGAZINE!
Fantastic Four
65¢
U.K. 30p
CAN. 75¢
280
JULY

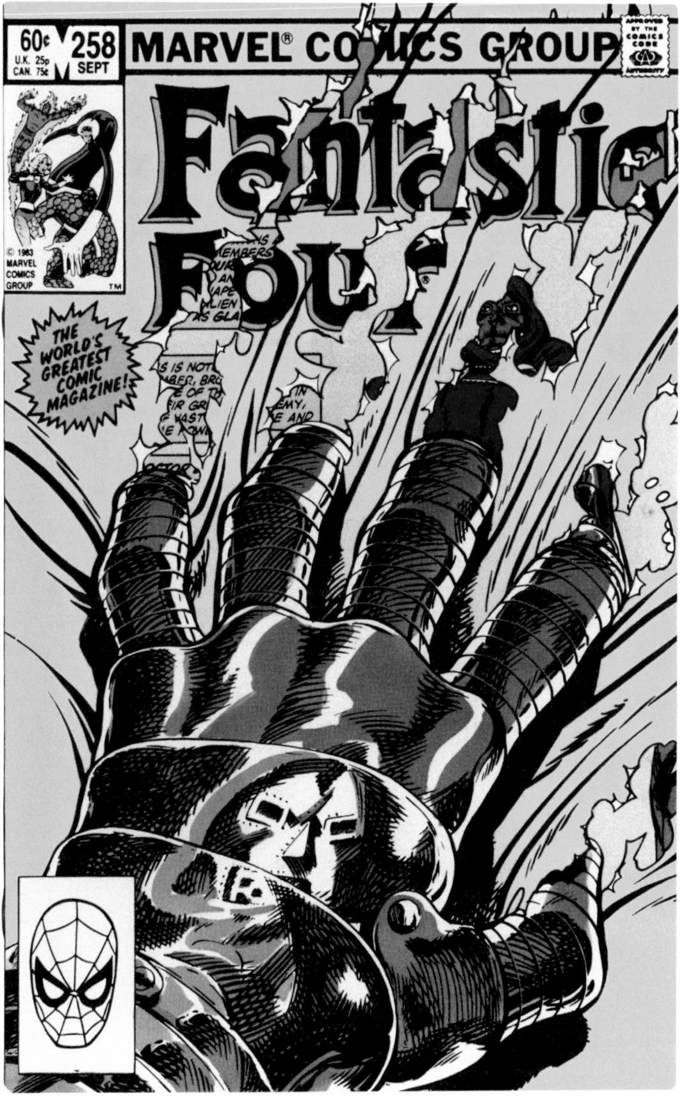
60¢
258
SEPT
U.K. 25p
CAN. 75¢
MARVEL® COMICS GROUP
APPROVED BY THE COMICS CODE AUTHORITY
Fantastic Four
© 1983 MARVEL COMICS GROUP
TM
THE WORLD'S GREATEST COMIC MAGAZINE!

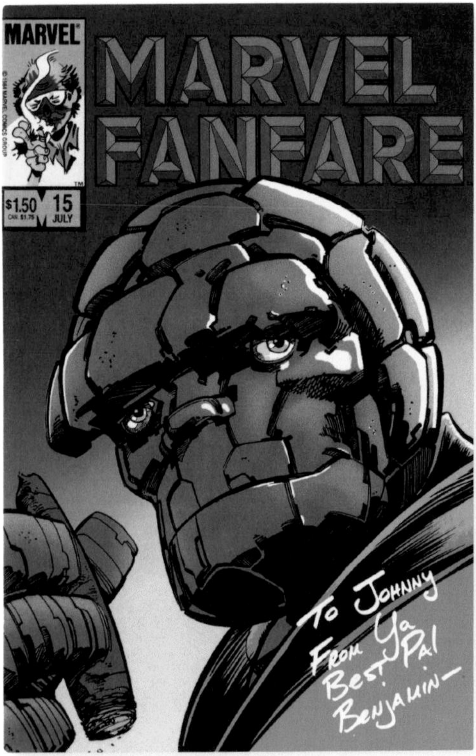
MARVEL
MARVEL FANFARE
$1.50
15
JULY
To Johnny
From Ya Best Pal
Benjamin—

MARVEL FANFARE No. 15

Above: *Cover; pencils and inks, Barry Windsor-Smith; July 1984.* *Marvel Fanfare* was a pricey bimonthly anthology printed on slick paper with no ads; each issue featured several short stories focusing on characters from all over the Marvel Universe, by industry superstars. This one features a striking cover by comics legend Barry Windsor-Smith.

THE SENSATIONAL SHE-HULK No. 31

Opposite: *Cover; pencils and inks, John Byrne; September 1991.* Byrne wrote and drew nearly thirty issues of *Sensational She-Hulk*. As seen on this cover, the series regularly broke the "fourth wall," having Shulkie aware that she was in a comic and interacting with her creators.

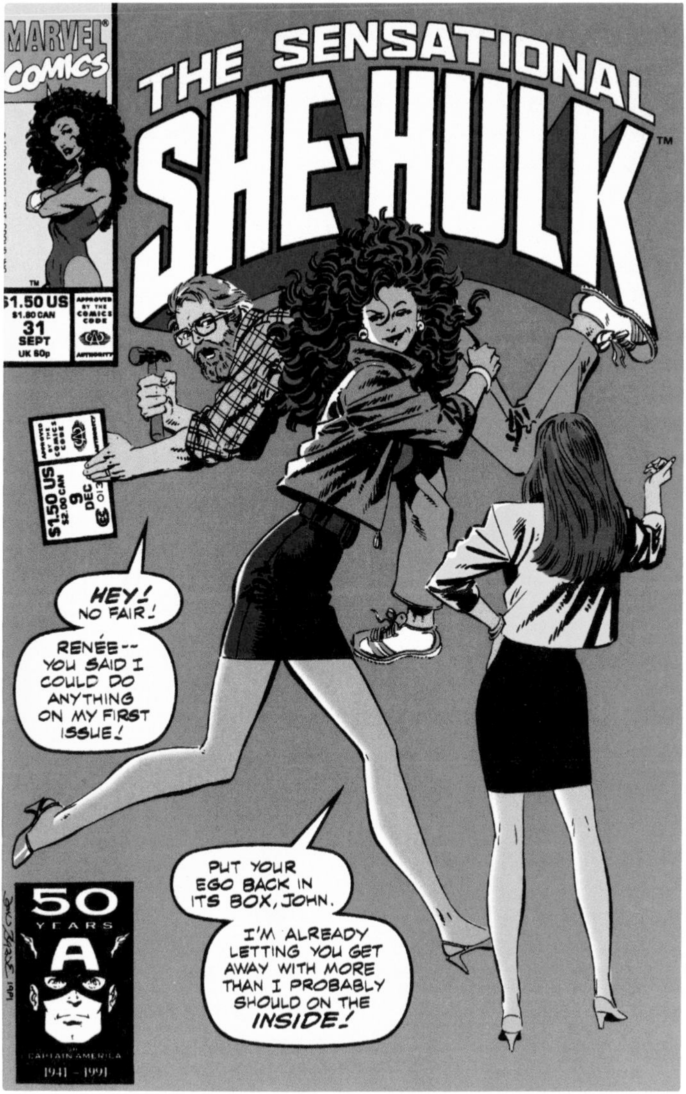
MARVEL COMICS
THE SENSATIONAL
SHE-HULK
$1.50 US
$1.80 CAN
31
SEPT
UK 60p
APPROVED BY THE COMICS CODE AUTHORITY
$1.50 US
$2.00 CAN
9
DEC
HEY! NO FAIR!
RENÉE-- YOU SAID I COULD DO ANYTHING ON MY FIRST ISSUE!
PUT YOUR EGO BACK IN ITS BOX, JOHN.
I'M ALREADY LETTING YOU GET AWAY WITH MORE THAN I PROBABLY SHOULD ON THE INSIDE!
50 YEARS
A
CAPTAIN AMERICA
1941 - 1991

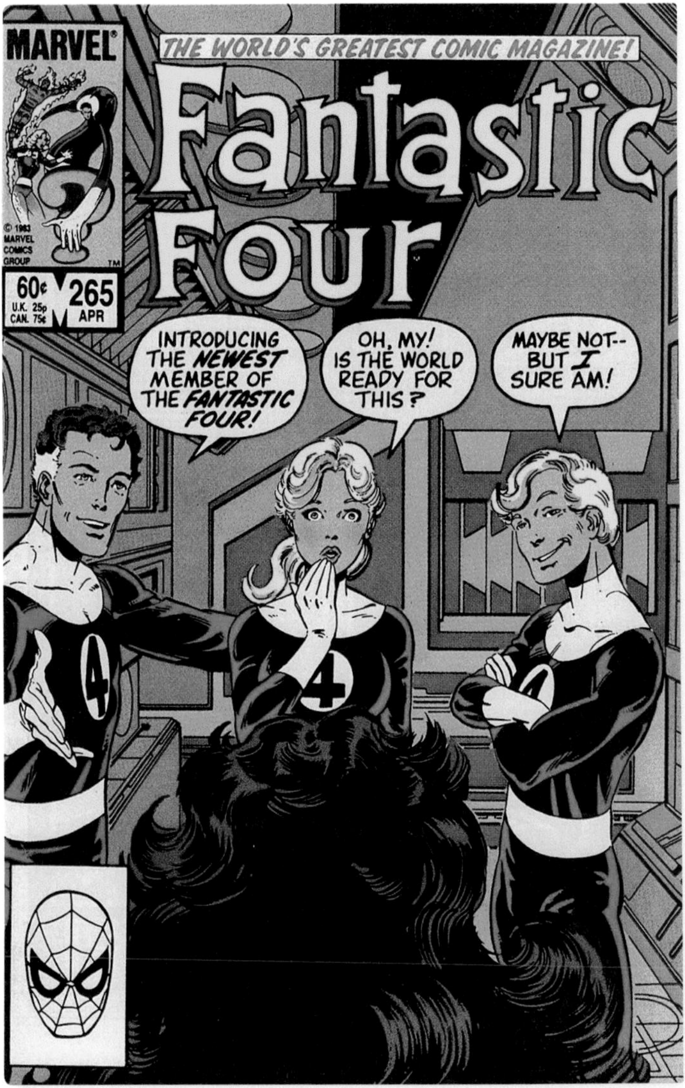
MARVEL
THE WORLD'S GREATEST COMIC MAGAZINE!
Fantastic Four
© 1983 MARVEL COMICS GROUP
TM
60¢ U.K. 25p CAN. 75¢
265 APR
INTRODUCING THE NEWEST MEMBER OF THE FANTASTIC FOUR!
OH, MY! IS THE WORLD READY FOR THIS?
MAYBE NOT-- BUT I SURE AM!

FANTASTIC FOUR No. 265

Opposite: *Cover; pencils and inks, John Byrne; April 1984.* The absent Thing is replaced with She-Hulk in this issue. The popular heroine's 35-issue run edged out Medusa for the longest of any non-original member.

SPECIAL SAVINGS TO YOU!!

Below: *House ad; 1984.* Subscriptions were cheap and convenient, but they were not wildly popular with collectors, since even after distributors stopped folding them *on purpose*, subscribers' comics tended to get wrinkled, dented, or ripped in transit!

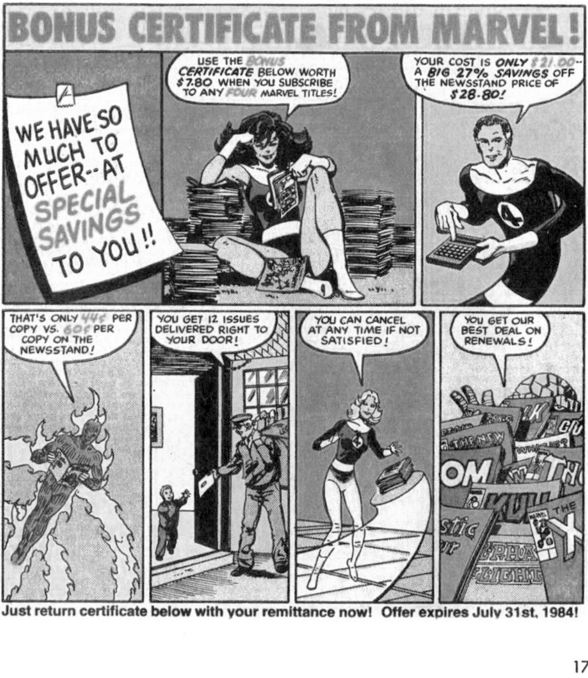

BONUS CERTIFICATE FROM MARVEL!
WE HAVE SO MUCH TO OFFER-- AT SPECIAL SAVINGS TO YOU!!
USE THE BONUS CERTIFICATE BELOW WORTH $7.80 WHEN YOU SUBSCRIBE TO ANY FOUR MARVEL TITLES!
YOUR COST IS ONLY $21.00-- A BIG 27% SAVINGS OFF THE NEWSSTAND PRICE OF $28.80!
THAT'S ONLY 44¢ PER COPY VS. 60¢ PER COPY ON THE NEWSSTAND!
YOU GET 12 ISSUES DELIVERED RIGHT TO YOUR DOOR!
YOU CAN CANCEL AT ANY TIME IF NOT SATISFIED!
YOU GET OUR BEST DEAL ON RENEWALS!
Just return certificate below with your remittance now! Offer expires July 31st, 1984!

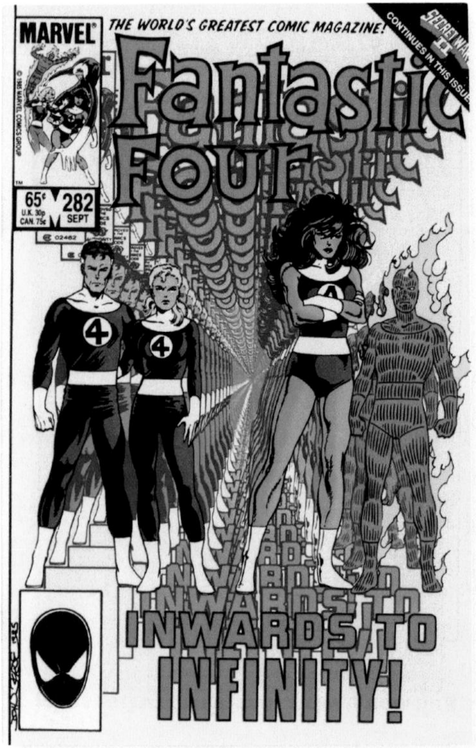
MARVEL
THE WORLD'S GREATEST COMIC MAGAZINE!
SECRET WARS II
CONTINUES IN THIS ISSUE
Fantastic Four
65¢
282
SEPT
U.K. 30p
CAN. 75¢
INWARDS TO INFINITY!

FANTASTIC FOUR No. 282

Above: *Cover; pencils and inks, John Byrne; September 1985.* Even the logo, cover copy, and corner boxes disappear into infinity in this spectacular cover — an old chestnut dating to comics' earliest days, but suitably '80s-ized here by Byrne.

FANTASTIC FOUR No. 375

Opposite: *Cover; pencils and inks, Paul Ryan; April 1993.* This cover checks off all the prerequisites for '90s super hero comics: foil cover, short jackets, tons of pouches, and gargantuan sci-fi rifles.

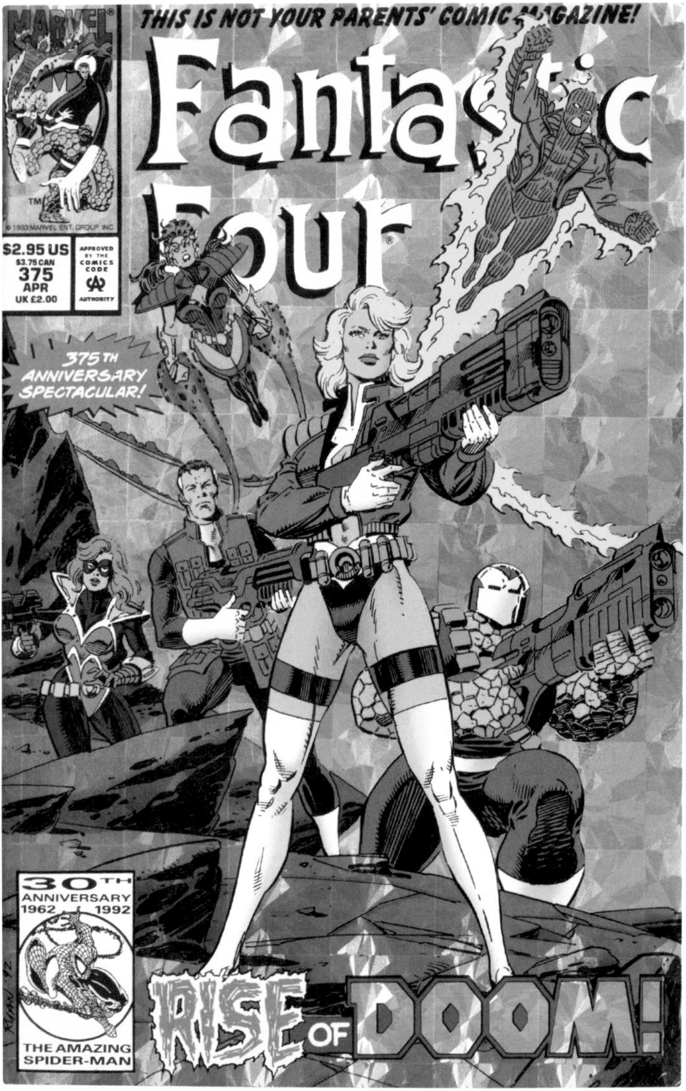
MARVEL
THIS IS NOT YOUR PARENTS' COMIC MAGAZINE!
Fantastic Four
© 1993 MARVEL ENT. GROUP, INC.
$2.95 US
$3.75 CAN
375
APR
UK £2.00
APPROVED BY THE COMICS CODE AUTHORITY
375TH ANNIVERSARY SPECTACULAR!
30TH ANNIVERSARY 1962 1992
THE AMAZING SPIDER-MAN
RISE OF DOOM!

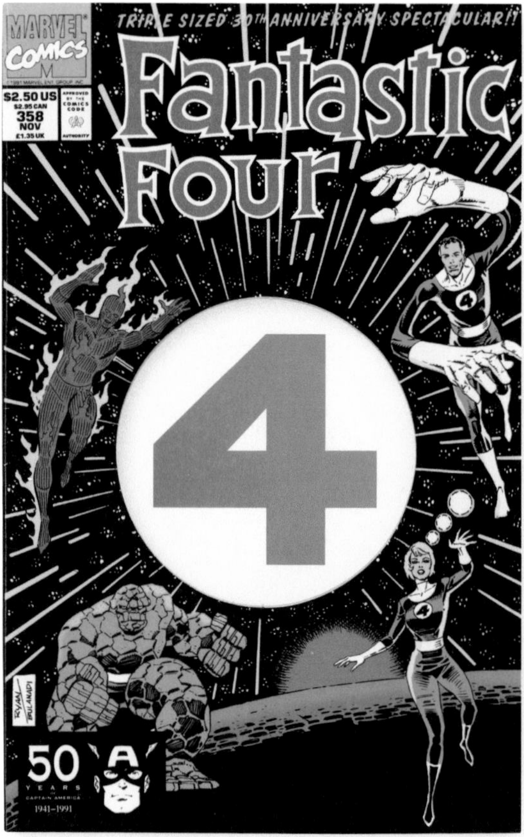
TRIPLE SIZED 30TH ANNIVERSARY SPECTACULAR!!
MARVEL COMICS
Fantastic Four
$2.50 US
$2.95 CAN
358
NOV
£1.35 UK
APPROVED BY THE COMICS CODE AUTHORITY
4
RYAN BULANADI
50 YEARS
CAPTAIN AMERICA
1941–1991

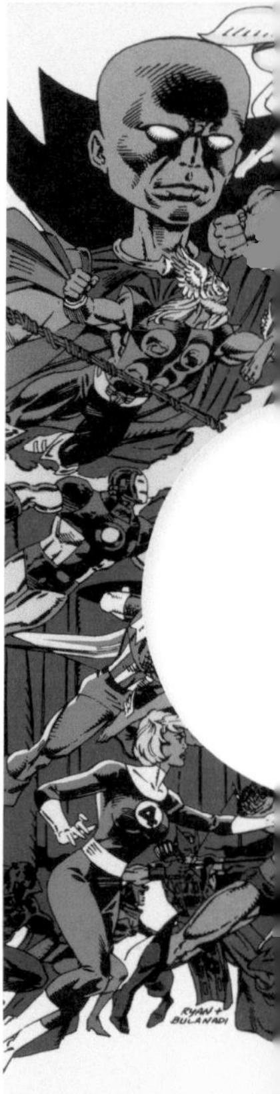
RYAN + BULANADI

FANTASTIC FOUR No. 358

Above: *Cover; pencils, Paul Ryan; inks, Danny Bulanadi; November 1991.* The Fantastic Four celebrated its 30th anniversary with a die-cut cover that opened to reveal a heroes vs. villains spread.

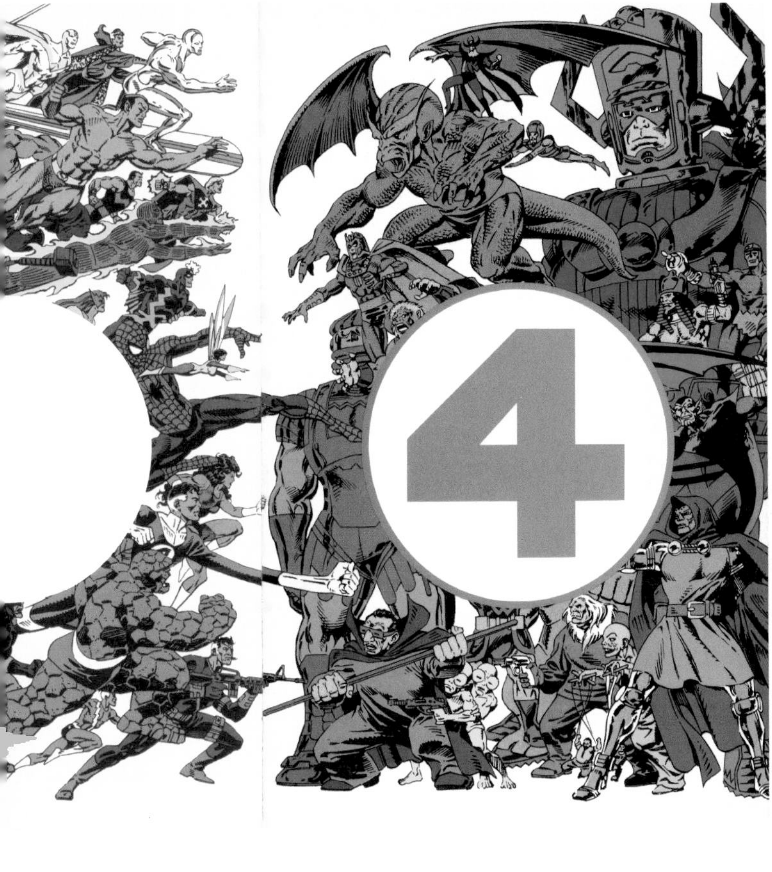
4

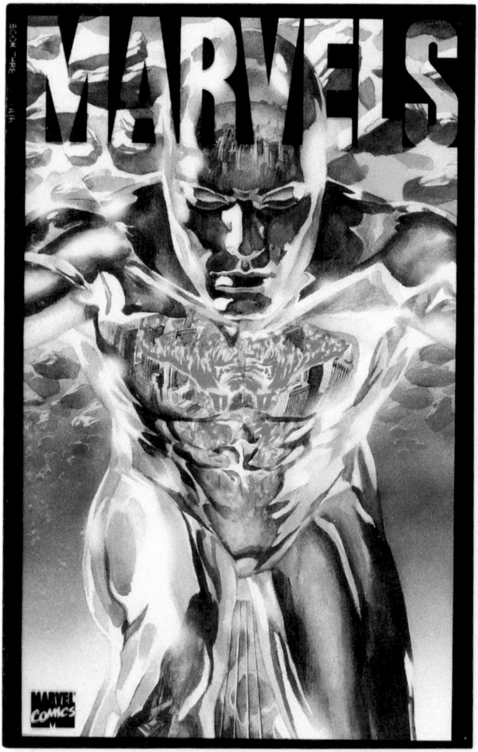
MARVELS
MARVEL COMICS

MARVELS No. 3

Above: *Cover; art, Alex Ross; March 1994.*

MARVELS No. 1

Opposite: *Cover; art, Alex Ross; January 1994.* Written by Kurt Busiek, *Marvels* was a miniseries that examined the Marvel Universe from the perspective of newspaper photographer Phil Sheldon. Alex Ross painted the interior art, as well as these stunning covers, which feature the Human Torch and Silver Surfer.

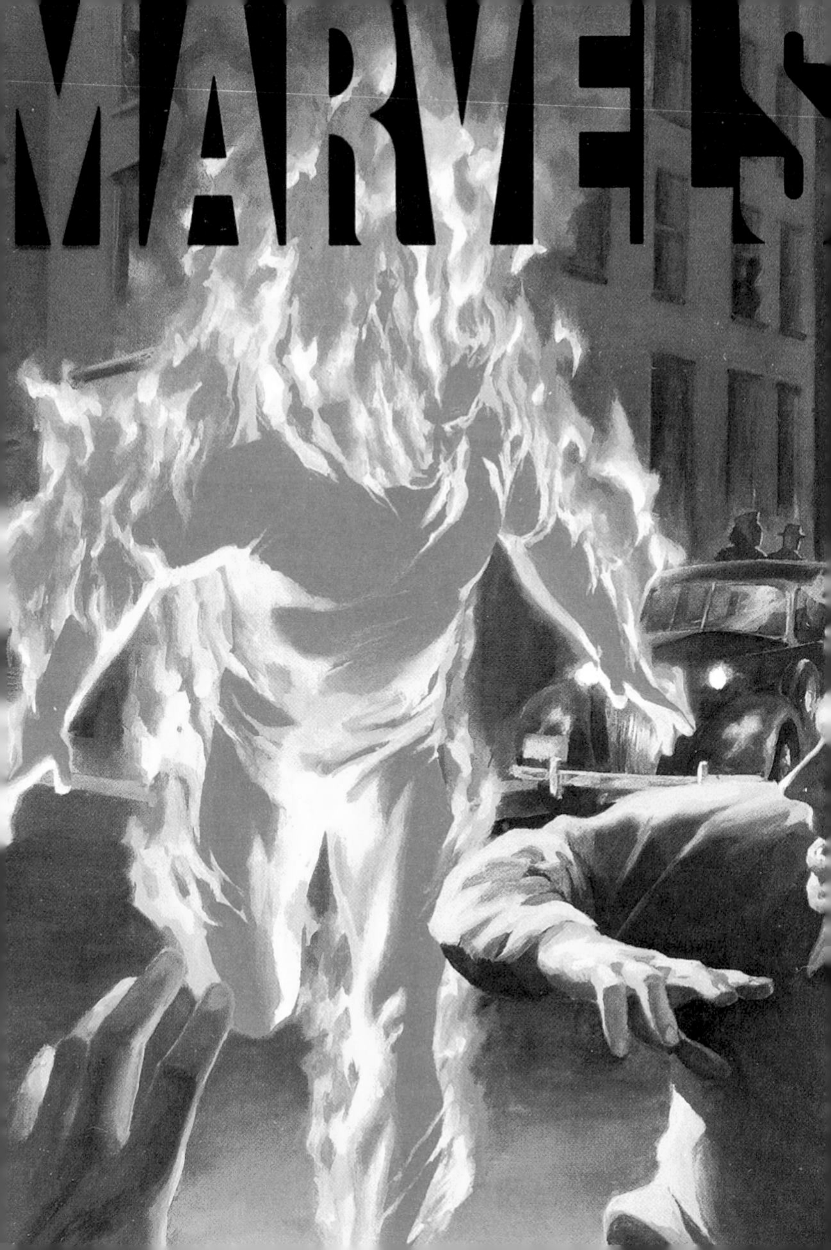
MARVELS

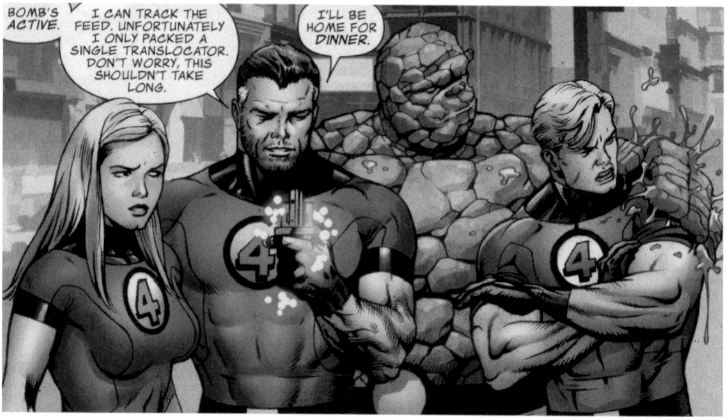
BOMB'S ACTIVE.
I CAN TRACK THE FEED. UNFORTUNATELY I ONLY PACKED A SINGLE TRANSLOCATOR. DON'T WORRY, THIS SHOULDN'T TAKE LONG.
I'LL BE HOME FOR DINNER.

FANTASTIC FOUR No. 570

Above: *Interior, "Solve Everything Part One"; script, Jonathan Hickman; pencils, Dale Eaglesham; October 2009.* Hickman's run on the series de-nerded Mister Fantastic a little bit, giving him short sleeves and Fury-esque stubble.

FF No. 1

Opposite: *Cover; art, Steve Epting; May 2011.* Here, FF stands for Future Foundation, with new-look white uniforms and a new member — Spider-Man — powering the concept of the Fantastic Four into the future.

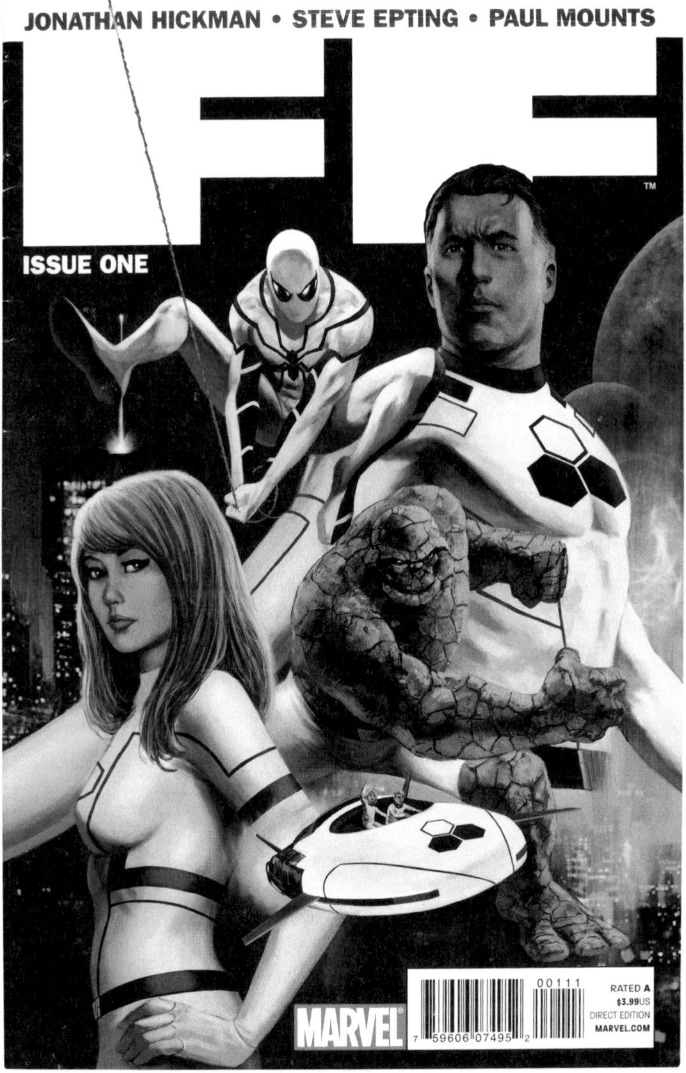
JONATHAN HICKMAN • STEVE EPTING • PAUL MOUNTS
FF
TM
ISSUE ONE
MARVEL
00111
7 59606 07495 2
RATED A
$3.99US
DIRECT EDITION
MARVEL.COM

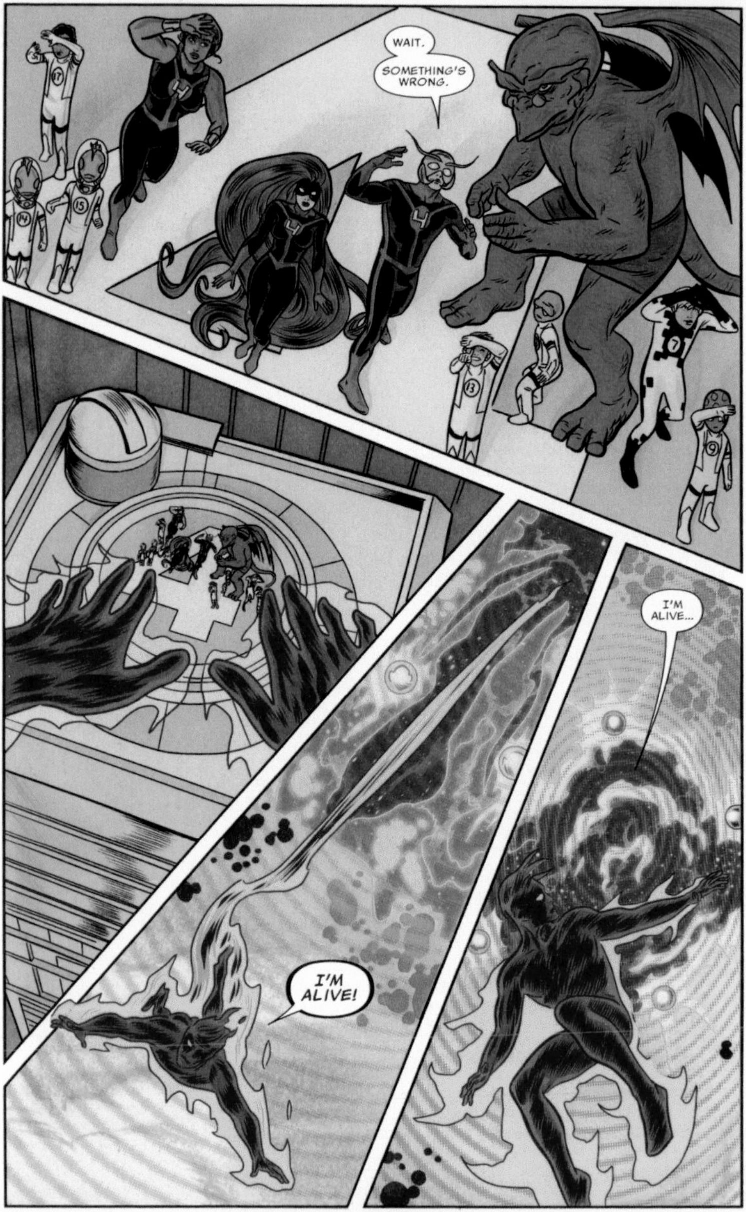
WAIT.
SOMETHING'S WRONG.
I'M ALIVE!
I'M ALIVE...

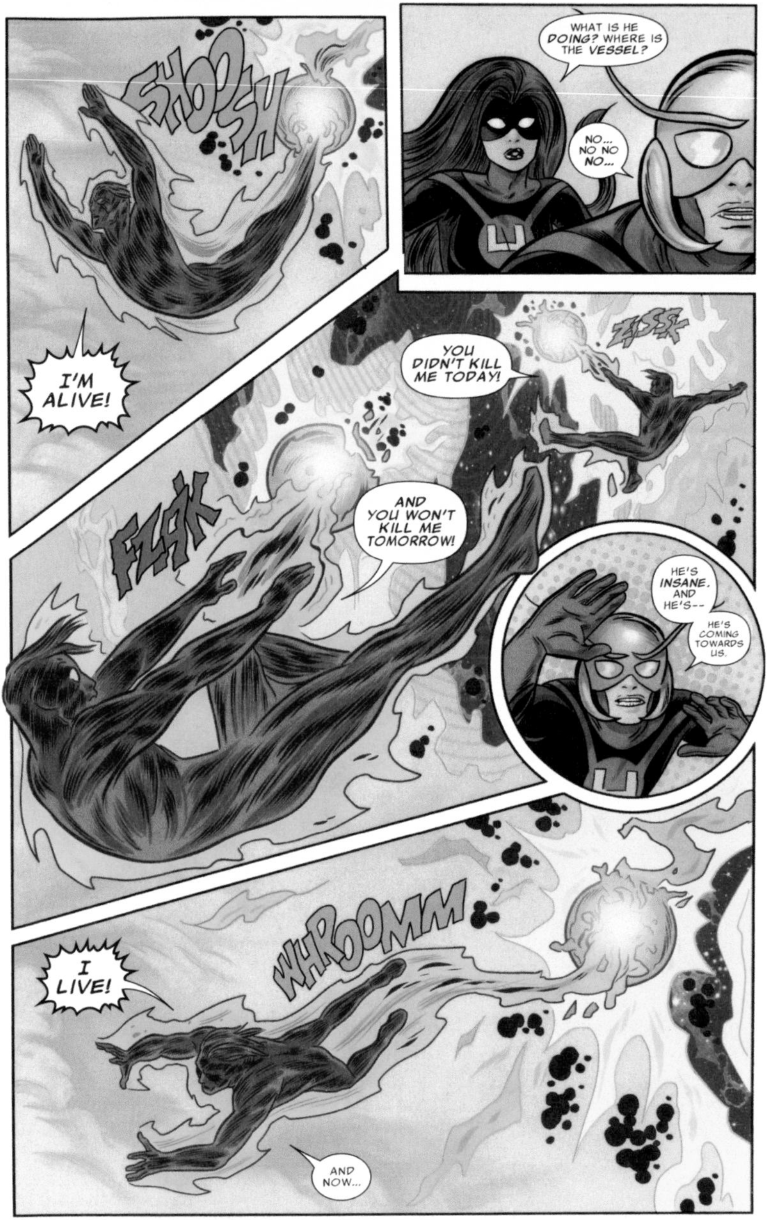
SHOOSH
I'M ALIVE!
WHAT IS HE DOING? WHERE IS THE VESSEL?
NO... NO NO NO...
ZISSK
YOU DIDN'T KILL ME TODAY!
FZAK
AND YOU WON'T KILL ME TOMORROW!
HE'S INSANE. AND HE'S--
HE'S COMING TOWARDS US.
WHROOMM
I LIVE!
AND NOW...

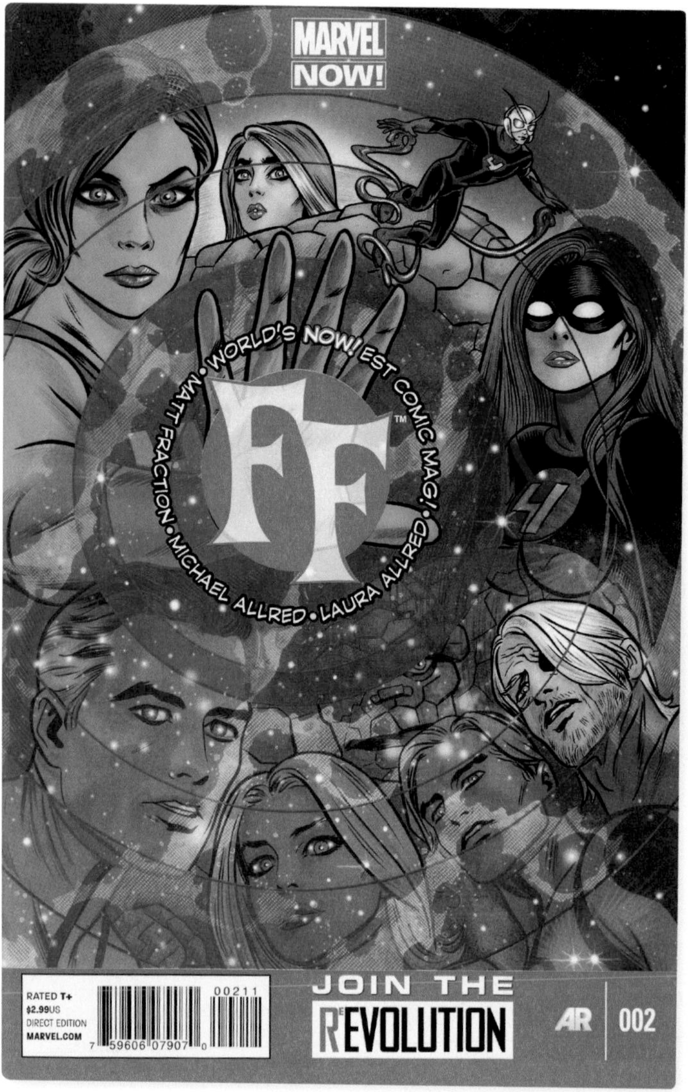

MARVEL NOW!
WORLD'S NOW! EST COMIC MAG!
FF™
MATT FRACTION • MICHAEL ALLRED • LAURA ALLRED
RATED T+
$2.99US
DIRECT EDITION
MARVEL.COM
JOIN THE REVOLUTION
AR
002

FF Vol. 2 No. 2

Pages 184–85 and opposite: *Interiors, "The Big Goodbye"; script, Matt Fraction; interior and cover pencils and inks, Michael Allred; February 2013.* Allred's clean, quirky style gave a new look to the franchise, as seen in this popular 2013 reboot, penned by Matt Fraction and simply titled *FF*.

BABY FF!

Below: *Cover variant,* FF *No. 1: pencils and inks, Skottie Young; January 2013.* Artist Skottie Young teamed up with writer Eric Shanower for several *Wizard of Oz*–related miniseries. His art style made him a sought-after cover artist, eventually doing more than 100 "Young variants," which became collectible in their own right.

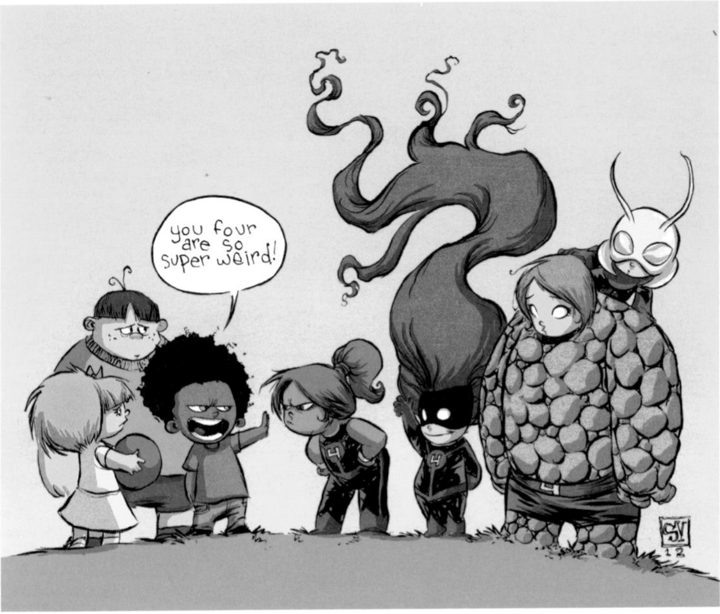
you four are so super weird!
SY 12

FANTASTIC FOUR FOREVER

Opposite: *Cover:* Fantastic Four Omnibus *No. 1; art, Alex Ross; 2005.* Ross painted this homage to Jack Kirby's cover to *Fantastic Four* No. 1 for the cover of the door-stopping, 848-page *Fantastic Four Omnibus*.

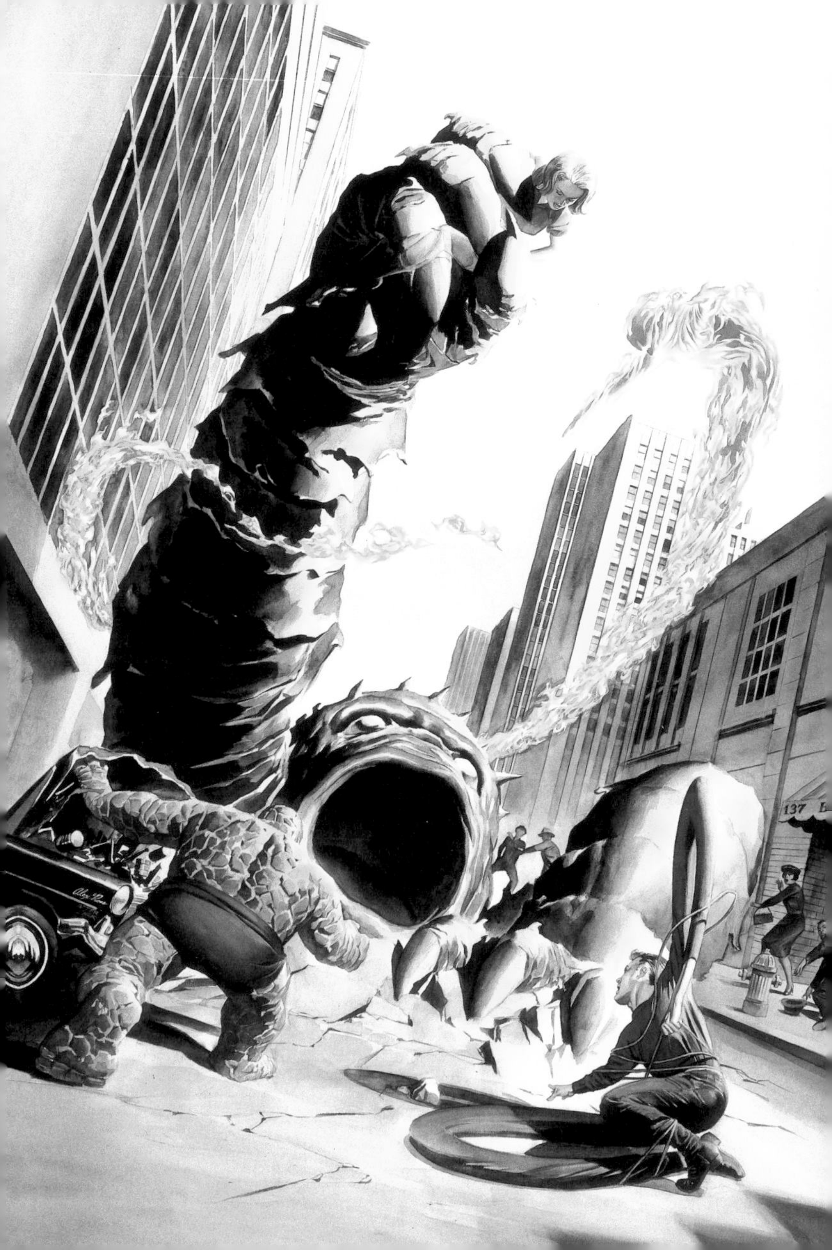
137

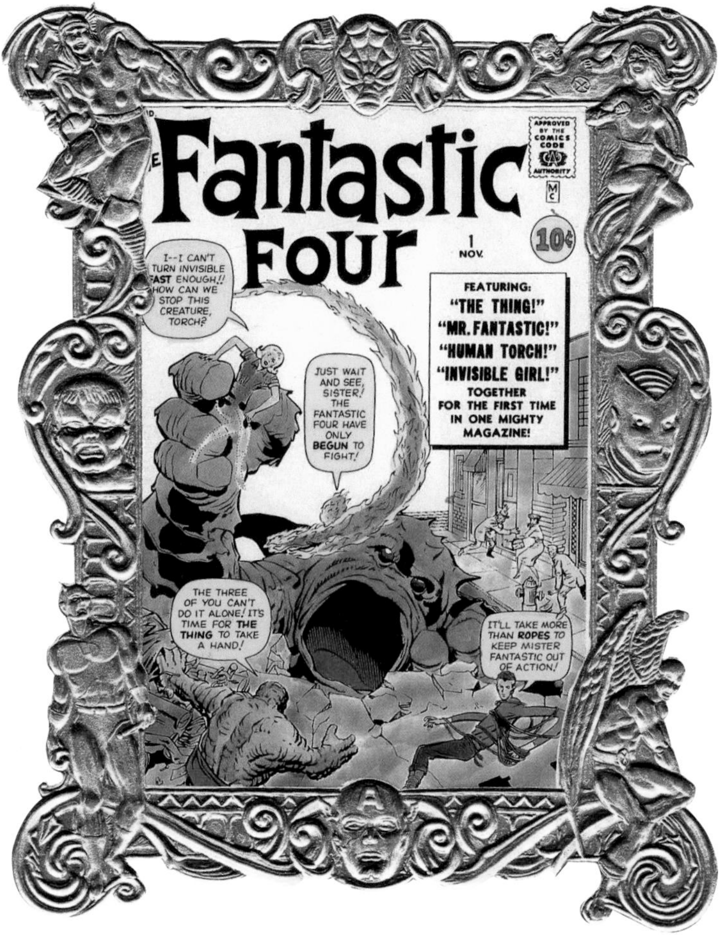

Fantastic Four
APPROVED BY THE COMICS CODE AUTHORITY
MC
1 NOV.
10¢
FEATURING: "THE THING!" "MR. FANTASTIC!" "HUMAN TORCH!" "INVISIBLE GIRL!" TOGETHER FOR THE FIRST TIME IN ONE MIGHTY MAGAZINE!
I--I CAN'T TURN INVISIBLE FAST ENOUGH!! HOW CAN WE STOP THIS CREATURE, TORCH?
JUST WAIT AND SEE, SISTER! THE FANTASTIC FOUR HAVE ONLY BEGUN TO FIGHT!
THE THREE OF YOU CAN'T DO IT ALONE! IT'S TIME FOR THE THING TO TAKE A HAND!
IT'LL TAKE MORE THAN ROPES TO KEEP MISTER FANTASTIC OUT OF ACTION!

FANTASTIC FOUR No. 45

Front cover: *Cover; pencils, Jack Kirby; inks, Joe Sinnott; December 1965.*

MARVEL MASTERWORKS

Opposite: *Cover; pencils, Jack Kirby; inks, attributed George Klein; November 1961.* The Masterworks line of hardcovers reprint the earliest tales of Spider-Man, Fantastic Four, and the X-Men.

FANTASTIC FOUR FOREVER

Back cover: *Cover; Fantastic Four Omnibus No. 1; art, Alex Ross; 2005.*

CREDITS

The majority of the comics included in this volume were photographed from the collections of Bob Bretall, Nick Caputo, Marvel, Barry Pearl, Michael J. Vassallo, and Warren Reece's Chamber of Fantasy. Also: Jesse and Sylvia Storob, John Chruscinski, Andrew Farago, Hake's, Robin Kirby, Colin Stutz, and Tellshiar. ™& © DC Comics. Used with permission: 8. Courtesy Glen David Gold: 10. © MARVEL/Photo Courtesy of Heritage Auctions, ha.com: 2, 121, 124, 125, 158–59, 164, 168, 180, 181. From the Collection of Metropolis Comics.com: 83. Courtesy NASA: 20. National Cartoonist Society: 76. Courtesy Joe Sinnott: 95. Topps ® Krazy Little Comics used courtesy of The Topps Company, Inc.: 106.

TASCHEN GMBH
Hohenzollernring 53, D-50672 Köln
taschen.com

Editor/art director: Josh Baker, Oakland
Design/layout: Nemuel DePaula, Los Angeles
Editorial coordination: Jascha Kempe, Cologne; Nina Wiener, New York
Production: Stefan Klatte, Cologne
German translation: Reinhard Schweizer, Freiburg
French translation: Éric Andret, Paris
Editorial consultants: Nick Caputo, Maurene Goo, Blake Hennon, Barry Pearl, Rhett Thomas, Michael J. Vassallo, Scott Bryan Wilson
Special consultant to Roy Thomas: Danny Fingeroth

EACH AND EVERY TASCHEN BOOK PLANTS A SEED!
TASCHEN is a carbon neutral publisher. Each year, we offset our annual carbon emissions with carbon credits at the Instituto Terra, a reforestation program in Minas Gerais, Brazil, founded by Lélia and Sebastião Salgado. To find out more about this ecological partnership, please check: *www.taschen.com/zerocarbon*
Inspiration: unlimited. Carbon footprint: zero.

To stay informed about TASCHEN and our upcoming titles, please subscribe to our free magazine at *www.taschen.com/magazine*, follow us on Twitter, Instagram, and Facebook, or e-mail your questions to *contact@taschen.com.*

Printed in Italy
ISBN 978-3-8365-6782-4